my World TEXAS

Social Studies®

Building Our Communities

PEARSON

Boston, Massachusetts
Chandler, Arizona
Glenview, Illinois
New York, New York

It's my story, too!

You are one of the authors of this book. You can write in this book! You can take notes in this book! You can draw in it too! This book will be yours to keep.

Fill in the information below to tell about yourself. Then write your autobiography. An autobiography tells about you and the kinds of things you like to do.

Name _____

School _____

City or Town _____

Autobiography _____

_____

_____

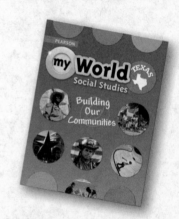

Front:

Top: L: Department of Public Safety officer in Austin; **R:** Independence Day parade in Texas
Center: L: Bullock Texas State History Museum, Austin; **C:** San Antonio firefighter;
R: Skateboarder at skate park near Houston **Bottom:** Children building a sand castle on the Texas Gulf Coast

Back:

Top: People canoeing at Caddo Lake State Park **Center: L:** Football; **R:** Chili festival in Conroe **Bottom: L:** Third grader gardening; **C:** DART train in Dallas

Credits appear on pages **R28–R30**, which constitute an extension of this copyright page.

Softcover: ISBN-13: 978-0-328-81351-3
ISBN-10: 0-328-81351-6
9 10 18 17 16

Hardcover: ISBN-13: 978-0-328-84906-2
ISBN-10: 0-328-84906-5
1 2 3 4 5 6 7 8 9 10 V011 19 18 17 16 15

Built for Texas

Pearson *Texas myWorld Social Studies* was developed especially for Texas with the help of teachers from across the state and covers 100 percent of the Texas Essential Knowledge and Skills for Social Studies. This story began with a series of teacher roundtables in cities across the state of Texas that inspired a program blueprint for *Texas myWorld Social Studies*. In addition, Judy Brodigan served as our expert advisor, guiding our creation of a dynamic Social Studies curriculum for TEKS mastery. Once this blueprint was finalized, a dedicated team—made up of Pearson authors, content experts, and social studies teachers from Texas—worked to bring our collective vision into reality.

Pearson would like to extend a special thank you to all of the teachers who helped guide the development of this program. We gratefully acknowledge your efforts to realize the possibilities of elementary Social Studies teaching and learning. Together, we will prepare Texas students for their future roles in college, careers, and as active citizens.

Program Consulting Authors

The Colonial Williamsburg Foundation
Williamsburg VA

Armando Cantú Alonzo
Associate Professor of History
Texas A&M University
College Station TX

Dr. Linda Bennett
Associate Professor, Department of
Learning, Teaching, & Curriculum
College of Education
University of Missouri
Columbia MO

Dr. James B. Kracht
Byrne Chair for Student Success
Executive Associate Dean
College of Education and Human
Development
College of Education
Texas A&M University
College Station TX

Dr. William E. White
Vice President for Productions,
Publications and Learning
Ventures
The Colonial Williamsburg
Foundation
Williamsburg VA

Reviewers and Consultants

ACADEMIC REVIEWERS

Kathy Glass
Author, *Lesson Design for
Differentiated Instruction*
President, Glass Educational
Consulting
Woodside CA

Roberta Logan
African Studies Specialist
Retired, Boston Public Schools/
Mission Hill School
Boston MA

Jeanette Menendez
Reading Coach
Doral Academy Elementary
Miami FL

Bob Sandman
Adjunct Assistant Professor of
Business and Economics
Wilmington College—Cincinnati
Branches
Blue Ash OH

PROGRAM CONSULTANT

Judy Brodigan
Former President, Texas Council
for Social Studies
Grapevine TX

Padre Island National Seashore

CONNECT

Master the TEKS with a personal connection.

myStory Spark

The **myStory Book** writing strand in the program begins with a **myStory Spark** activity. Here you can record your initial ideas about the **Big Question**.

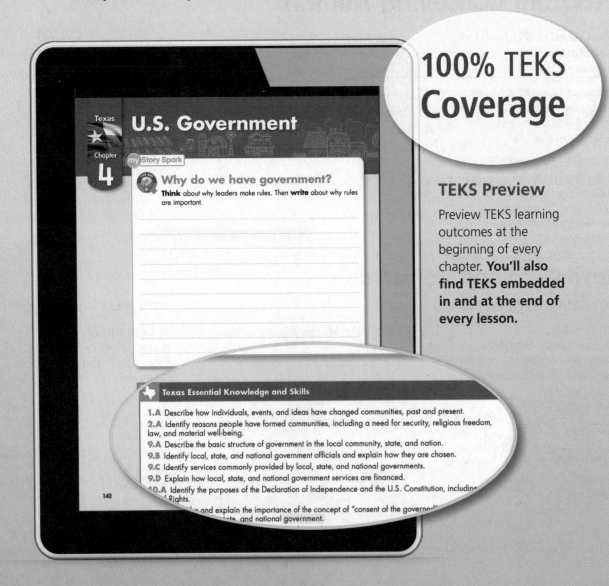

100% TEKS Coverage

TEKS Preview

Preview TEKS learning outcomes at the beginning of every chapter. **You'll also find TEKS embedded in and at the end of every lesson.**

Texas

U.S. Government

Chapter 4

myStory Spark

Why do we have government?

Think about why leaders make rules. Then **write** about why rules are important.

Texas Essential Knowledge and Skills

1.A Describe how individuals, events, and ideas have changed communities, past and present.
2.A Identify reasons people have formed communities, including a need for security, religious freedom, law, and material well-being.
9.A Describe the basic structure of government in the local community, state, and nation.
9.B Identify local, state, and national government officials and explain how they are chosen.
9.C Identify services commonly provided by local, state, and national governments.
9.D Explain how local, state, and national government services are financed.
10.A Identify the purposes of the Declaration of Independence and the U.S. Constitution, including Rights.
 and explain the importance of the concept of "consent of the governed" and national government.

140

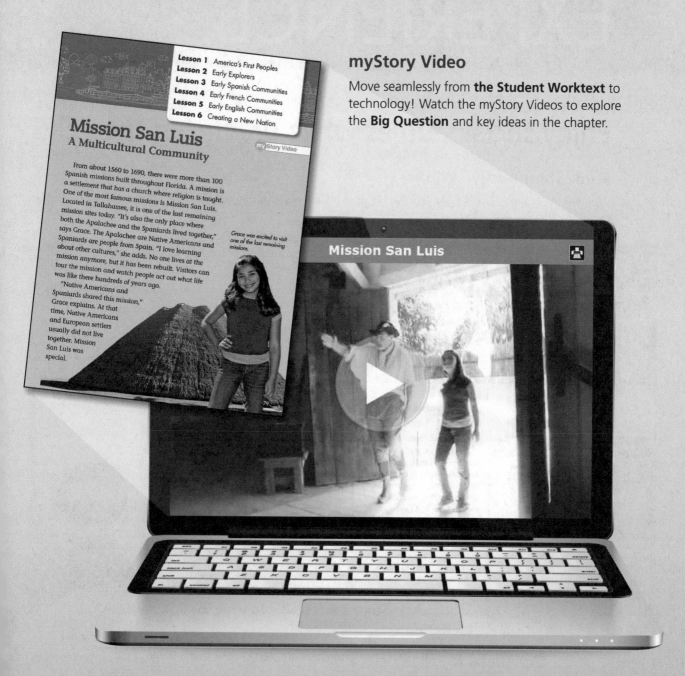

myStory Video

Move seamlessly from **the Student Worktext** to technology! Watch the myStory Videos to explore the **Big Question** and key ideas in the chapter.

Lesson 1 America's First Peoples
Lesson 2 Early Explorers
Lesson 3 Early Spanish Communities
Lesson 4 Early French Communities
Lesson 5 Early English Communities
Lesson 6 Creating a New Nation

Mission San Luis
A Multicultural Community

myStory Video

From about 1560 to 1690, there were more than 100 Spanish missions built throughout Florida. A mission is a settlement that has a church where religion is taught. One of the most famous missions is Mission San Luis. Located in Tallahassee, it is one of the last remaining mission sites today. "It's also the only place where both the Apalachee and the Spaniards lived together," says Grace. The Apalachee are Native Americans and Spaniards are people from Spain. "I love learning about other cultures," she adds. No one lives at the mission anymore, but it has been rebuilt. Visitors can tour the mission and watch people act out what life was like there hundreds of years ago.

"Native Americans and Spaniards shared this mission," Grace explains. At that time, Native Americans and European settlers usually did not live together. Mission San Luis was special.

Grace was excited to visit one of the last remaining missions.

Access the TEKS

Texas *myWorld Social Studies* covers the TEKS in all formats. Access the content through the printed worktext, eText, or online with the digital course on Realize.

 **PEARSON realize** **Go online at:** www.PearsonTexas.com

Every lesson is supported by digital activities, myStory Videos, vocabulary activities, and myStory Book on Tikatok.

EXPERIENCE

Enjoy social studies while practicing the TEKS.

Student Interactive Worktext

With the Texas *myWorld Social Studies* worktext, you'll love writing, drawing, circling and underlining in your own book.

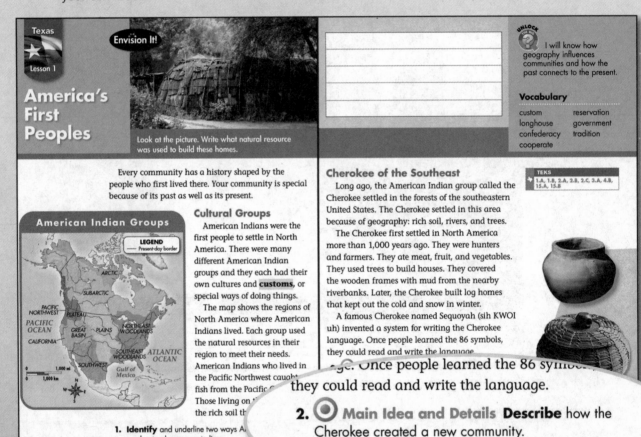

Texas

Envision It!

Lesson 1

America's First Peoples

Look at the picture. Write what natural resource was used to build these homes.

Every community has a history shaped by the people who first lived there. Your community is special because of its past as well as its present.

Cultural Groups

American Indians were the first people to settle in North America. There were many different American Indian groups and they each had their own cultures and **customs**, or special ways of doing things.

The map shows the regions of North America where American Indians lived. Each group used the natural resources in their region to meet their needs. American Indians who lived in the Pacific Northwest caught fish from the Pacific Ocean. Those living on the rich soil th...

1. **Identify** and underline two ways A... used natural resources to live.

American Indian Groups

LEGEND
Present-day border

ARCTIC
SUBARCTIC
PACIFIC NORTHWEST
PLATEAU
PACIFIC OCEAN
GREAT BASIN
PLAINS
CALIFORNIA
NORTHEAST WOODLANDS
SOUTHEAST WOODLANDS
ATLANTIC OCEAN
SOUTHWEST
Gulf of Mexico

1,000 mi
1,000 km

UNLOCK
I will know how geography influences communities and how the past connects to the present.

Vocabulary

custom   reservation
longhouse   government
confederacy   tradition
cooperate

Cherokee of the Southeast

Long ago, the American Indian group called the Cherokee settled in the forests of the southeastern United States. The Cherokee settled in this area because of geography: rich soil, rivers, and trees.

The Cherokee first settled in North America more than 1,000 years ago. They were hunters and farmers. They ate meat, fruit, and vegetables. They used trees to build houses. They covered the wooden frames with mud from the nearby riverbanks. Later, the Cherokee built log homes that kept out the cold and snow in winter.

A famous Cherokee named Sequoyah (sih KWOI uh) invented a system for writing the Cherokee language. Once people learned the 86 symbols, they could read and write the language.

TEKS
1.A, 1.B, 2.A, 2.B, 2.C, 3.A, 4.B, 15.A, 15.B

...ge. Once people learned the 86 symbo... they could read and write the language.

2. **Main Idea and Details** **Describe** how the Cherokee created a new community.

Target Reading Skills

The worktext enables you to practice important **Target Reading Skills**—essential skills you'll need when reading informational texts. Reinforce your ELA TEKS during the social studies block of time.

realize Go online at: www.PearsonTexas.com

Every lesson is supported by digital activities, myStory Videos, vocabulary activities, and myStory Book on Tikatok.

Leveled Readers

Engaging leveled readers are available in print and digital formats on Realize.

Digital Activities

Every lesson includes a **Digital Activity** that helps support the Big Idea.

UNDERSTAND

Assess TEKS and demonstrate understanding.

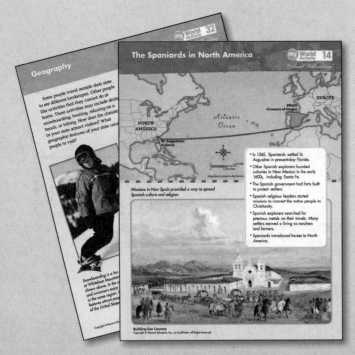

myWorld Activities

Work together in small groups on activities that range from mapping, graphing, and role playing, to read-alouds and analyzing primary sources. Digital versions of innovative hands-on activities for each chapter can be found on Realize.

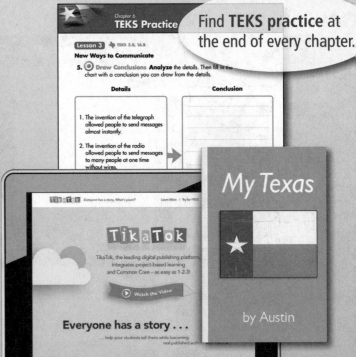

Find **TEKS practice** at the end of every chapter.

myStory Book

The **myStory Book** final writing activity gives you the exciting opportunity to write and illustrate your own digital book. Go to **www.Tikatok.com/myWorldSocialStudies** to learn more.

PEARSON realize Go online at: www.PearsonTexas.com | Every lesson is supported by digital activities, myStory Videos, vocabulary activities, and myStory Book on Tikatok.

Celebrating Texas and the Nation

Our Communities

PEARSON realize Go online at:
www.PearsonTexas.com

▶ **Interactive eText**

▶ **Big Question Activity**
What makes a good community?

▶ **myStory Video**
Different Communities: Exploring
Nearby Communities

▶ **Vocabulary Preview**

▶ **Lesson Introduction**

▶ **Digital Skill Lessons**
Generalize
Latitude and Longitude

▶ **Digital Got it? Activity**

▶ **Vocabulary Review**

▶ **myStory Book on Tikatok**
www.tikatok.com/
myWorldSocialStudies

▶ **Chapter Tests**

? **What makes a good community?**

A suburban street

Texas

Our Environment

Chapter 2

How do we interact with our planet?

Go online at:
www.PearsonTexas.com

- ▶ **Interactive eText**
- ▶ **Big Question Activity**
  How do we interact with our planet?
- ▶ **myStory Video**
  Jacques-Ives Cousteau: Underwater Adventurer
- ▶ **Vocabulary Preview**
- ▶ **Lesson Introduction**
- ▶ **Digital Skill Lessons**
  Interpret Maps
  Cause and Effect
- ▶ **Digital Got it? Activity**
- ▶ **Vocabulary Review**
- ▶ **myStory Book on Tikatok**
  www.tikatok.com/
  myWorldSocialStudies
- ▶ **Chapter Tests**

Jack rabbit

Communities Build a Nation

How does our past affect our present?

PEARSON
realize **Go online at:**
www.PearsonTexas.com

▶ **Interactive eText**

▶ **Big Question Activity**
How does our past affect our present?

▶ **myStory Video**
Mission San Luis: A Multicultural Community

▶ **Vocabulary Preview**

▶ **Lesson Introduction**

▶ **Digital Skill Lessons**
Sequence
Timelines

▶ **Digital Got it? Activity**

▶ **Vocabulary Review**

▶ **myStory Book on Tikatok**
www.tikatok.com/
myWorldSocialStudies

▶ **Chapter Tests**

An early American flag

Texas

Chapter 4

U.S. Government

PEARSON realize Go online at:
www.PearsonTexas.com

- ▶ Interactive eText
- ▶ Big Question Activity
  Why do we have government?
- ▶ myStory Video
  George Washington: America's
  First President
- ▶ Vocabulary Preview
- ▶ Lesson Introduction
- ▶ Digital Skill Lessons
  Summarize
  Compare Viewpoints
- ▶ Digital Got it? Activity
- ▶ Vocabulary Review
- ▶ myStory Book on Tikatok
  www.tikatok.com/
  myWorldSocialStudies
- ▶ Chapter Tests

Mount Rushmore

Texas

Chapter

5

Citizenship

Go online at:
www.PearsonTexas.com

- ▶ **Interactive eText**
- ▶ **Big Question Activity**
  How can I participate?
- ▶ **myStory Video**
  Volunteering: Mentor, Tutor, Friend
- ▶ **Vocabulary Preview**
- ▶ **Lesson Introduction**
- ▶ **Digital Skill Lessons**
  Conflict and Resolution
  Fact and Opinion
- ▶ **Digital Got it? Activity**
- ▶ **Vocabulary Review**
- ▶ **myStory Book on Tikatok**
  www.tikatok.com/
  myWorldSocialStudies
- ▶ **Chapter Tests**

THE BIG ? How can I participate?

People helping others in their community

A Growing Nation

 How does life change throughout history?

Go online at:
www.PearsonTexas.com

- ▶ **Interactive eText**
- ▶ **Big Question Activity**
  How does life change throughout history?
- ▶ **myStory Video**
  Benjamin Franklin: A Man Who Changed History
- ▶ **Vocabulary Preview**
- ▶ **Lesson Introduction**
- ▶ **Digital Skill Lessons**
  Primary and Secondary Sources
  Draw Conclusions
- ▶ **Digital Got it? Activity**
- ▶ **Vocabulary Review**
- ▶ **myStory Book on Tikatok**
  www.tikatok.com/
  myWorldSocialStudies
- ▶ **Chapter Tests**

Henry Ford's Model T car

Texas

Chapter

7

Working in Our Communities

PEARSON realize **Go online at:**
www.PearsonTexas.com

- ▶ **Interactive eText**

- ▶ **Big Question Activity**
  How do people get what they need?

- ▶ **myStory Video**
  Farmers Market: Meet Me at Third and Fairfax

- ▶ **Vocabulary Preview**

- ▶ **Lesson Introduction**

- ▶ **Digital Skill Lessons**
  Main Idea and Details
  Line Graphs

- ▶ **Digital Got it? Activity**

- ▶ **Vocabulary Review**

- ▶ **myStory Book on Tikatok**
  www.tikatok.com/
  myWorldSocialStudies

- ▶ **Chapter Tests**

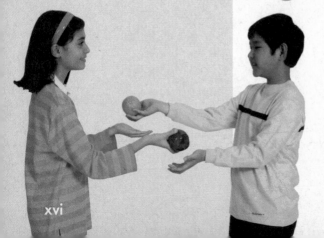

Friends exchanging fruit

Celebrating Our Communities

How is culture shared?

PEARSON **realize** **Go online at:**
www.PearsonTexas.com

▶ **Interactive eText**

▶ **Big Question Activity**
How is culture shared?

▶ **myStory Video**
Joseph Bruchac: Storyteller

▶ **Vocabulary Preview**

▶ **Lesson Introduction**

▶ **Digital Skill Lessons**
Compare and Contrast
Research

▶ **Digital Got it? Activity**

▶ **Vocabulary Review**

▶ **myStory Book on Tikatok**
www.tikatok.com/
myWorldSocialStudies

▶ **Chapter Tests**

A cultural celebration

Keys to Good Writing

The Writing Process

Good writers follow steps when they write. Here are five steps that will help you become a good writer!

Prewrite
- Choose a topic that you like.
- Gather details about your topic.

Draft
- Get all your ideas down on paper.
- Don't worry about making it perfect.

Share
- Share your writing with others.

Revise
- Review your writing and share it with a friend.
- Look for the traits of good writing.
- Change parts that are unclear or incomplete.

Edit
- Check your spelling, capitalization, and punctuation.
- Make a final copy.

The Writing Traits

Good writers look at six qualities of their writing to make it the best work possible.

Ideas	Ideas are your thoughts and the message you want to share. Choose ideas that are interesting to you.
Organization	Organization means you put your thoughts in order. Make your writing and your ideas easy to follow.
Voice	Voice means your writing sounds natural. Write as if you were telling someone your story.
Word Choice	Word choice means you choose your words carefully. Make a clear picture for your readers.
Sentence Flow	Sentence flow means your writing is easy to read. Use sentences of different lengths and with different beginnings.
Conventions	Conventions are the rules of writing, such as spelling, capitalization, and punctuation. Correct any errors you find.

21st Century Learning Online Tutor

You can go online to www.PearsonTexas.com to practice the skills listed below.
These are skills that will be important to you throughout your life.
After you complete each skill tutorial online, check it off here in your worktext.

◉ Target Reading Skills

- ☐ Main Idea and Details
- ☐ Cause and Effect
- ☐ Classify and Categorize
- ☐ Fact and Opinion
- ☐ Draw Conclusions
- ☐ Generalize
- ☐ Compare and Contrast
- ☐ Sequence
- ☐ Summarize

Collaboration and Creativity Skills

- ☐ Solve Problems
- ☐ Work in Cooperative Teams
- ☐ Resolve Conflict
- ☐ Generate New Ideas

Graph Skills

- ☐ Interpret Graphs
- ☐ Create Charts
- ☐ Interpret Timelines

Map Skills

- ☐ Use Longitude and Latitude
- ☐ Interpret Physical Maps
- ☐ Interpret Economic Data on Maps
- ☐ Interpret Cultural Data on Maps

Critical Thinking Skills

- ☐ Compare Viewpoints
- ☐ Use Primary and Secondary Sources
- ☐ Identify Bias
- ☐ Make Decisions
- ☐ Predict Consequences

Media and Technology Skills

- ☐ Conduct Research
- ☐ Use the Internet Safely
- ☐ Analyze Images
- ☐ Evaluate Media Content
- ☐ Deliver an Effective Presentation

Celebrate Freedom

TEKS 10.A, 11.A, 11.B, 11.C, 17.E, 18.B

Vocabulary

constitution

segregate

The United States of America has always been a nation that has fought for and celebrated freedom. Before it was a free nation, the United States was made up of 13 British colonies. Many people in the colonies did not like how the British government treated them.

The Declaration of Independence

In 1775, the colonies began a war with Great Britain. A group of leaders from each of the 13 colonies met and decided to write a formal statement to declare freedom from British rule.

Thomas Jefferson wrote the Declaration of Independence. He listed the reasons why the colonies should break away from Great Britain. He also listed the rights all people have and explained how the government protects those rights. The Declaration of Independence was approved on July 4, 1776. Today, Americans celebrate Independence Day on July 4.

1. **Identify** and underline the rights of all people as listed in the Declaration of Independence. **Discuss** with a partner what those rights mean to you.

"We hold these Truths to be self-evident, that all Men are created equal, that they are endowed by their Creator with certain unalienable Rights, that among these are Life, Liberty and the Pursuit of Happiness— That to secure these Rights, Governments are instituted among Men, deriving their just Powers from the Consent of the Governed."

Read the passage from the Declaration of Independence aloud.

1

The United States Constitution

The United States Constitution explains how our national government is set up. A **constitution** is a written plan for a government. Our constitution also lists the rights and freedoms of United States citizens. The first three words of the Constitution are "We the People."

United States Constitution

The Bill of Rights

The first ten amendments to the Constitution are called the Bill of Rights. They are the basic rights and freedoms of all American citizens. These rights include freedom of speech, religion, and the press. Other rights guarantee citizens the right to a fair and speedy trial with a jury of their peers.

2. **Explain** why the Declaration of Independence, the United States Constitution, and the Bill of Rights are important to United States citizens.

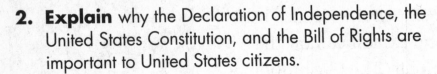

This boy is singing "The Star-Spangled Banner." It is a patriotic song that shows love for freedom and our country.

Sing About Freedom

Patriotic songs are songs that celebrate our nation. Some celebrate our freedom.

- Explain what freedom means to you.
- Write a song about freedom.
- Perform your song for your class.

Understanding Civic Responsibility

Civic responsibilities are the actions citizens take to participate in their government or community. Good citizens discuss and read about important issues. They serve on juries and vote for leaders. After elections, good citizens send e-mails or speak to leaders to thank them for taking action on an issue or to remind them to follow through on a promise made before an election. When citizens take these actions, they make our country strong. Below are some characteristics of good citizenship.

- ☐ Being truthful and trustworthy
- ☐ Working toward justice for all citizens
- ☐ Working toward equality for all citizens
- ☐ Showing respect for yourself and others
- ☐ Showing responsibility in daily life
- ☐ Educating yourself about issues
- ☐ Holding elected leaders to their word
- ☐ Serving on a jury
- ☐ Voting for government officials

3. **Compile** a classroom list of ways to respectfully hold public officials to their word.

4. Explain why the actions in the checklist, such as serving on a jury, are important.

   ....

   ....

5. **Discuss** with a partner an issue that is important in your community. How could you educate yourselves about the issue?

Helen Keller

Helen Keller was a citizen who worked for justice for all people. She was born in 1880 in Alabama. She was sick as a child. That sickness caused her to be blind and deaf. Anne Sullivan worked with Keller to teach her how to communicate. Later, Keller went to schools to learn to speak and to read, using Braille.

Keller wrote about and worked for better treatment of and justice for the blind and deaf. She helped improve the lives of many people.

Ruby Bridges

Ruby Bridges was born in 1954 in Mississippi. At the time, schools in the South were segregated. To **segregate** is to separate. African Americans had to go to different schools.

When Bridges was six years old, she was chosen to attend an all-white school. Many people protested as she walked to school. Bridges was the only African American student in her class. Bridges's courage and actions helped end segregation.

Good citizens like these women live in your community and your state. You can use word processing software to write about them and computer technology to make visuals. If you draw a picture or take a photo, you can scan it.

6. Use the Internet to **research** a person in your community or state who is a good citizen. Use computer software to make a picture that shows how that person is a good citizen.

Helen Keller

Ruby Bridges

What Makes a Hero?

Heroes are people who bravely help others. Many are normal people who do extraordinary things.

Vocabulary

chaplains

entrepreneur

Military Heroes

Many heroes serve in the military. These members of the Army, Navy, Air Force, Marines, and Coast Guard take risks to protect our freedoms.

During World War II, four chaplains, Lt. George Fox, Lt. Alexander Goode, Lt. Clark Poling, and Lt. John Washington, served aboard the U.S.A.T. *Dorchester.* **Chaplains** are religious leaders who support people in the military. On February 3, 1945, their ship was hit by a German torpedo.

The Four Chaplains

The men, now known as the Four Chaplains, guided wounded men to rescue boats. Each chaplain gave his life jacket to another man because there were not enough. The chaplains died when the ship sank. For their heroic deeds, the president awarded them a special medal of heroism.

To learn more about events or people in history, such as the Four Chaplains, you can look at illustrations. The details in illustrations and other visuals can enhance what you read and add to your understanding.

7. **Identify** the heroic deeds of the Four Chaplains. **Examine** the illustration to **analyze** why their actions were heroic deeds. **Discuss** with a partner.

First Responders

First responders are community heroes. First responders are police, firefighters, and emergency medical technicians, or EMTs. They are often the first people who come to help during an emergency or after an accident.

Police officers, firefighters, and EMTs have many responsibilities. They help others and keep people safe. Police officers make sure people follow the laws. Firefighters put out fires in the community. EMTs give medical help to people during an emergency. They may also take injured people to a hospital. First responders sometimes visit schools and other community centers to teach people about safety.

Some first responders teach bicycle safety.

Sometimes first responders are injured or killed while helping others. In April 2013, a fertilizer plant in West, Texas, exploded. Fourteen people died in the explosion. Twelve of them were first responders.

8. **Identify** and **analyze** the heroic actions of first responders.

....

....

....

....

A first responder helps a woman to safety after a hurricane hit Galveston, Texas, in 2008.

Heroic Texans

Dr. Héctor Pérez García was a Texan hero. He was born in Mexico in 1914 but later moved to Texas. At this time, Mexican Americans were not always treated fairly. They went to separate schools. Most Mexican Americans could only find work as farm laborers. They were not allowed to vote unless they paid a poll tax.

After graduating from medical school, García joined the army. He fought in World War II. When he came back to Texas, García began working for equal rights for Hispanics. García founded the American G.I. Forum. It started as a group to help Mexican American veterans but soon grew to help all Mexican Americans.

Héctor Pérez García

As a result of García's work, life for Mexican Americans improved. There were no more separate schools. Mexican Americans could vote without paying the poll tax.

Today, Texans continue to be heroes. For more than 20 years, the Texas State Board of Education has given an award called the Heroes for Children award. Fifteen people receive the award each year. Any citizen who works to support public schools and students in Texas can be nominated for the award.

The Texas Flag

9. **Compare** the heroic deeds of García and the deeds of a Heroes for Children award recipient.

....

....

....

United States astronauts are heroes, too. Many astronauts train at the Lyndon B. Johnson Space Center in Houston, Texas.

James Lovell Jr. was an astronaut. He joined the National Aeronautics and Space Administration, or NASA, in about 1963. At the time, NASA was working on sending an American to the moon. Lovell went on space flights and missions that helped NASA reach that goal.

In 1970, Lovell was the commander of the *Apollo 13* mission to the moon. During the mission an accident damaged the spacecraft. Lovell worked with NASA mission control in Houston to get his crew home safely.

John "Danny" Olivas is an engineer and astronaut. He grew up in El Paso, Texas. Olivas studied engineering in college and went to work for a chemical company. In 1998, NASA picked him to train to become an astronaut. Olivas went on many missions, including a mission to the International Space Station.

Ellen Ochoa was the first female Hispanic American astronaut. She went on four space flights and spent over 950 hours in space. Today, Ochoa is the director of the Johnson Space Center in Houston.

10. Compare the heroic deeds of James Lovell Jr., John Olivas, and Ellen Ochoa.

....

....

....

James Lovell Jr.

John "Danny" Olivas

Ellen Ochoa

National Heroes

Juliette Gordon Low helped young girls around the world. Low was born and grew up in Savannah, Georgia. Low decided that she wanted to make a difference and help others. She started the Girl Scouts.

In the Girl Scouts, girls learn outdoor skills, like hiking and camping, as well as homemaking skills. They also learn skills that will help them in the arts, sciences, and business.

Todd Beamer is a hero whose actions saved lives. On September 11, 2001, Beamer was among the passengers on United Flight 93. Terrorists hijacked the plane to try to crash it into the White House. The passengers realized that terrorists had hijacked the plane. When they made cell phone calls for help, they learned that other planes had crashed.

Beamer and other passengers bravely fought the terrorists to try to take control of the plane. The plane crashed in an empty field in Pennsylvania. Everyone on board the plane died when it crashed. The passengers of Flight 93 were hailed as heroes for their heroic actions.

Today, millions of girls enjoy learning new skills and helping others through the Girl Scouts.

11. Choose a hero. With a partner, **compare** the heroic actions of the hero you each chose.

....

....

....

Todd Beamer

Dana Vollmer is an Olympic gold medalist in swimming. She was born in Syracuse, New York. Later, her family moved to Granbury, Texas. Vollmer, at only 12 years old, was the youngest person to compete at the 2000 Olympic Trials. She did not make the team, but she did make the team four years later. In the 2012 Olympic games, she won three gold medals.

As a child, Vollmer suffered from heart problems. Even with that challenge, she always worked hard to reach her goals. Vollmer is a supporter of the American Heart Association. She has spoken at events to raise awareness about heart disease.

Doctors and nurses are often heroes to the people they take care of. The Heroes of Military Medicine award is given out every year. Each year a few people are honored with this award. Some of the honorees are military medical professionals who are still on active duty. These heroes are recognized for improving medicine and the health of service members, veterans, and their families.

12. Identify your own hero. Use a keyword search to find out more about your hero. **Create** a poster about your hero. Share your poster with a partner.

Dana Vollmer

A veteran visits the World War II Memorial in Washington, D.C.

Success in Science and Technology

Maria Mitchell was born in 1818. At the time, there were few colleges that women could attend.

Mitchell had a telescope that she used to study the night sky. In 1847, she was looking through her telescope and discovered a comet. A comet is an object made of rock and ice that orbits around the sun.

Mitchell became the first American female professional astronomer and only the second woman in the world to discover a comet. She made it possible for other women to become astronomers.

Bill Gates is a leader in computer technology. Gates started a company called Microsoft in college. His company became a leader in operating systems for computers and software, such as word processing, spreadsheets, and Web browsers.

Mitchell became a professor at Vassar College.

Gates is more than a technology leader. He also founded the Bill and Melinda Gates Foundation in 1994. Its mission is to help people live healthy and productive lives and get an education. Funding worldwide health programs and creating a foundation to build libraries helps achieve these goals.

13. Identify how Maria Mitchell and Bill Gates changed how we think about science and technology today.

The Bill and Melinda Gates Foundation works to improve health around the world.

....

....

....

....

Success in Business

Entrepreneurs decide what products or services to provide. An **entrepreneur** is a person who starts a business.

Milton Hershey was born in 1857. At first, Hershey started several candy businesses that failed. Finally, he started a new company called Hershey Chocolate. It became very successful. Later, Hershey founded the city of Hershey, Pennsylvania, for his workers.

Hershey started the Milton Hershey School for orphans.

Sam Walton believed in good customer service. Walton wanted to open stores in rural areas where there were few stores. In 1962, he opened his first Wal-Mart store. Today, there are thousands of Wal-Mart stores all over the world.

In 1963, Mary Kay Ash opened a small store in Dallas, Texas. She sold five products. Ash believed in treating her employees well. Her business grew in Texas and around the country. Today, Mary Kay Cosmetics sells more than 200 products.

Mary Kay Ash

When Wallace Amos was a child, he enjoyed baking cookies with his aunt. As an adult, Amos started baking and selling chocolate chip cookies. In 1975, he opened his first Famous Amos store. The business grew and became very successful.

14. Identify an entrepreneur who was successful in starting a business. **Explain** why this person was successful.

....

....

Wallace Amos

Research and Writing Skills
Organizing Information

TEKS 1.A, 3.A, 11.B, 14.A, 17.A, 17.B, 17.D, 17.E, 18.B, 18.C

Vocabulary

current events
physical geography

Writers use tables and charts to organize or categorize information. By using visuals, information can be categorized to show a sequence or similarities and differences.

Tables are often used to show information with numbers. A table is organized into rows and columns. Rows or columns in tables have labels to describe the information shown.

Some charts are organized like tables with rows and columns. A flowchart can be used to show the order of events. The table below shows information about civil rights leaders.

You can make your own charts and tables to organize information. You can create a table or chart on your computer. You can type in text and add photos, too.

15. Choose three people you read about on pages 5–12. **Research** these people. Then **create** a table or chart on the computer to categorize the information.

Name	Year Born	Place Born	Civil Rights Work
Héctor García	1914	Tamaulipas, Mexico	Worked to end segregation in Texas schools
Ruby Bridges	1954	Tylertown, Mississippi	Worked to end segregation in schools in the South

Writing and Word Processing

TEKS 18.B, 18.C

You can use word processing software to write a poem, story, essay, or report. This software makes it easy to edit your work. If you make a mistake, you can delete it. It's fast and easy.

Word processing software also has tools that help you change the margins, move the text, and use different font sizes and colors. You can also create tables, charts, and other graphics.

Use this checklist as you read what you wrote.

- ☐ Is your grammar correct? Did you use the correct form of the verb?
- ☐ Are all your sentences complete?
- ☐ Do all your sentences end with a period and your questions with a question mark?
- ☐ Did you use other punctuation, such as commas or quotation marks?
- ☐ Did you spell words correctly? Did you check commonly misspelled words such as *red* and *read*?
- ☐ Is your writing clear and easy to understand? Are any of your sentences too long?

16. Choose one of the people you researched in Question 15. **Write** a story about this person. **Create** your final draft using word processing software. Make sure you use correct grammar, spelling, sentence structure, and punctuation.

Researching Current Events

Current events are things that happen in the present, or now. You can research current events around the world, in our country, in Texas, and in your own community. You can use print, oral, visual, or Internet resources.

Resources such as reference materials include encyclopedias, dictionaries, almanacs, and atlases. They can be both print and electronic.

Books often have tools to help you find information in them. A table of contents lists the chapters or sections in a book and their page numbers. A glossary gives meanings of key terms. An index lists key terms and page numbers.

The best way to do research on the Internet is to use a keyword search in a search engine. The keywords should describe what you are looking for.

17. **Identify** and **research** a current event in your community and the world. Use print, electronic, visual, and oral resources. **Present** your findings on a poster. Give an oral report to your class about the current event.

Resources for Research			
Print	**Oral**	**Visual**	**Internet**
newspaper	community member interview	works of art	valid Web sites (look for sites ending with .gov, .edu, or .org)
books	museum tour guide	video	online dictionaries
magazines	speech	photographs	online encyclopedias

Understanding the Community and World

Physical geography refers to land, water, and other resources of an area. It includes climate, too. Physical geography plays an important role in communities here and around the world.

A community located in an area with snow and mountains might have businesses that sell ski supplies. Farming might be an important activity in a community that has a warm climate and flat land.

The western part of the state is a good area for farming and raising livestock, such as cows, sheep, and goats.

Buenos Aires, Argentina, is a port city. It is located near the Atlantic Ocean. The city's location makes it easy for goods to move in and out of the area.

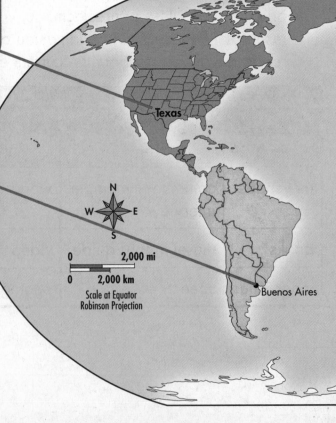

N
W   E
S

0   2,000 mi
0   2,000 km
Scale at Equator
Robinson Projection

Texas

Buenos Aires

Physical geography affects how people live. You can research these effects using print, oral, visual, and Internet resources. You can use library resources, talk to people who have traveled, and use keywords to do Internet searches. Use these methods to answer questions 18 and 19.

18. Research the geographic features of your community and a community in another state. **Organize** your findings in a Venn diagram.

19. Choose a part of the world you would like to visit. **Research** the physical geography of the area and how it affects daily life there. **Write** a journal entry from the point of view of someone who lives in or travels to that area.

In the Netherlands, some people ride bicycles rather than drive cars. As a result, cities in the Netherlands are building more bike lanes.

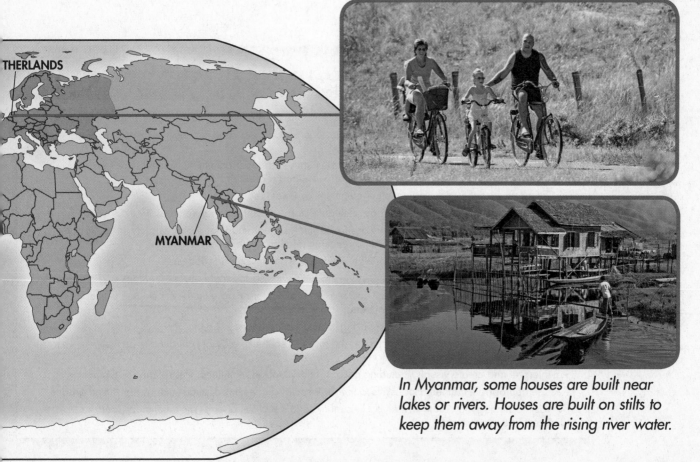

THERLANDS

MYANMAR

In Myanmar, some houses are built near lakes or rivers. Houses are built on stilts to keep them away from the rising river water.

Our Communities

What makes a good community?

Think about your community. Then write about people and places you see around you and what you do on a typical day in your community.

....

....

....

....

....

....

....

Texas Essential Knowledge and Skills

1.A Describe how individuals, events, and ideas have changed communities, past and present.

2.A Identify reasons people have formed communities, including a need for security, religious freedom, law, and material well-being.

2.B Identify ways in which people in the local community and other communities meet their needs for government, education, communication, transportation, and recreation.

2.C Compare ways in which various other communities meet their needs.

3.A Use vocabulary related to chronology, including past, present, and future times.

5.A Use cardinal and intermediate directions to locate places on maps and globes such as the Rocky Mountains, the Mississippi River, and Austin, Texas, in relation to the local community.

5.B Use a scale to determine the distance between places on maps and globes.

5.C Identify and use the compass rose, grid system, and symbols to locate places on maps and globes.

5.D Create and interpret maps of places and regions that contain map elements, including a title, compass rose, legend, scale, and grid system.

6.A Identify ways of earning, spending, saving, and donating money.

17.D Use various parts of a source, including the table of contents, glossary, and index as well as keyword Internet searches, to locate information.

17.E Interpret and create visuals, including graphs, charts, tables, timelines, illustrations, and maps.

17.F Use appropriate mathematical skills to interpret social studies information such as maps and graphs.

18.B Use technology to create written and visual materials such as poems, pictures, maps, and graphic organizers to express ideas.

Different Communities

Exploring Nearby Communities

my Story Video

"I guess I live in a suburban neighborhood!" says Casey. "I never really thought about the difference." Casey lives in Arizona. He has been learning a lot in school about different types of communities. Some are urban communities, or areas in large cities. Then there are suburban communities, or smaller towns that are located near large cities. Farther away in the countryside where there is a lot of open space, there are rural communities. Now that Casey has learned about all of these communities, he wants to see for himself what they are like.

The first stop on Casey's community tour of Arizona is an urban community. Casey loves the downtown area. "There's always something to do," he says as he walks downtown with his mother. Casey looks around and sees people shopping, going to work, visiting museums, and walking their dogs. There are so many tall buildings. It seems like there are buses, cars, taxis, and trains everywhere!

Casey visited three different types of communities in Arizona.

19

Casey enjoys looking at all of the tall buildings.

Suburban communities, like Chandler, Arizona, have many houses with yards and driveways.

Casey climbs on the playground equipment in Chandler, Arizona.

More than 1 million people live in this urban community. Casey understands why so many people enjoy living in the city. Everything is so close! There are also many ways to have fun. "When it's hot, I can cool off in the city fountains!"

The next stop on Casey's tour is Chandler, a suburb that is also his hometown. Chandler is very close to the city. It is only about 25 miles away. Almost 250,000 people live in Chandler. Many people like living there because it is very easy to travel into the city. There are nearby highways that lead right into the city, or people can take a bus or train. "When we go downtown, it doesn't take very long," Casey says, walking around his suburban neighborhood. "But staying close to home is fun, too."

The streets of Chandler are much different from the streets in the city. The buildings are not as close together, and there are not a lot of crowds. Only a few people are crossing the street. Some people are walking in and out of the small shops. Casey then notices some children riding their bicycles toward a park. As Casey and his mother walk toward the playground, he sees a family playing with their dog in their front yard. There is definitely a lot more space here to run around!

Some rural communities have farms with many animals, like horses.

Casey and his grandpa like taking walks around the farm.

The final stop on Casey's tour is a rural community. This community is in the countryside, where towns are very small. Fewer than 1,500 people live there. Many people live and work on farms. People in cities and suburbs depend on these farms for fresh fruits and vegetables. "My grandpa lives in a rural community," says Casey. "He has the best peaches I've ever tasted! And lots of horses I can pet."

Casey and his grandpa take a walk toward the horses. As he sees the horses in the distance, Casey is amazed by all of the open space. Many people enjoy living here because there is so much peace and quiet. "I have more elbow room," says Casey's grandpa. "I like to relax and slow down out here." But his grandpa does enjoy visiting the suburbs or the city every now and then, too.

So, which community does Casey like best? "I liked touring all of these communities," says Casey. "They all have something special. They all have what it takes to make a good community!"

Casey always enjoys petting the horses on his grandpa's farm.

Think About It Based on this story, do you think you would like to live in a community different from your own? As you read the chapter ahead, think about what makes your community special.

PEARSON
realize Go online to access your interactive digital lesson.

21

What Makes a Community?

Envision It!

These are pictures of the same community. Think about which picture is from the past and which is from the presen

Communities near Lake Michigan have water resources for fishing.

Where do you live? That's easy! You live in a community. A **community** is a place where people live, work, and have fun together. Communities are alike in many ways. People in communities help each other. They care about the safety of their communities. They follow laws, or rules, to make their communities safe places to live, work, and play. Many people have jobs or businesses. For fun, people join clubs and sports teams, go shopping, and see movies.

Why Communities Are Formed

People have settled in communities for many reasons. Some communities were formed so that people could be safe and have rules to follow. As new areas of our country were settled, people created laws and set up governments. Austin was formed to be the capital of the Republic of Texas. Other communities were formed so that people could be free to practice their religion. The Pilgrims came to this land to practice their religion freely.

People have also formed communities looking for material well-being, or the chance to live comfortably. Some settlers settled communities

UNLOCK
THE BIG
?
I will know ways in which communities are the same and different.

Vocabulary

community   mineral
location   diverse
natural   culture
  resource
region

Label the picture from the past with a 1. Label the picture from the present with a 2.

because of their **location**, or where they were. They chose areas with good **natural resources**, or something in nature that is useful to people. Having bodies of water nearby offered food and enjoyment. Farmers settled where there was good soil to help them grow crops and raise animals.

Trees were also an important land resource. People used trees for building homes, schools, and stores. As people kept building, their communities continued to grow. All of these things contributed to their material well-being.

TEKS
1.A, 2.A, 2.B, 3.A, 6.A, 17.D

1. ◎ **Main Idea and Details** **Identify** two more details to support the main idea. Then fill in the chart.

> **People settle in communities where there are good natural resources for their material well-being.**

	Farmers can work in communities that have good soil.	

Communities in Regions

Communities have been settled in all 50 states of the United States. Some states are located in the North, the South, the East, or the West. Some states are in the middle of our country, too! Different groups of states are located in different regions. A **region** is an area with common features that set it apart from other places.

Some states are located in regions where there are many mountains. The Rocky Mountains are some of the highest in the United States. People like to settle near the mountains because of some of the activities they can enjoy there. They can ski and sled in winter. In summer, they can go camping, hiking or mountain climbing.

A community in the mountains

Beach communities can be found in some regions along the shoreline, near the coasts. Some people settle there because they enjoy swimming or surfing. Others settle near the shoreline because of jobs they can do there. People can work in restaurants that serve the seafood from the ocean.

Some regions have communities located near mineral resources such as coal or iron. A **mineral** is a resource that does not come from an animal or a plant. Businesses that produce items made with minerals are located in these communities.

A community near a beach

24

People in Communities

People all over the world form communities. Many people in communities have jobs to earn money. Some work as doctors, teachers, car mechanics, police officers, or mail carriers. When people are not working, they enjoy different activities. People might participate in their favorite activities, such as gardening, riding bicycles, or playing a sport. Others might try new activities they have never done before.

The Powwow is a dance from the American Indian culture.

Many communities have **diverse**, or different, cultures. **Culture** is the way of life of a group of people. Some communities hold festivals, parades, and fairs to honor these cultures. San Marcos, Texas, is proud of its diverse community. Every year it hosts the Sacred Springs Powwow. This celebrates American Indian culture, through food, dancing, and the arts.

2. Fill in the chart with examples that **describe** your community.

My Community

Land Resources	Water Resources	Work	Activities

Communities Change Over Time

Communities change over time. What was once an open field may be a parking lot in the present, or today. A small town could grow into a big city as more people settle there. New and different businesses open. A shop that sold farm supplies in the past may now be a computer store.

One thing has not changed over time: people in every kind of community want to make the community a better place. They might work at food banks or pick up litter to improve their communities.

You can find out how your community was settled and how it has changed. Read about your community. Compare and contrast visuals, such as images or maps, from the past and present. Interview people who have lived in your community for a long time.

3. **Compare** the maps. **Describe** how events or ideas may have changed the Capitol area from the past to the present.

....

....

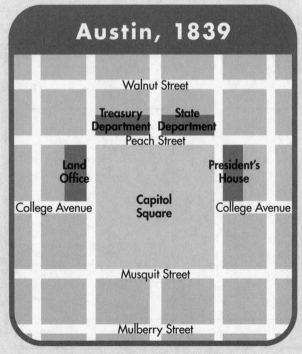

Capitol Square, Austin, Texas

Capitol Complex, Austin, Texas

4. ◉ **Generalize Identify** one fact that supports this generalization: Individuals in a community have ideas to help make it a better place.

....

....

....

....

Got it?

🔸 TEKS 1.A, 2.B, 6.A, 17.D

5. ◉ **Main Idea and Details Describe** two ways that communities can grow and change over time.

....

....

....

....

6. ❓ **Identify** three jobs people in your community have to earn money. **Describe** how these jobs make your community a better place.

my Story Ideas

....

....

....

7. Use a keyword search to **research** communities with green spaces in Texas. Use the information you find to make a video or podcast that describes how technology and programs have changed these communities.

Generalize

A generalization is a broad statement that tells how different ideas or facts are alike in some way. Look at the chart below and read the three facts. Each fact tells a different way people use trees to meet their needs. Now read the generalization. The generalization is a statement made about all of the facts. It tells how the facts are alike: people use trees to meet their needs.

Fact

People use trees to get food they need.

Fact

People use trees for fuel they need.

Fact

People use trees to build houses they need.

Generalization
People use trees to meet their needs.

Learning Objective

I will know how to generalize based on facts.

 TEKS

SS 2.B Identify ways in which people in the local community and other communities meet their needs for government, education, communication, transportation, and recreation.

ELA 2.B Locate facts and details about stories and other texts and support answers with evidence.

ELA 13.A Identify the details or facts that support the main idea.

 **Try it!**

Read the newspaper article about Maple City.
Then answer the questions.

Maple City News

Soccer season starts this Saturday in Maple City! The town just finished building a new soccer field. Now there are two large soccer fields: one for the girls' team and one for the boys' team. Since there are two fields, each team has enough time to practice. People in the community also raised money to pay for new equipment and uniforms for both teams. Maple City is a great place to play soccer!

A soccer game in Maple City

---

1. **Identify** and underline two facts about soccer in Maple City.

2. **Identify** and circle the generalization in the article that tells how these facts are alike.

3. Write three facts to support this generalization: My community is a great place to live.

....

....

....

....

PEARSON realize Go online to access your interactive digital lesson.

29

Where Communities Are Located

Look at the map. Draw a line to show how the bus gets to the library.

People can use maps or a globe to find a community's location. Satellites in space take pictures of Earth that are used by global positioning systems (GPS) that help drivers find places.

Maps and Globes

A globe is a three-dimensional model of Earth. It shows the land and the oceans. Because a globe is shaped like a ball, you can only see one half of it at a time.

Maps are two-dimensional images of Earth. Some maps show the whole Earth. Some maps only show parts of Earth. There are many kinds of maps used for different purposes. Some maps show you where different streets are. Other maps show you where different types of landforms are.

When you take the round surface of Earth and make it flat on a map, distortion happens. When something is distorted, it looks different from its real size and shape.

1. Look at a map of the United States and a globe. **Locate** Texas on both.

....

We live here!

30

Vocabulary

cardinal direction
intermediate direction
symbol
relative location
absolute location
hemisphere

Elements of Maps and Globes

TEKS
5.A, 5.B, 5.C, 5.D, 17.E, 17.F, 18.B

Maps and globes have many elements. The title of a map tells what the map shows. The title of the map on this page is Texas. Compass roses show directions on both maps and globes. The compass rose on this map shows **cardinal directions:** north (N), south (S), east (E), and west (W). It also shows intermediate directions. **Intermediate directions** are northeast (NE), southeast (SE), northwest (NW), and southwest (SW).

Maps and globes can have symbols, too. Each **symbol** stands for something. The key, or legend, explains what the symbols stand for. A scale shows how to measure the real distance between two places on a map or globe.

2. **Identify** and circle the map elements. Then **identify** the same elements on a globe.

3. **Locate** and **label** your community on the map. Then find it on a globe. Use cardinal and intermediate directions to write how to get from your community to Austin, Texas.

Texas

Amarillo

0 · · · · · 200 mi
0 · · · · · 200 km

Lubbock

Fort Worth · Dallas

Odessa

El Paso

Austin ★

Houston

San Antonio ·

Galveston

LEGEND
★ Capital city
· City

Laredo

Gulf of Mexico

South Padre Island

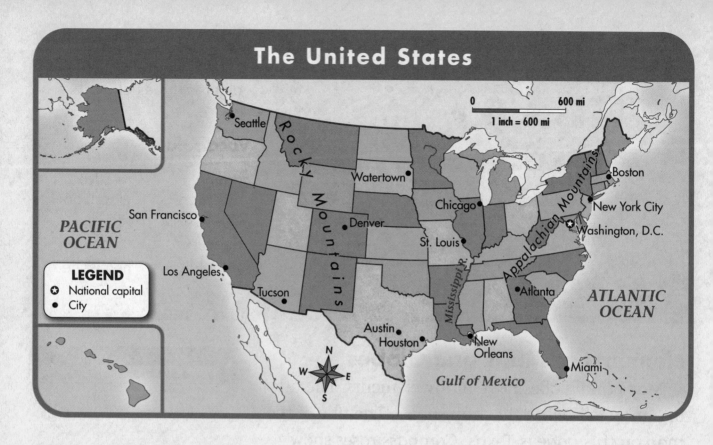

The United States

LEGEND
- ✪ National capital
- • City

PACIFIC OCEAN

ATLANTIC OCEAN

Gulf of Mexico

0 ——— 600 mi
1 inch = 600 mi

Rocky Mountains

Appalachian Mountains

Mississippi R.

Seattle, San Francisco, Los Angeles, Tucson, Denver, Watertown, Chicago, St. Louis, Austin, Houston, New Orleans, Atlanta, Miami, Boston, New York City, Washington, D.C.

Measuring Distance

A scale allows you to measure the real distances between places on a map or globe. Here's how. First, put a ruler or tape measure just below the line on a map or globe scale. Find out how many inches long the line is. Then, read the number on the map or globe scale to tell how many miles 1 inch stands for. Next, use the ruler or tape measure to determine the distance between the two cities. Then, count the number of inches between them. Finally, do the math. On the map, 1 inch stands for 600 miles. If there are 2 inches between cities, multiply 600 miles per inch by 2 inches. The actual distance between cities is 1,200 miles.

4. **Use** the map scale to **determine** the distance between Houston and Washington, D.C. Then find the scale on a globe. **Determine** the distance between Austin and New York City on the globe.

Grid Maps

You can use a grid to find places on a map. A grid is a pattern of lines that forms squares. Each row of squares on a grid map has a letter, and each column of squares has a number.

Look at the grid map of San Antonio, Texas. It shows old buildings and monuments called landmarks, museums, and other places in the city. You can use the grid to help find these places. Put your finger on the letter C. Then move your finger to the right into Box 1. The location of the River Walk is C1.

5. Locate the Alamo. ....

Absolute and Relative Location

You can describe the location of a place in two ways. You can use the directions in the compass rose. You can say that San Antonio is southwest of Austin. This is the **relative location,** or a description of where a place is in relation to other places. To describe the **absolute location,** you tell exactly where a place is located on Earth. You can find the absolute location of a place by using latitude and longitude on a map or globe. These imaginary lines create a grid on a globe. The equator is a line of latitude that divides Earth into two parts, or **hemispheres,** called the Northern and Southern hemispheres.

6. Use the map on the previous page and a globe to **describe** to a partner how to **locate** the Rocky Mountains and the Mississippi River in relation to your community. Use cardinal and intermediate directions.

San Antonio

LEGEND
- Attraction
- 35 Interstate highway
- 368 State highway

Fort Sam Houston

San Antonio Zoo

Witte Museum

River Walk

San Antonio Museum of Art

The Alamo

Tower of the Americas

Regions Maps

A region is an area with common features that set it apart from other areas. The world is made up of different regions. A country can be made up of different regions, too. Cartographers use software to create maps of regions with the same elements they use to make maps of places: title, compass rose, legend, scale, and grid system. Look at the map below. It shows the five regions of the United States.

7. Read the title and use the legend to **locate** and circle the region that includes Texas.

8. **Plan** a trip to three regions and **draw** the route on the map. Use the scale to **measure** the distances and use the compass rose to **determine** the directions you would travel. **Write** the directions and distances on the route.

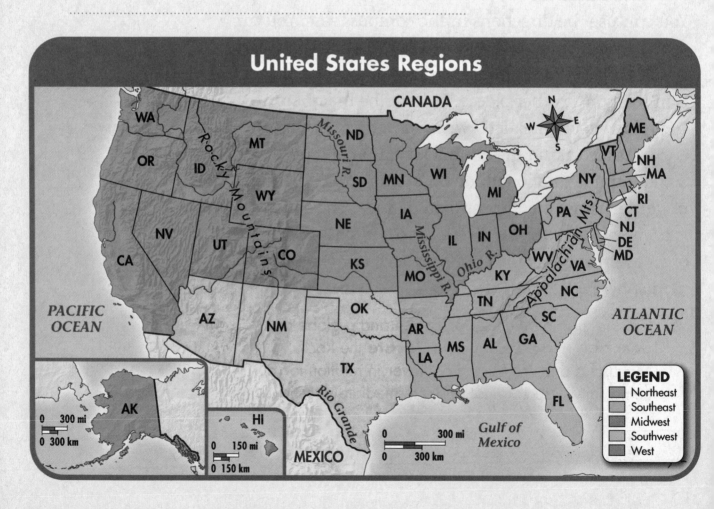

United States Regions

LEGEND
- Northeast
- Southeast
- Midwest
- Southwest
- West

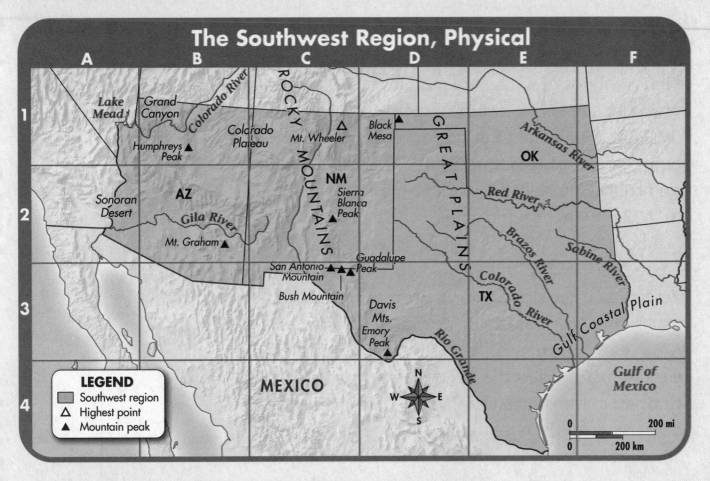

The Southwest Region, Physical

LEGEND
- Southwest region
- △ Highest point
- ▲ Mountain peak

Some maps of regions show the different places that make up the region. Others can show the geographic features of the region, such as mountains. The Grand Canyon is a well-known geographic feature in the Southwest. See if you can locate it on the map above.

9. **Use** the grid system and legend to **locate** the highest point in the Southwest region. ....
   Describe its location in relation to other geographic features.

   ....

   ....

   ....

10. **Create** a map of the Northeast region. Be sure to include map elements, including a title, compass rose, legend, scale, and grid system.

Different Types of Maps and Globes

As you have seen in this lesson, there are many kinds of maps and they are used for many different purposes. One type of map or globe is a political map or globe. A political map can show country and state boundaries, or borders. You can also find major cities and capitals on a political map. The maps on pages 31 and 32 are political maps.

Another type of map or globe is a physical map or globe. You can find valleys, mountains, plains, and deserts on a physical map. You can also find bodies of water, such as rivers, lakes, and oceans. Different colors are used on the map to show different land heights, or elevations. For example, valleys have lower elevations than mountains. Therefore, valleys are shaded in a different color than mountains. The map legend tells which colors show lower and higher elevations. When you read an elevation, it is read from a whole number at the bottom range shown on the legend to the whole number minus 1 at the top of the range. Find Austin on the map. It is shaded light green. That tells us that Austin has an elevation between 500 and 999 feet.

11. Think about a map you would like to create. **List** the title and the symbols you would add to the legend. **Describe** the other elements you would include.

....

....

....

Rocky Mountains

12. Locate and circle the region of Texas with the highest elevation. Then **determine** the distance between Austin and Lubbock using the scale.

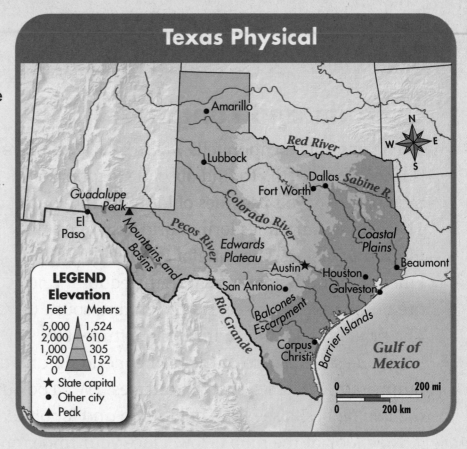

Texas Physical

LEGEND
Elevation

Feet	Meters
5,000	1,524
2,000	610
1,000	305
500	152
0	0

★ State capital
● Other city
▲ Peak

0   200 mi
0   200 km

Amarillo

Lubbock

Red River

Guadalupe Peak

El Paso

Dallas   Sabine R.

Fort Worth

Pecos River   Colorado River

Edwards Plateau

Mountains and Basins

Coastal Plains

Beaumont

Austin★   Houston

San Antonio   Galveston

Rio Grande

Balcones Escarpment

Corpus Christi

Barrier Islands

Gulf of Mexico

Got it?

TEKS 5.A, 5.D, 17.E, 18.B

13. Generalize Different maps are used for different purposes. Write a sentence **describing** what you learned that supports this generalization.

....

....

14. Suppose someone was looking for your community on a map. **Describe** the relative location of your community.

my Story Ideas

....

....

15. Use an online map-building tool to **create** a map of Texas. Include all map elements, such as title, compass rose, legend, grid, and scale. Show your town or city, the state capital, and at least three physical features that are important to the state.

Latitude and Longitude

The absolute location tells where exactly a place is located on Earth. To find absolute location on a map or globe, you use lines of latitude and longitude. These imaginary lines form a grid system on maps and globes. The equator is a line of latitude. Lines of latitude start at zero at the equator and are numbered in degrees north (N) and south (S). The prime meridian is a line of longitude. Lines of longitude start at zero at the prime meridian and are numbered in degrees east (E) and west (W). Look at the two globes to see lines of latitude and longitude.

Now look at the map below. Place your finger on New Orleans. Now look to see which lines of latitude and longitude are nearest to the city. That is New Orleans's absolute location. It is 30° N and 90° W.

Latitude

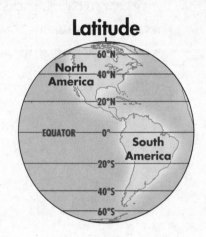

Longitude

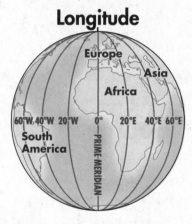

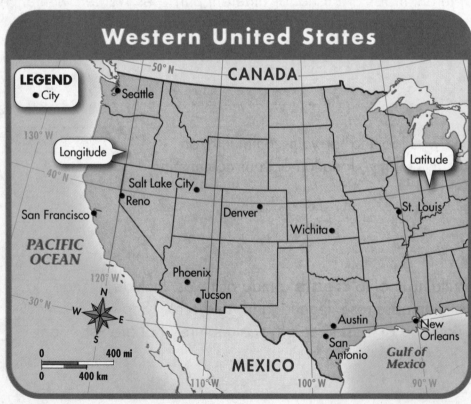

Western United States

TEKS

SS 5.C Identify and use the grid system to locate places on maps and globes.
SS 17.E Interpret visuals, including maps.
ELA 15.B Locate and use specific information in graphic features of text.

Try it!

Review the map below. Then answer the questions.

1. **Locate** and circle the city on the map below that is closest to 30° N and 80° W.

2. **Identify** which lines of latitude and longitude you would cross if you traveled along the route from Boston to Little Rock.

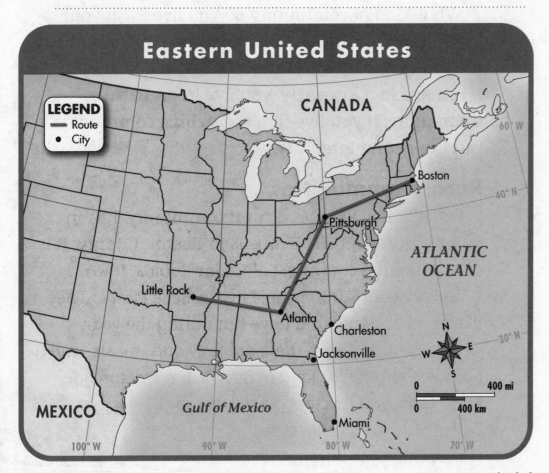

Eastern United States

3. **Identify** which lines make up the grid system on maps and globes.

4. On a globe, **determine** whether Dallas or Houston is closer to 30° N latitude.

PEARSON **realize** Go online to access your interactive digital lesson.

39

Three Types of Communities

What kind of community do you live in? If your community is in the countryside where there is plenty of open space, then you live in a **rural** community. If you live in a large city, you live in an **urban** community. If you live in a **suburban** community, you live near a large city.

Rural Communities

Belle Plaine, Iowa, is a rural community. It is in the countryside. Belle Plaine is in Benton County. It is about 40 miles southwest of Cedar Rapids, Iowa.

Today about 3,000 people live in Belle Plaine. They like to get together and have fun during the year. On the Fourth of July, there are fireworks, music, and a parade. One special kind of parade is a tractorcade. More than 500 tractors parade through Belle Plaine and other rural communities in Iowa!

A tractorcade moves through a rural community.

40

UNLOCK THE BIG ?

I will know what rural, suburban, and urban communities are like.

Vocabulary

rural
urban
suburban

Rural communities have their own mayors and other government officials to make and enforce laws, or rules, for their community. Local governments also provide services, such as schools, for their towns. Some towns have their own schools, while others share schools. Many rural communities have the technology to connect to the Internet quickly or use cell phones, but others do not. People in these communities use slower dial-up phone lines to connect to the Internet. Rural communities have local newspapers that share information.

Some people in rural communities are farmers. Farmers grow crops like corn that people in larger towns and cities depend on.

People in rural communities depend on other communities, too. They travel to suburban or urban communities to buy the things that they need. In some places, people can travel by bus. In others, people need to drive their own cars.

TEKS
2.B, 2.C, 17.D, 17.E

1. **Describe** what you might see in a rural community.

....

....

You often see farms in rural communities.

Suburban Communities

   Alamo Heights, Texas, is a suburban community. It is surrounded by the city of San Antonio. Today about 7,300 people live in Alamo Heights.

   In Alamo Heights and other suburban communities, there are many houses with yards lining the streets. You might also expect to see a library, a post office, schools, stores, a movie theater, and parks there. Take a short drive, and you will find a large shopping mall.

   Suburban communities have their own governments to make their local laws. People in suburban communities are often proud of where they live. When there is litter on the streets of Alamo Heights, for example, people help clean it up. They cut the grass and clean streets, just like people in other suburban communities do.

People work together to keep their community clean.

There are plenty of activities to keep children busy in suburban communities. They can go for a swim at the community pool or play basketball in a local park. They can also join a soccer or baseball team.

People in suburban communities get news about their town from local newspapers, on the Internet, or on television.

Many people who live in suburban communities work in a nearby city. Some people who live in Alamo Heights work in San Antonio. While some drive their cars or trucks on busy highways, others choose to take an express bus to work.

People began moving to suburban communities to get away from the crowded cities. New highways helped suburban communities grow. People could get to the city safely and quickly, so living in the suburbs became more popular.

2. ⊙ **Generalize** **Identify** and list two facts that support this generalization: There are many activities that children in suburban communities can enjoy.

....

....

....

People in suburbs use highways to get to and from the city.

Urban Communities

Many people live, work, and play in urban communities like San Francisco, California. About 800,000 people live in San Francisco. Most live in apartment buildings and row houses. Row houses share walls.

In San Francisco and other cities, people work in tall buildings, or skyscrapers. Many people from suburban communities travel to cities to work. Once inside the city, people can use public transportation to get around. The city of San Francisco has cable cars. Other cities may use subways.

There are many things to do for fun in a city. People can shop in stores or visit museums. In urban areas, people have access to technology. Internet and cell phones help make communication easier.

San Francisco

Features of Communities

	Rural	Suburban	Urban
Location	in the countryside	near a large city	in a large city
Population	small population	medium-sized population	large population
Buildings	farmhouses, barns	houses, shopping malls	apartment buildings, row houses, skyscrapers

Like other communities, an urban community has its own local government and schools. In a city, a mayor and a city council are elected to make laws.

3. ⊙ **Compare and Contrast Analyze** the chart on the previous page. Then underline the words in the chart that show how the population in each type of community is different.

TEKS 2.B, 2.C, 17.D

4. ⊙ **Generalize** Write a generalization about transportation in an urban community. Then **identify** two facts to support your generalization.

....

....

....

5. **Describe** the type of community you live in. **Explain** how your community is similar to and different from one of the other types of communities.

my Story Ideas

....

....

....

6. In this lesson, you learned what makes up different communities. **Use a keyword search** to **research** your community and the community of Fort Yukon, Alaska. **Compare** how each community meets its needs, such as education, government, and natural resources. Draw a Venn diagram comparing the two communities.

What Makes a Community?

1. Draw a picture that **describes** how a community can change over time.

Then   **Now**

2. Identify and write three reasons why people formed and settled communities.

....

....

....

Where Communities Are Located

3. Look at the political map below. **Identify** and underline the map scale. **Use the map legend** to **identify** and **locate** the state capital. Circle the capital. **Identify** the title of the map and draw a star next to it.

4. **Use** symbols to **locate** and **identify** two cities in North America on a globe.

....

5. **Describe** the relative location of your community using cardinal and intermediate directions to two other cities in Texas.

....

Lesson 3 ⭐ **TEKS 2.B, 2.C**

Three Types of Communities

6. **Compare** how the different types of communities meet their needs.

   ....

   ....

   ....

   ....

7. **List** three activities people can do for fun in a suburban community.

   ....

   ....

   ....

   ....

8. **Read** the question and **circle** the best answer.

   Identify one way people in communities meet their need for communication.

   A movie theaters

   B public transportation

   C local newspapers

   D highways

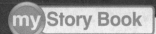
Go online to write and illustrate your own **myStory Book** using the **myStory Ideas** from this chapter.

 **What makes a good community?**

🔻 TEKS

SS 1.A

ELA 17

In this chapter, you have learned about communities and where they are located. People live in rural, suburban, and urban communities. In each type of community, people work together to make it a better place to live.

Think about your community. **Write** about what you can do to make it a better place to live.

....

....

....

....

Now **draw** a picture of people in your community who work to make it a better place to live.

Our Environment

How do we interact with our planet?

Think about your surroundings. Then **describe** the land and water features and the weather.

....

....

....

....

....

Texas Essential Knowledge and Skills

2.C Compare ways in which various other communities meet their needs.

4.A Describe and explain variations in the physical environment, including climate, landforms, natural resources, and natural hazards.

4.B Identify and compare how people in different communities adapt to or modify the physical environment in which they live such as deserts, mountains, wetlands, and plains.

4.C Describe the effects of physical processes such as volcanoes, hurricanes, and earthquakes in shaping the landscape.

4.D Describe the effects of human processes such as building new homes, conservation, and pollution in shaping the landscape.

4.E Identify and compare the human characteristics of various regions.

5.C Identify and use the compass rose, grid system, and symbols to locate places on maps and globes.

5.D Create and interpret maps of places and regions that contain map elements, including a title, compass rose, legend, scale, and grid system.

12.B Identify examples of actions individuals and groups can take to improve the community.

17.B Sequence and categorize information.

17.C Interpret oral, visual, and print material by identifying the main idea, distinguishing between fact and opinion, identifying cause and effect, and comparing and contrasting.

17.E Interpret and create visuals, including graphs, charts, tables, timelines, illustrations, and maps.

18.A Express ideas orally based on knowledge and experiences.

18.B Use technology to create written and visual material such as stories, poems, pictures, maps, and graphic organizers to express ideas.

18.C Use standard grammar, spelling, sentence structure, and punctuation.

19.A Use a problem-solving process to identify a problem, gather information, list and consider options, consider advantages and disadvantages, choose and implement a solution, and evaluate the effectiveness of the solution.

19.B Use a decision-making process to identify a situation that requires a decision, gather information, identify options, predict consequences, and take action to implement a decision.

Jacques-Yves Cousteau
Underwater Adventurer

my Story Video

People need oceans, lakes, and rivers to live. People rely on them for fresh drinking water, food, and transportation. Even though people have always used these bodies of water, few people knew much about what was beneath the surface of the water until the 1930s. Jacques-Yves Cousteau [zhahk eev koo STOH] changed that.

In the 1930s, Cousteau began to examine the sea life underwater. He put on his goggles, held his breath, and swam. However, Cousteau wanted to go deeper into the ocean. He also wanted to swim for longer periods of time. Cousteau worked with Émile Gagnan to make an underwater breathing machine called the Aqua-Lung™. It could be worn on a person's back while swimming. It allowed Cousteau to swim into deeper waters and breathe for longer periods of time.

Cousteau soon traveled to different oceans. He wanted to share what he found underwater. With help, he developed an underwater camera that could take pictures of what he saw.

Cousteau wore a diving suit and a breathing machine.

51

Cousteau helped develop underwater cameras so that he could film the wonders he found.

Cousteau even explored the water in and around Antarctica.

Cousteau felt it was important for people to learn about the plants and animals that are underwater. He wrote books and made films about his work. He also starred in a television series called *The Undersea World of Jacques Cousteau*. Cousteau started several research centers, too. He wanted more people to study and learn about the many different bodies of water around the world.

Over time, Cousteau noticed that the underwater world was changing. He realized that some of the things that people did affected sea life. He wanted to protect the oceans. He also wanted to take action to repair some of the damage people had done.

Cousteau and his crew traveled underwater in what was called a diving saucer.

Cousteau began to see changes that showed that the underwater world was being harmed.

Cousteau told world leaders that we need to protect our oceans.

In the early 1970s, Cousteau started The Cousteau Society. He organized this group to help protect the sea life that was being harmed by people's actions. Today, there are more than 50,000 members. The Cousteau Society continues to study the oceans and to work to protect them. It also teaches others about the oceans.

All over the world, there are natural and man-made landmarks that help keep Cousteau's vision alive. The Barrier Reef Reserve System in Belize is home to many threatened animals. People continue to explore sea life there. At the Vancouver Aquarium in Canada, people protect sea life and help sick or injured animals become healthy again.

Think About It Based on this story, why do you think it is important to protect the oceans? As you read the chapter ahead, think about how people can affect and change the land and water.

PEARSON realize Go online to access your interactive digital lesson.

53

Land and Water

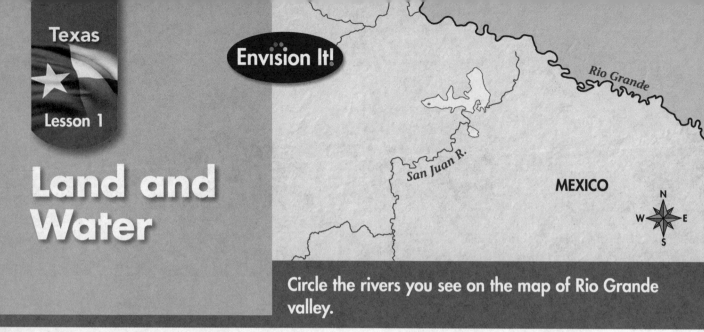

Rio Grande

San Juan R.

MEXICO

N
W E
S

Circle the rivers you see on the map of Rio Grande valley.

Glacier

Island

Peninsula

Geography is the study of Earth and its people. Earth is made up of both land and water. The largest land areas on Earth are the seven **continents:** North America, South America, Europe, Africa, Asia, Australia, and Antarctica. The four oceans are the Pacific Ocean, the Atlantic Ocean, the Indian Ocean, and the Arctic Ocean.

Landforms and Bodies of Water

There are many different landforms on each of the seven continents. A **landform** is the form or shape of part of Earth's surface.

Glaciers, mountains, hills, islands, and peninsulas are landforms. Glaciers are made up of ice and snow. Mountains are land masses that rise above the surrounding land. Some mountains are rounded at the top while others form a rocky peak. Hills are usually lower than mountains and have rounded tops. Islands are areas of land surrounded on all sides by water. Peninsulas are connected to a mainland and are nearly surrounded by water. There is usually water on only three sides of a peninsula.

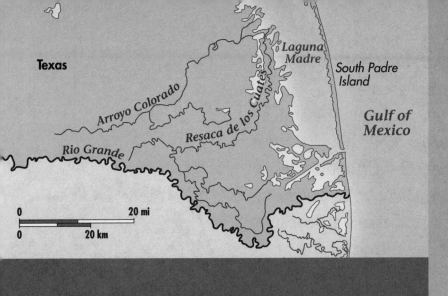

Texas

Laguna Madre

Arroyo Colorado

Resaca de los Cuates

South Padre Island

Rio Grande

Gulf of Mexico

0 ——— 20 mi
0 ——— 20 km

Vocabulary

continent
landform
mine
adobe

Just like landforms, bodies of water are all different shapes and sizes. On the map, find the four oceans. Oceans are the largest bodies of salt water on Earth. Lakes and rivers provide people with freshwater. The Great Lakes in the United States are the largest freshwater lakes in the world. These lakes include Lake Superior, Lake Michigan, Lake Huron, Lake Erie, and Lake Ontario.

TEKS
4.A, 5.C, 5.D

1. **Identify** and circle a landform in North America.
   Locate and underline the body of water north of Asia.

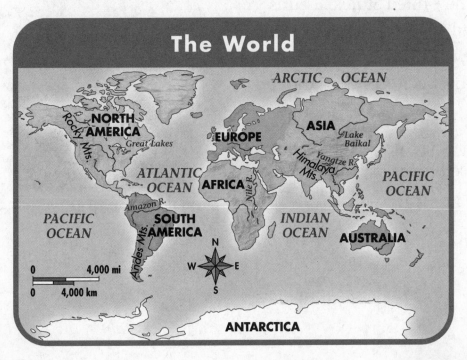

The World

ARCTIC OCEAN

NORTH AMERICA

Rocky Mts.

Great Lakes

EUROPE

ASIA

Lake Baikal

Yangtze R.

Himalaya Mts.

ATLANTIC OCEAN

AFRICA

Nile R.

PACIFIC OCEAN

Amazon R.

PACIFIC OCEAN

SOUTH AMERICA

Andes Mts.

INDIAN OCEAN

AUSTRALIA

N
W E
S

0 ——— 4,000 mi
0 ——— 4,000 km

ANTARCTICA

Land and Water in the United States

Geographers who study land areas often organize the United States into regions. The states in each region are grouped based on their location and the landforms they share. The United States is organized into five regions: the West, the Midwest, the Northeast, the Southeast, and the Southwest.

Many different landforms are found in the regions of the United States. The Appalachian Mountains stretch across the Southeast and Northeast regions. In between mountains there are low areas called valleys. Plains, such as the Great Plains, are also low areas. They tend to be very flat. The Great Plains cover parts of the Midwest, Southwest, and West regions. Plateaus, such as the Columbia Plateau located in the West region, are high areas that have steep sides and flat tops. Mountains are also found in the West region.

The West region

The largest bodies of water in the United States are rivers and lakes. Locate the Mississippi River on the map. More than 2,000 miles long, it is the second longest river in the United States. It runs through the Midwest and Southeast regions. The Great Lakes, in the Midwest and Northeast regions, form part of the border between Canada and the United States.

2. **Review** the map on the next page. Label the states in each of the five United States regions. **Identify** the region you live in.

The Southwest region

The Northeast region

The Midwest region

United States Regions

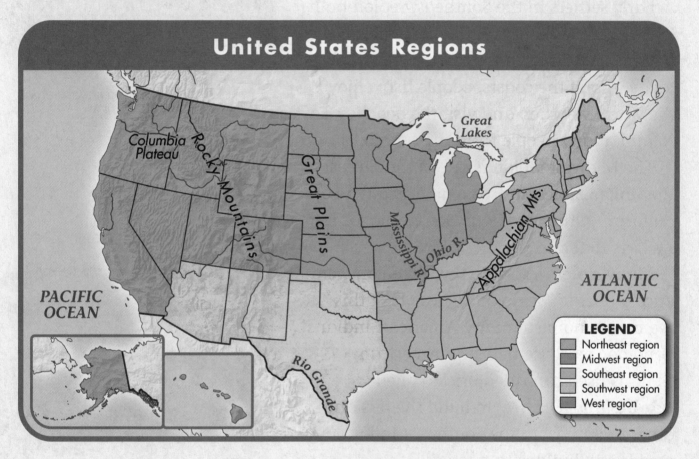

Columbia Plateau

Rocky Mountains

Great Plains

Great Lakes

Mississippi R.

Ohio R.

Appalachian Mts.

PACIFIC OCEAN

ATLANTIC OCEAN

Rio Grande

LEGEND
- Northeast region
- Midwest region
- Southeast region
- Southwest region
- West region

The Southeast region

Five Regions of the United States

The Northeast region has some of the largest cities in the United States, such as New York City in New York, and Philadelphia, Pennsylvania. This region has areas of hills, rocky coastlines, and farmland. Many people also fish along the coast. Coasts are areas of flat land that are located near water.

This plantation home was built in the Southeast region in the early 1800s.

Early settlers in the Southeast region built large farms called plantations. However, the region is best known for its long coastlines today. Along the coasts, people fish, enjoy the warm weather, and visit the beaches. Farther inland, many people farm the rich soil.

The Midwest region is one of the flattest areas in the United States. In this region, many people work on farms. Other people **mine,** or dig for materials, such as coal and iron.

Many states in the Southwest region were once a part of Mexico. The deserts of this region are home to many American Indians. Long ago, early settlers and American Indians used sun-dried bricks called **adobe** [uh DOH bee] to build shelters and other buildings. In the Southwest today, people still build with adobe.

Homes made of adobe are found in the Southwest region.

The West is a region of mountains. The Rocky Mountains are in this region. They are some of the tallest mountains in the United States. Other mountain ranges include the Coast Ranges and the Alaska Range. The West region also has a long coast. Many people visit the West to hike, fish, and camp. People also come to visit the beaches.

3. ◉ **Cause and Effect** **Explain** what might cause people in a region to work as farmers.

....

....

....

....

....

Most of the corn in the United States is grown in the Midwest region.

Got it?

TEKS 4.A, 5.D

4. ◉ **Cause and Effect** Choose one region of the United States. **Explain** how the landforms may affect some of the activities people do. **Identify** clues in the maps and photographs.

....

....

....

5. ❓ **Describe** the landforms and bodies of water that you live near. **Identify** how they affect the activities you do.

my Story Ideas

....

....

....

6. In this lesson, you have learned about the regions of the United States. With a partner, use a mapping tool on the Internet to **create** a map of the regions of Texas. Show the Gulf Coastal Plains, Interior Lowlands, Great Plains, and Basin and Range. Include your town or city. Your map should have a title, compass rose, grid, legend, and scale.

Weather, Climate, and Forces of Nature

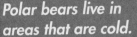
Envision It!

Polar bears live in areas that are cold.

Alligators live in areas that are wet.

Draw an animal you like. Add details that show the weather where the animal lives.

This rain forest is in a warm and wet climate. Plants grow here all year.

What is the weather today? When you explain the **weather**, you tell about the daily conditions outside. It may be hot, rainy, or cold. **Climate** is the weather that a place has over a long period. There are three parts that make up the climate of a region: temperature, precipitation, and wind. Temperature is how hot or cold it is. Precipitation is the amount of rain or snow that falls.

Climate Regions

Climates are different from region to region. In fact, the climate of a region depends on its location on Earth. Places located close to the equator get more direct sunlight. Places far from the equator get less direct sunlight.

Bodies of water shape the climate of places near them. They affect the amount of rain that falls. Bodies of water also change the temperature since they warm and cool more slowly than land. In summer, winds that blow from the water cool the land. In winter, the winds that blow from the water warm the land. The **elevation**, or the height of land above sea level, affects climate, too. High places and mountains are cool most of the year.

UNLOCK
THE BIG
?
I will know how climate affects the land, plants, and animals.

Vocabulary

weather   vegetation
climate   ecosystem
elevation

The map of North America shows the different climate regions on the continent. Arctic climates are cool or cold most of the year. Tropical climates are wet and hot most of the year. Temperate climates are not as cold as arctic climates or as hot as tropical climates. Most of the United States is in a temperate climate region. However, parts of the West have dry desert climates. In the desert, there is little rainfall. The temperature during the day can be hot while the temperature at night can be cold.

TEKS
4.A, 4.B, 4.C, 18.B, 18.C

1. **Review** the map of North America. **Identify** the climates found in most of Texas.

....

....

North America, Climate Regions

GREENLAND
(Denmark)

0   1,000 mi
0   1,000 km

CANADA

PACIFIC
OCEAN

UNITED STATES

ATLANTIC
OCEAN

Gulf of
Mexico

MEXICO

Caribbean
Sea

LEGEND
- Tropical
- Temperate
- Desert
- Arctic

N
W   E
S

Climate and Plants

The climate of a place affects the plants that grow there. Both the temperature and the amount of rainfall determine the types of **vegetation,** or kinds of plant life, that grow. In the United States, there are four main types of vegetation: forests, grasslands, tundra, and deserts. Different animals depend on the vegetation that grows in an area.

In climate regions that have plenty of rainfall, large forests are found. Forests grow in many parts of the United States. In fact, not long ago, forests covered most of North America! Many forests today are found in parts of the West region, near the Great Lakes, and in the eastern United States. Animals such as bears, deer, and raccoons live in forests.

Grasslands cover much of the plains in the United States. Some parts of the Great Plains get enough rain for tall grasses, berry bushes, and even small trees to grow. However, in the western Great Plains, there is less rain. Short grasses are found here. The prairie dogs that live in this region dig underground and eat the grasses.

Both tundra and desert vegetation are found in places that have dry climates. In the arctic climates of Alaska, the land is called tundra. In the tundra, the ground is frozen nearly all year long. It is too cold for trees to grow. However, moss, lichens, and some shrubs grow. Deer called caribou use their hooves to scrape away snow and eat the moss and lichens off the frozen land.

In parts of Alaska, shrubs and moss grow in the tundra.

In desert climates, the only plants that can survive are those that can live with little water. In some deserts, grasses and shrubs are found. In the deserts of the West region, there are large cactuses called saguaros [suh GWAR ohs]. Saguaros grow in Mexico, too. Saguaros have long roots that allow them to get water from a wide area. A saguaro can grow to be 50 feet high. That is nearly as tall as a five-story building!

Animals that live in deserts can survive the hot temperatures during the day. Some animals, such as desert tortoises, keep cool by spending much of their time underground. Other animals only come out at night when it is cooler.

2. ◎ **Main Idea and Details** **Identify** two details about each type of vegetation, then fill in each box.

Forests	Grasslands

Tundra	Desert

The plants that grow in the desert need only small amounts of water.

Plants and Animals Work Together

Forests, deserts, and grasslands each have different ecosystems. In an **ecosystem**, all living things, such as the plants and animals, interact with each other.

In both forest and rain forest ecosystems, birds, squirrels, and other animals depend on trees. Some of the seeds the animals eat drop into the soil and grow into new trees. The vegetation in these ecosystems needs animals to help spread the seeds.

In the desert, cactuses are important to many animals. Bats, such as the lesser long-nosed bats, drink nectar from the cactus flowers. By doing this, the bats spread pollen from cactus to cactus. This helps the cactus fruit grow. Other animals, including jack rabbits, eat parts of the cactus.

Lesser long-nosed bat

Places with similar vegetation can have different ecosystems. The grasslands in the middle of the United States do not have the same ecosystem as the grasslands on the continent of Africa. Some of the grasslands in Africa get more rainfall.

In the lake and swamp ecosystems in the southeastern United States, alligators dig large pond-like holes. Alligators use the holes as a place to rest. The holes also provide shallow water for birds and fish.

3. **◉ Cause and Effect Explain** the effect the animals have on the vegetation in an ecosystem.

Jack rabbit

....

....

....

Natural Hazards

Have you ever watched a weather forecast? On a forecast, you may have heard about events in nature, called natural hazards. Some examples of natural hazards are volcanoes, hurricanes, and earthquakes. These physical processes can cause changes to the land. Some physical processes such as these are dramatic and happen quickly. Other physical processes, like erosion, happen slowly.

A volcano is a mountain that erupts in an explosion of molten rock (lava), gases, and ash. The lava, gases, and ash are forced out of the volcano. Hot lava flows down the side of the volcano. When it cools, it changes the land. The ash that falls down can make the soil rich, which helps plants grow. Volcanic eruptions have helped form some of the greatest mountain chains around the world.

A hurricane is a big storm with strong winds and a lot of rainfall. Heavy rains and wind from hurricanes can cause flooding. These factors shape and change the land.

An earthquake is a violent shaking of the earth. Many earthquakes strike along faults, or cracks in Earth's crust. The crust is the outer layer of Earth. Earthquakes can cause landslides and mudslides, which can change the landscape.

Volcanic eruption

Hurricane

Earthquake

Natural Disasters

Natural hazards can change the land in the environment. When they cause damage, they are natural disasters. A disaster is something that can cause damage to human-made structures such as buildings and bridges. It can wipe out land or form new land.

In 1900, a big hurricane hit Galveston. A wave caused by the hurricane came over Galveston like a blanket. The water level rose. Soon, about 15 feet of water covered the whole city. Severe storms like hurricanes have even split an island into two pieces of land.

Earthquakes have caused major damage around the world. More earthquakes strike California than any other state in our country. In Texas, earthquakes have caused little damage or changes to the land.

Galveston before the hurricane hit in 1900

Galveston after the hurricane hit in 1900

4. Describe the effects of volcanoes, hurricanes, and earthquakes on the land.

....

....

....

....

....

Got it?

TEKS 4.A, 18.B, 18.C

5. ◉ **Cause and Effect** **Explain** the effect the climate has on vegetation that grows in a region.

....

....

6. ❓ **Describe** how the weather or climate affects how you live.

my Story Ideas

....

....

....

....

7. Research and **identify** the climate, plants, and animals in your community. Use a word processing program to write a story about the information you learned. Refer to page 14 for help. Draw a map and pictures for your story.

....

....

Interpret Maps

Maps can show different types of information. Maps that show details about the land are physical maps. On elevation maps, colors are used to show how high the land is above the surface of the sea, or sea level.

On the elevation map, place your finger on the West Coast. Move your finger across the map toward the East. The Rocky Mountains are mostly shaded in purple and brown. The legend shows that land shaded in purple has an elevation higher than 10,000 feet above sea level. Land shaded in brown has an elevation between 6,000 and 10,000 feet above sea level.

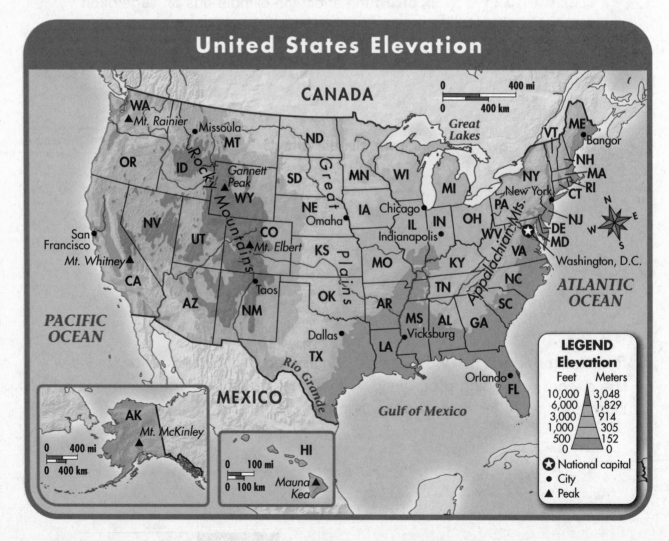

United States Elevation

LEGEND
Elevation

Feet	Meters
10,000	3,048
6,000	1,829
3,000	914
1,000	305
500	152
0	0

⭐ National capital
• City
▲ Peak

TEKS

SS 17.E Interpret visuals, including maps.

ELA 15.B Locate and use specific information in graphic features of text.

ELA 20.C Write responses to expository texts that demonstrate an understanding of the text.

The Great Plains is mostly shaded in yellow. This means that the elevation is 1,000 to 3,000 feet above sea level. On the East Coast, most of the land is shaded dark green. Therefore, the elevation of the land is between 0 and 500 feet above sea level.

Read the elevation map. Then answer the questions.

1. **Analyze** the map legend. Write the color that shows elevation between 500 and 1,000 feet above sea level.

   ....

2. **Identify** the Appalachian Mountains in the East. Write the elevation of most of the Appalachian Mountains.

   ....

   ....

3. **Identify** Orlando, Florida. Then write its elevation.

   ....

   ....

4. **Explain** how you can tell the elevation of an area of land.

   ....

   ....

   ....

   ....

PEARSON realize Go online to access your interactive digital lesson.

69

Using Earth's Resources

Envision It!

Water is important to all living things. Write how you use water.

People need rich soil to grow food.

Earth has many different natural resources. Some natural resources, such as soil and trees, are found on the land. Other natural resources are minerals like gold and iron. Water is another important natural resource. People use water to meet many of their needs.

Natural Resources

There are many natural resources in North America. Canada has many minerals, forests, and rich soil. Iron and gold are natural resources found in Mexico. Oil can be found in Trinidad and Tobago, and there are forests and rich soil throughout the Caribbean islands.

In parts of the West region of the United States, there are forests. In other parts, there is rich soil. Animals can eat the grasses that grow in the drier areas. The West also has minerals such as gold.

In the Southwest region, the land is used for mining and to raise animals such as cows. Oil, a natural resource used for fuel, is also found in the region. This natural resource is found in parts of Oklahoma and Texas.

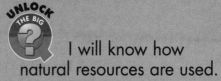

Vocabulary

agricultural region

industrial region

renewable resource

nonrenewable resource

conserve

erosion

recycle

There is rich soil in parts of the Midwest, Northeast, and Southeast regions. Many crops are grown in these regions. You can see on the map that coal is also found in all three of these regions. Iron is found in the northern part of the Midwest region.

TEKS

4.A, 4.B, 4.D, 5.C, 5.D, 17.B, 18.A, 19.A, 19.B

1. **Identify** and circle three resources in the Southwest.

United States Resources

Northeast Region

Midwest Region

West Region

Southwest Region

Southeast Region

West Region

400 mi
400 km

0   100 mi
0   100 km

0   250 mi
0   250 km

LEGEND

Agricultural area
Industrial area
Other uses
Region border
Oil
Coal
Iron
Gold
Timber

PEARSON realize   Go online to access your interactive digital lesson.

71

Agriculture and Products

People use natural resources to make products they need. In an **agricultural region,** or a place where there is much flat land and rich soil, people use the land and soil to farm.

Farmers grow many different crops. The top five crops grown in the United States are corn, soybeans, hay, wheat, and cotton. Some crops are grown for people to eat, and some are made into products. Cotton is made into fabric for clothing. People buy plastic containers and car seats made from soybeans.

Cotton

In other agricultural regions, vegetable and fruit crops are grown for people to eat. People also use grasses to feed animals such as cows and sheep.

People make other products from the natural resources that grow on the land. In some forest regions, people cut down trees. The trees are then sent to mills and made into timber, or lumber, for building. Wood from trees is also turned into pulp to make paper products.

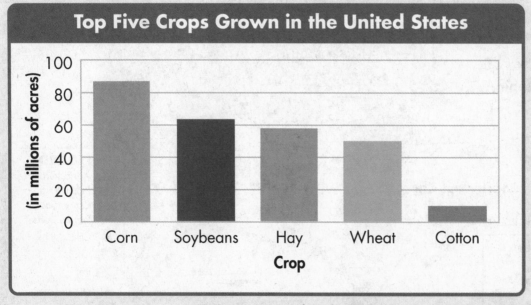

Top Five Crops Grown in the United States

(in millions of acres)

Crop: Corn, Soybeans, Hay, Wheat, Cotton

Source: U.S. Department of Agriculture, National Agricultural Statistics Service, 2007

Industry and Products

People make products from the resources found underground, too. Many of these products are made in industrial regions. An **industrial region** is a place where many kinds of factories are located. In the United States, many industrial regions are located near large cities such as Chicago, Illinois, and Detroit, Michigan.

Gasoline is made from oil.

In many places with oil and natural gas, people pump them from underground. The oil is then made into fuel such as gasoline. Oil can also be heated to make plastic. Then the plastic is used to make many different products such as telephones, plastic bags, and even toys! Most people use gasoline to power automobiles. They also use gas or oil to heat their water and their homes. People mine coal, copper, zinc, and iron. Coal is used to help make electricity. Coins, including pennies, are made from copper and zinc. Iron is used to make steel. Steel is used in making automobiles and building materials.

Minerals are melted to make items such as coins.

2. You can **create** a chart to show products made from natural resources. **Identify** the natural resource used.

Products	vegetables wheat	lumber paper	telephones toys
Natural Resource			

Protecting Resources

Some resources people use, such as trees and soil, are renewable resources. A **renewable resource** is one that can be replaced in a short time. Many of the resources found underground are nonrenewable resources. **Nonrenewable resources** are those that take a long time to replace or cannot be replaced after they are used. Coal, oil, and natural gas are all nonrenewable resources. In order to make sure that everyone has enough natural resources to live, people find ways to **conserve,** or to save and protect, them.

Recycled materials can be used again.

One way people conserve resources is by using less of them. Many people try to use less natural gas or water. People also conserve resources when they use them more carefully. Some farmers plant trees near their crops or strips of grass in between rows of crops. These plants help prevent **erosion,** or the washing away of soil by rain, wind, and nearby rivers. The plants help to hold the soil down.

Another way to protect natural resources is by recycling them. To **recycle** means to use an item again. Plastic bottles, newspapers, aluminum cans, and glass bottles are all items that people recycle every day. In many neighborhoods, trucks pick up these items from bins that line the streets. Many factories use recycled materials instead of natural resources to make new products.

People conserve water when they turn off the faucet while they brush their teeth.

While many people work hard to protect natural resources, sometimes people's actions can harm them. Chemicals used in factories and on farms can pollute the air and nearby waterways. Smoke from burning fires can also pollute the air.

3. ◉ **Cause and Effect** **Analyze** the section. Write an effect of recycling items you use every day.

....

....

....

Got it?

⬛ TEKS 4.A, 4.D, 19.A

4. ◉ **Cause and Effect** **Describe** a cause of pollution.

....

....

5. ❓ Think about your daily routine. **Describe** which natural resources you use the most.

my Story Ideas

....

....

6. Research the natural resources of Texas. Make a chart to categorize the resources as renewable or nonrenewable. Then use problem-solving steps to **identify** ways to conserve resources. Consider different options. Make a list of your solutions.

Reading Skills

Cause and Effect

One way to learn more about what you have read is to identify a cause and its effect. A cause makes something happen. An effect is the outcome, or the result of what happens. Clue words such as *because, if, then, now,* and *since* help you identify examples of cause and effect. You can also study visuals, such as photographs, to identify causes and effects.

Read the passage below aloud to a partner. Prepare to tell the causes and effects.

Cause

Lily sees that a storm is coming! Soon, she sees lightning and hears a loud "pop." Lightning has struck the electricity pole on the street. Now there is no electricity in her house. Since the electricity is out, the television and refrigerator are off. Hours later, Lily wants a snack. She opens the refrigerator. "Oh no!" she says. Because the electricity went out, the refrigerator was off. Now the ice cream has melted!

Effect

In your own words, tell your partner the causes and effects. When you express ideas orally, speak clearly. Use what you've learned about clue words and what you already know about causes and effects in your explanation. Look at the phrases and sentences that are highlighted. The causes are highlighted orange. The effects are highlighted purple.

Learning Objective

I will know how to recognize a cause and its effect.

TEKS

SS 17.C Interpret oral, visual, and print material by identifying cause and effect.
SS 18.A Express ideas orally based on knowledge.
ELA 13.A Identify the details or facts that support the main idea.
ELA 13.C Identify explicit cause and effect relationships among ideas in texts.

Read aloud the passage below with a partner. Then answer the questions.

For many years, groups of people drilled for oil at Spindletop in Texas. Then one group of workers got a new part for their drill. They were now able to dig deeper into the ground. On January 10, 1901, mud began to bubble up from the well. Then suddenly a stream of oil shot up more than 100 feet high! The nearby city of Beaumont was changed forever. Since oil had been found near it, people from all over the country rushed to Beaumont in search of oil. The number of people living in Beaumont rose from 10,000 to 50,000 people. Now that there was plenty of oil, automobiles and factories started to use more of this natural resource.

1. **Identify** the causes in the passage as your partner reads it aloud.

2. **List** words that you hear that help you identify the causes.

3. **Identify** the effects in the passage as your partner reads it aloud.

4. **Present** the causes and effects from the passage to your class. As you express your ideas orally, remember to state clearly information you learned as you read.

Interacting With the Environment

Envision It!

Write some of the ways people use lakes and the land near lakes.

In arctic climates, people drive snowmobiles to get from place to place.

Think about what makes up your environment. Landforms, bodies of water, vegetation, natural resources, and climate are all things that make up the environment of a place.

The Environment Affects People

The environment affects where people live, work, and play. Most communities develop in regions where there is plenty of land and fresh water. People also settle communities near natural resources. People live near forests to cut and plant trees. Other people live near the coast to fish. In the mountains and in desert areas, there are fewer settlements. These places do not always have flat land or enough water to grow crops.

People adapt to the environment to fit their needs. To **adapt** is to change the way you do something. People may change the way they dress or how they travel. In arctic climates, people dress in warm clothes to protect themselves from the cold. They ski or sled to travel down snow-covered hills. People drive snowmobiles in areas where it is difficult or unsafe to drive automobiles.

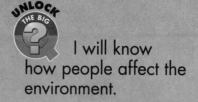
People in states such as Texas and Florida, and in the countries of Central America, have changed how they make buildings. In these areas, heavy rains and hurricanes can bring strong winds and a quick rise in the water level. Many people in these places use building materials that can stay up in strong winds. Other people in these areas settle farther inland to avoid rising waters.

In Arizona, American Indians called Havasupais [hah vah SOO pyez] live in a village in the Grand Canyon. This environment affects how they travel in and out of their village. People cannot drive automobiles down the canyon. Mail and other supplies are carried into the village on horseback or are flown in by helicopter.

TEKS

2.C, 4.A, 4.B, 4.C, 4.D, 4.E, 12.B, 19.B

1. ◉ **Cause and Effect** **Describe** an effect of living in a cold, snowy climate.

   ....

   ....

   ....

The Havasupais live in the Grand Canyon.

PEARSON realize™ Go online to access your interactive digital lesson.

79

Climate Affects People

As you have learned, the environment affects people and how they live. People who live in desert communities must adapt in different ways than people who live in wetlands do. They have different climates, resources, and challenges. Mountain and plains communities also have different environments. People adapt to their environment to best meet their needs.

In desert climates, conditions are often dry and hot, but they can be cool at night. Water can be limited. In a desert, there can be little shade to escape the heat and sun. People build homes that will stay cool in the day and warm at night. They may practice conservation to make sure that there is always a water supply.

People who live in wetland climates may have to live with a lot of rainfall, humidity, and little farmland. Unlike in desert climates, wetlands often have a lot of water. Sometimes the land is waterlogged from having too much water. This can make it difficult to grow crops. People can change the direction of the flow of water by building dams. People who live in wetlands have to consider the kind of homes they build. They must make sure that the land is solid.

2. **Cause and Effect** Some wetlands in East Texas flood. **Interpret** the visual. What do you think causes these floods? **Explain** one effect on people's lives in East Texas.

....
....
....
....
....
....
....

In mountain climates, people also adapt their way of life. Mountain climates are different from desert climates because they often are cool and wet. Farming can be difficult in mountain climates because of the elevation. There is less oxygen at high elevations. Without enough oxygen, living things cannot grow. The climate in a mountain community may be harsh in winter. People may need to collect food, water, blankets, and firewood to prepare for a winter storm.

Living on the plains has its own set of challenges. The climate on the plains is often cold in winter and warm in the summer. The plains may have low rainfall, but they do have some sources of water such as rivers. The land in this environment can be good for growing crops. However, it can be very windy on the plains. Wind can wear away the soil. Poor soil or no soil makes it hard to grow crops. These areas, however, can work well for herding cattle and ranching.

People have used the land for herding cattle.

3. **Compare** how people adapt to different environments to meet their needs.

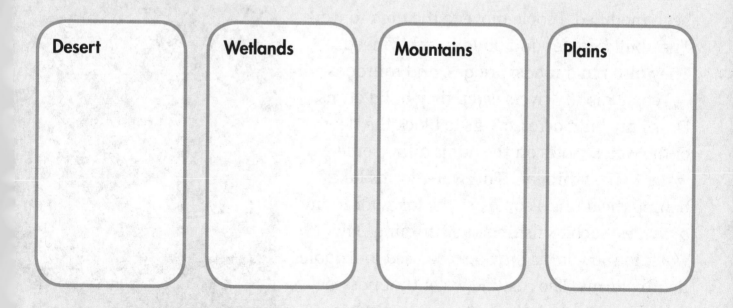

Desert	Wetlands	Mountains	Plains

People Modify Environments

People interact with, or act on, their environment in many ways. One way is to modify their environment to fit their needs. To **modify** is to change something, such as the physical environment. In areas with dry land, farmers may not have enough water for their crops. These farmers **irrigate**, or bring water in through pipes. Other farmers break up the soil to expose it to the air. This helps to kill weeds and to keep the soil rich. Farmers may add chemicals to the soil. Some are fertilizers that help farmers grow more crops. Other chemicals get rid of insects.

People modify the land when they use other natural resources, too. Large machines pump oil from the earth. In Pennsylvania and West Virginia, miners dig tunnels deep underground to reach minerals. Miners also carry away soil and rock to uncover coal. Land in some forests is cleared as workers cut down trees to sell as lumber. In some countries, people also burn forest areas to clear land. This land is used for farms or homes.

The areas near these resources have also been modified. People move to the area to work. They build homes and buildings they need. They also build roads, bridges, and railroads.

People modify rivers when they build dams. Dams are built across rivers to block the flow of the water. Gates on the dams allow some water to flow through. This water forms lakes behind the dams. People use the lakes for many activities, such as fishing or swimming. The water in these lakes may also be used to irrigate nearby farms. The rushing water that passes through some dams is used to make electricity.

In the United States, water from the Hoover Dam on the Colorado River is used to make electricity.

Effects of Population

The number of people who live in an area can also affect the physical environment. In the late 1800s and early 1900s, new tools and equipment made farming easier. Fewer farm workers were needed. Many people began to move to cities in the East to work in factories. As more people moved to cities, more space was needed for people to live.

As newcomers arrived, people built out from the center of the city. People built homes and other buildings they needed. They laid railroad tracks and built roads so people could travel in and out of the city. People also built upwards. They built tall buildings called skyscrapers. Over time, people used improved materials to build skyscrapers that were much taller.

Today, in areas with large populations, people modify the land to meet the changing needs in a community. As more people move to a city, more methods of transportation are added. The city may work on roads to make them wider so they can fit more cars, trucks, and buses. It might also build more rail lines so that more trains can travel into and out of the city. Builders may also build taller buildings so more people can live in the area.

4. **Explain** two ways that people modify the land.

....

....

....

More people can live and work in large skyscrapers than in smaller buildings.

People and the Land

Some of the activities that people do can help or harm the environment. Scientists and others look for ways to improve the environment and how resources are used. Over the years, farmers learned that planting the same crops every year can harm the soil. As a result, many farmers today rotate, or take turns, growing different crops. Farmers also plan for a period of rest when they do not plant any crops. By doing so, the soil is moist and better able to grow crops.

Miners also work to help the environment. After they carve out soil in search of minerals, the land has little or no vegetation left. Miners then work to plant trees and other vegetation on the land.

Community leaders help the environment with some of the decisions they make. Leaders pass laws to prevent people from throwing garbage on the ground. They also pass laws to keep the drinking water clean. Some laws protect the oceans. These laws do not allow companies to dump materials that can harm the ocean or sea life.

Other people help the environment by their actions every day. Some people buy automobiles that do not pollute the air. People also use the heat from the sun or the wind to power things. Others organize groups to help clean up beaches, parks, and lakes. When people clean up the land, they make it safe for people and animals.

Cleaning up the land is one way people help the environment.

Another way people help the environment is by conserving land. People conserve land when they set aside some of it in state parks or national parks. The first national park was created in 1872. Today, there are more than 350 national parks in the United States. This land is protected. People may not build or settle on this land.

Yellowstone was the first national park.

5. List three ways people help the environment.

....

....

....

 **Got it?**

🤚 TEKS 4.B, 12.B, 19.B

6. ◎ **Cause and Effect Explain** the effect of a law that helps the environment.

....

....

....

7. ❓ **Describe** ways the land has been modified in your community.

 my Story Ideas

....

....

....

8. Work in a small group to **research** a local organization that has worked to stop pollution. Gather information and evaluate the work it has done. Then **identify** a plan of action to help support the organization. **Present** your action plan to the class. Make sure your plan offers a solution. Put your plan into action in your community.

Lesson 1   TEKS 4.A, 5.C

Land and Water

1. Identify the name of each landform under its picture.

....

2. Label the continents and oceans on the map below.

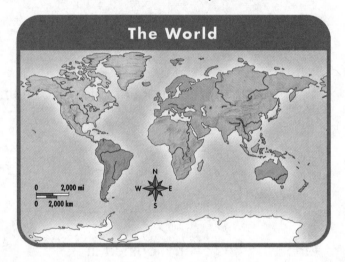

Lesson 2   TEKS 4.B

Weather, Climate, and Forces of Nature

3. Describe and **compare** two ways people can adapt to
the desert climate in the Southwest and plains climate in
the Midwest.

....

....

....

Using Earth's Resources

4. Describe what many people do for work in an agricultural region.

....

....

....

5. ◉ **Cause and Effect** Factories use natural resources to make products. **Describe** one effect of factories on the environment.

....

....

6. Draw a picture of something you have at home that is made from a natural resource. Then **identify** the natural resource used to make it.

....

Lesson 4 TEKS 4.A, 4.C

Interacting With the Environment

7. Describe how people in Texas and Florida have changed how they make buildings.

....

....

....

8. Explain why people may settle near a dam.

....

....

....

9. Analyze what might happen if people cut down trees but did not plant new ones.

....

....

....

....

10. Read the question and circle the best answer.

Which sentence **describes** what happens when there is a volcanic eruption, hurricane, or earthquake?

A People move from the farm to the city.

B People tear down bridges.

C The landscape is unchanged.

D The landscape may change.

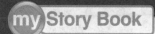
Go online to write and illustrate your own **myStory Book** using the **myStory Ideas** from this chapter.

 # How do we interact with our planet?

⬇ **TEKS**

SS 4.B

ELA 17

Every day, people modify their environment. In some ways, people may harm the land. In other ways, they help the land.

Think about how you interact with your environment. Then write about activities you can do to use fewer natural resources.

....

....

....

....

Draw a picture of someone doing an activity to help the environment.

 PEARSON realize | Go online to access your interactive digital lesson.

89

Communities Build a Nation

How does our past affect our present?

Describe something about your community that is special.

....

....

....

....

....

Texas Essential Knowledge and Skills

1.A Describe how individuals, events, and ideas have changed communities, past and present.

1.B Identify individuals, including Pierre-Charles L'Enfant, Benjamin Banneker, and Benjamin Franklin, who have helped to shape communities.

1.C Describe how individuals, including Daniel Boone, Christopher Columbus, the Founding Fathers, and Juan de Oñate, have contributed to the expansion of existing communities or to the creation of new communities.

2.A Identify reasons people have formed communities, including a need for security, religious freedom, law, and material well-being.

2.B Identify ways in which people in the local community and other communities meet their needs for government, education, communication, transportation, and recreation.

2.C Compare ways in which various other communities meet their needs.

3.A Use vocabulary related to chronology, including past, present, and future times.

3.B Create and interpret timelines.

3.C Apply the terms year, decade, and century to describe historical times.

4.A Describe and explain variations in the physical environment, including climate, landforms, natural resources, and natural hazards.

4.B Identify and compare how people in different communities adapt to or modify the physical environment in which they live such as deserts, mountains, wetlands, and plains.

10.A Identify the purposes of the Declaration of Independence and the U.S. Constitution, including the Bill of Rights.

14.A Identify and compare the heroic deeds of state and national heroes, including Hector P. Garcia and James A. Lovell, and other individuals such as Harriet Tubman, Juliette Gordon Low, Todd Beamer, Ellen Ochoa, John "Danny" Olivas, and other contemporary heroes.

15.A Identify various individual writers and artists such as Kadir Nelson, Tomie dePaola, and Phillis Wheatley and their stories, poems, statues, and paintings and other examples of cultural heritage from various communities.

15.B Explain the significance of various individual writers and artists such as Carmen Lomas Garza, Laura Ingalls Wilder, and Bill Martin Jr. and their stories, poems, statues, and paintings and other examples of cultural heritage to various communities.

17.B Sequence and categorize information.

17.E Interpret and create visuals, including graphs, charts, tables, timelines, illustrations, and maps.

Mission San Luis
A Multicultural Community

my Story Video

From about 1560 to 1690, there were more than 100 Spanish missions built throughout Florida. A mission is a settlement that has a church where religion is taught. One of the most famous missions is Mission San Luis. Located in Tallahassee, it is one of the last remaining mission sites today. "It's also the only place where both the Apalachee and the Spaniards lived together," says Grace. The Apalachee are American Indians and Spaniards are people from Spain. "I love learning about other cultures," she adds. No one lives at the mission anymore, but it has been rebuilt. Visitors can tour the mission and watch people act out what life was like there hundreds of years ago.

"American Indians and Spaniards shared this mission," Grace explains. At that time, American Indians and European settlers usually did not live together. Mission San Luis was special.

Grace was excited to visit one of the last remaining missions.

91

Squash and beans are some of the crops that the Apalachee used to grow.

The Spaniards built a fort to protect their settlement.

People working at the mission wear clothing from the time period as part of their teaching about life long ago.

The Apalachee were the first Americans to settle in this area. There was a river nearby and rich soil, which made it a good place to live. Over the years, the Apalachee learned a lot about farming and grew crops including corn, beans, and squash. "*Mi abuela* grows these crops, too!" says Grace. "Sorry, *abuela* means 'Grandma' in Spanish!" Grace and her family are originally from Puerto Rico, so English is Grace's second language. She uses a lot of Spanish words when she speaks. "Grandma says that our family has grown these crops for a long time, too," Grace tells us.

When the Spaniards came to the Florida coast, they were looking for a place where they could create a community, build a fort to protect the settlement, and spread their Christian religion. The Apalachee wanted to learn about Christianity, and they felt that the Spaniards could help protect them. So, the Apalachee welcomed the Spaniards to the area. By living together, both groups shared different ways of doing things and grew to respect each other's differences. "My family and I also learned a lot of new things when we came to America," Grace says. While most missions began to shrink during that time, San Luis grew.

This bedroom is decorated with Spanish fabrics.

Grace saw several Spanish artifacts in this dining area.

In 1656, the Spaniards chose the present-day location of Mission San Luis to build their fort. This area is on a hilltop and has a clear view of the land below. "The area reminds me of our family's farm in Puerto Rico," said Grace's mother. "Oh yeah... It's also on a hilltop!" remembers Grace. It was very important that their fort be on a hilltop, because the Spaniards needed to be able to see if anyone was coming to attack them.

Today, visitors to Mission San Luis can experience what it was like to live among the Apalachee and the Spaniards. "This place is amazing," says Grace. As Grace walks to the central area known as the plaza, she says, "I bet this is where they held special ceremonies and played games." The church and the Apalachee chief's house are just a few of the many buildings that have been rebuilt to look the way they did hundreds of years ago. Grace also enjoys looking at all of the artifacts from Spanish households. The past really does come alive at Mission San Luis!

The tour guides and others who work at Mission San Luis enjoy helping visitors learn about the past.

Think About It Based on this story, why do you think it is important to visit places like Mission San Luis? As you read the chapter ahead, think about how learning about the past affects your life today.

PEARSON realize Go online to access your interactive digital lesson.

93

America's First Peoples

Look at the picture. Write what natural resource was used to build these homes.

Every community has a history shaped by the people who first lived there. Your community is special because of its past as well as its present.

American Indian Groups

LEGEND
— Present-day border

ARCTIC

SUBARCTIC

PACIFIC NORTHWEST

PLATEAU

PACIFIC OCEAN

CALIFORNIA

GREAT BASIN

PLAINS

NORTHEAST WOODLANDS

SOUTHEAST WOODLANDS

ATLANTIC OCEAN

SOUTHWEST

Gulf of Mexico

0   1,000 mi
0   1,000 km

N
W   E
S

Cultural Groups

American Indians were the first people to settle in North America. There were many different American Indian groups and they each had their own cultures and **customs**, or special ways of doing things.

The map shows the regions of North America where American Indians lived. Each group used the natural resources in their region to meet their needs. American Indians who lived in the Pacific Northwest caught fish from the Pacific Ocean. Those living on the Plains used the rich soil there for farming.

1. **Identify** and underline two ways American Indians used natural resources to live.

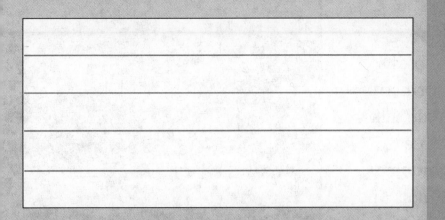

Vocabulary

custom   reservation
longhouse   government
confederacy   tradition
cooperate

Cherokee of the Southeast

TEKS
1.A, 1.B, 2.A, 2.B, 2.C, 3.A, 4.B, 15.A, 15.B, 17.B

Long ago, the American Indian group called the Cherokee settled in the forests of the southeastern United States. The Cherokee settled in this area because of geography: rich soil, rivers, and trees.

The Cherokee first settled in North America more than 1,000 years ago. They were hunters and farmers. They ate meat, fruit, and vegetables. They used trees to build houses. They covered the wooden frames with mud from the nearby riverbanks. Later, the Cherokee built log homes that kept out the cold and snow in winter.

A famous Cherokee named Sequoyah (sih KWOI uh) invented a system for writing the Cherokee language. Once people learned the 86 symbols, they could read and write the language.

2. ◉ **Main Idea and Details** **Describe** how the Cherokee created a new community.

....

....

....

The Cherokee used natural resources to make pottery and to weave baskets.

PEARSON realize. Go online to access your interactive digital lesson.

95

Iroquois of the Northeast

The Iroquois settled in the forests of what is now central and northern New York and southern Canada. Like the Cherokee, the Iroquois chose this area to settle because of geography. The forests had plenty of animals and plants. The Iroquois used rivers for fishing and traveling.

An Iroquois village

Like the Cherokee, the Iroquois used trees to build their houses. However, Iroquois houses had a different shape than Cherokee houses. They were up to 200 feet long! Since these homes were longer than they were wide, they were called **longhouses.** Longhouses could be home to as many as ten families. Each family had its own living space. Fires were built down the middle of the longhouse, and families on each side shared a fire.

Hiawatha was an Onondaga chief and a member of the Iroquois Confederacy.

More than 500 years ago, the Iroquois formed a confederacy. A **confederacy** is a formal agreement, or treaty, between groups to work together. The Iroquois Confederacy had five groups: the Mohawk, Oneida, Onondaga, Cayuga, and Seneca peoples all shared a similar culture. The Confederacy was also called the Five Nations. It had rules to protect the rights of each of the five groups. Each group voted on important Iroquois decisions.

3. **Describe** how the idea to form a confederacy changed communities.

....

....

....

Group Cooperation

As the Iroquois Confederacy shows, some American Indian groups **cooperated**, or worked together. Even though the Confederacy allowed each group to rule itself, the Five Nations felt it was best to come together so they could be stronger and more powerful. The main purpose of the Iroquois Confederacy was the *Great Law of Peace*. This law said that all decision making had to be done peacefully. No one was allowed to hurt anyone if groups disagreed.

American Indian groups not only worked with one another, but they also cooperated with the first settlers from England. When these settlers came about 300 years ago, some American Indians taught them how to plant crops such as pumpkin, squash, beans, and corn. They also taught settlers different ways to fish in the shallow water.

At times, however, American Indian groups went to war against each other. About 400 years ago, the Iroquois fought wars against the Huron, Erie, and Algonquin groups. The Iroquois had traded beaver furs with European settlers for guns and other supplies. When the beaver population began to die out, the Iroquois traveled west into other American Indian lands to look for beaver. Because the Iroquois had better weapons than the groups they were fighting against, they won what were called the Beaver Wars.

American Indians bring beaver furs to English settlers.

4. ◎ **Cause and Effect**
Identify and underline the effects of the Iroquois groups working together.

97

American Indians Today

Today, there are about 2 million American Indians living in the United States. About 1 million American Indians live in Canada.

Some American Indians in the United States live on **reservations**, or lands that the United States government set aside for them many years ago. Each reservation has its own **government.** A government is a system of ruling people. American Indians who live on reservations have to obey the laws created by this government. They not only have to follow the laws set up by their reservation's government, but they also have to follow the laws made by the United States government.

Ben Nighthorse Campbell wears traditional American Indian clothing to a United States government meeting.

Ben Nighthorse Campbell is part of the Northern Cheyenne group and serves as a member of the group's Council of Chiefs. He also served as a member of the United States government for 18 years.

American Indians have traditions. A **tradition** is a special way that a group does something that is passed down over time. Some Cherokee traditions include games, dances, songs, and clothing. Some American Indians wear traditional clothing, such as feathered headdresses. The photograph shows Ben Nighthorse Campbell wearing a headdress that stands for bravery and courage.

5. **Identify** who creates the laws on American Indian reservations.

....

....

6. ⊙ **Main Idea and Details** **Compare** American Indian settlements. Then, fill in the chart with details that support the main idea.

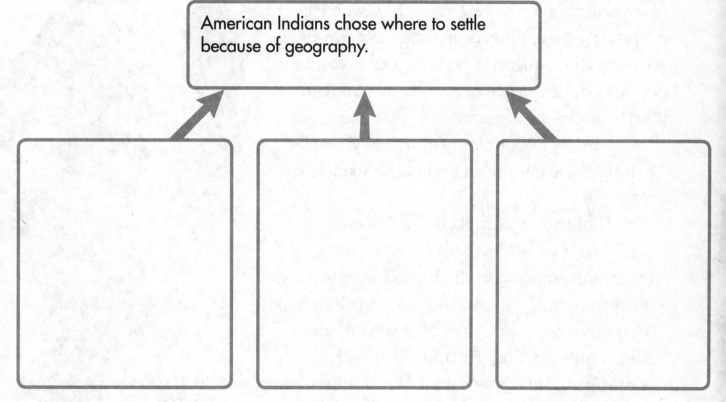

American Indians chose where to settle because of geography.

7. ❓ **Describe** traditions in your family or community that came from the past.

my Story Ideas

....

....

....

8. Identify a local American Indian artist or writer whose work reminds people about their culture and helps to keep it alive. Choose a visual artist or a writer. Share an example of the artist's work with your class. **Explain** how the artist's work is part of their culture.

....

....

Sequence

Sequence is the order in which events take place. Words such as *first, second, third, then, after, next, finally, past, future, now,* and *later* can help you find the sequence of events. Dates can help you find the sequence of events, too. Look for days, months, and years.

Read below about Ben Nighthorse Campbell. Then read the chart that shows the sequence of events.

Ben Nighthorse Campbell was born in California in 1933. About 50 years later, he began working in the United States government. Then in 2004, Campbell arrived at a government meeting in his traditional Cheyenne clothing. During his speech, Campbell said, "It was a bit of a tight schedule. I didn't know if I could change before I got to the floor."

Ben Nighthorse Campbell

Ben Nighthorse Campbell

Ben Nighthorse Campbell was born in California in 1933.

About 50 years later, he began working in the United States government.

Then in 2004, Campbell arrived at a government meeting in his traditional Cheyenne clothing.

Read the passage about Sequoyah. Then fill in the sequence of events in the chart below. **Circle** the words or dates in the passage that helped you find the correct sequence.

Sequoyah made a very important contribution to Cherokee culture. In 1821, he developed a set of symbols to go with all 86 syllables of the Cherokee language. Then the language was taught in all Cherokee schools. Finally, the Cherokee began to print books and newspapers in the Cherokee language.

Sequoyah

Sequoyah

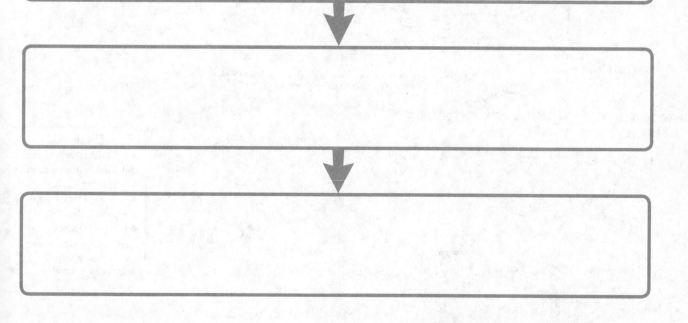

PEARSON realize   Go online to access your interactive digital lesson.

101

Early Explorers

Envision It!

Suppose you traveled to the place in the picture. Describe what you might find when you get there.

Do you like going to new places and meeting new people? An explorer does! An **explorer** is a person who travels looking for new lands and discoveries.

Explorers Sail From Europe

Explorers from Europe thought traveling to Asia by water might take less time than traveling by land. They all wanted to be the first to find a water route to Asia. A **route** is the course you take to get somewhere.

Routes of European Explorers

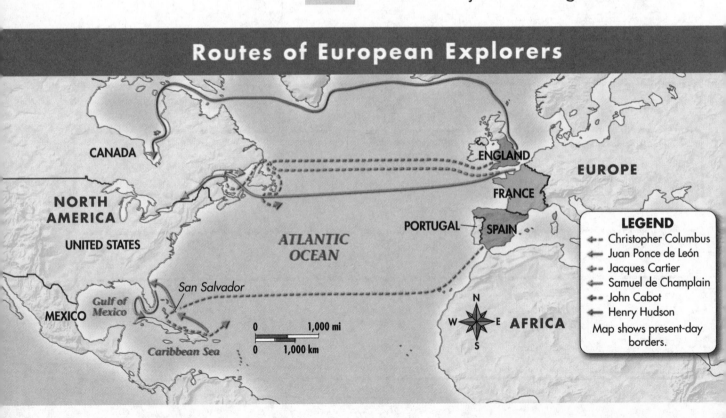

CANADA

ENGLAND

EUROPE

FRANCE

NORTH AMERICA

PORTUGAL — SPAIN

UNITED STATES

ATLANTIC OCEAN

San Salvador

Gulf of Mexico

MEXICO

Caribbean Sea

0   1,000 mi
0   1,000 km

AFRICA

LEGEND
- Christopher Columbus
- Juan Ponce de León
- Jacques Cartier
- Samuel de Champlain
- John Cabot
- Henry Hudson

Map shows present-day borders.

UNLOCK THE BIG ? I will know the causes and effects of European exploration.

Vocabulary

explorer
route

More than 500 years ago, in the 1480s, explorers from Portugal began to search for a water route to Asia by sailing east around Africa. In the early 1490s, Spain was the first country to send explorers west across the Atlantic Ocean. These explorers were looking not only for a way to travel to Asia by water, but also for spices and herbs needed for cooking and medicine. In addition, they hoped to find gold, silk, and other riches.

Late in the 15th century, English explorers were also trying to find a water route to Asia. The English explorers wanted to own land in the Americas, so they sent explorers there, too.

By the early 1500s, France was also searching for a water route to Asia. During the search, French explorers built settlements and traded with American Indians in what is now Canada.

TEKS
1.A, 1.C, 3.A, 3.C, 17.B

Spices, gold, silk, gems

1. **⊙ Sequence Analyze** the section. Then list the countries in Europe in the order that they began searching for a water route to Asia.

....

....

PEARSON realize Go online to access your interactive digital lesson.

103

Spanish Explorers

Long ago, spices were very valuable. People used spices to keep food from spoiling. Spain hired Christopher Columbus, an explorer born in Italy, to sail to China to search for spices.

Columbus began his trip to China in the year 1492. He thought he could reach China by sailing west from Spain. He did not find China. He landed on an island off the coast of present-day Florida instead. When he first saw the people living there, he called them "Indians." That is because he thought he had reached the East Indies near southern China. Next, Columbus sailed to more islands. He set up a settlement on an island called Hispaniola (hihs pun YOH luh).

A group called the Taino (TYE noh) already lived on the island of Hispaniola. Their lives changed after the Spaniards, or people from Spain, arrived. Many Taino people died of diseases brought by the Spaniards.

Amerigo Vespucci was another explorer who sailed for Spain. He explored many places, including what is known today as Venezuela. North and South America were named in his honor.

Columbus had three ships: the Niña, the Pinta, and the Santa Maria.

French Explorers

After the French arrived in North America in the 1520s, they began to explore the land. They traveled north by river through the center of North America. Jacques Cartier sailed the St. Lawrence River in 1535.

Samuel de Champlain explored the St. Lawrence region and the Great Lakes. He founded Quebec City in 1608. Champlain learned a lot from the American Indians and formed good relationships with them.

In 1634, Jean Nicolet tried to find the Northwest Passage to India, a water route that would link the Atlantic and Pacific oceans. He did not find it, but he explored Lake Michigan. Robert de La Salle explored the Great Lakes and the Mississippi River.

2. Describe how Christopher Columbus contributed to the creation of new communities.

....

....

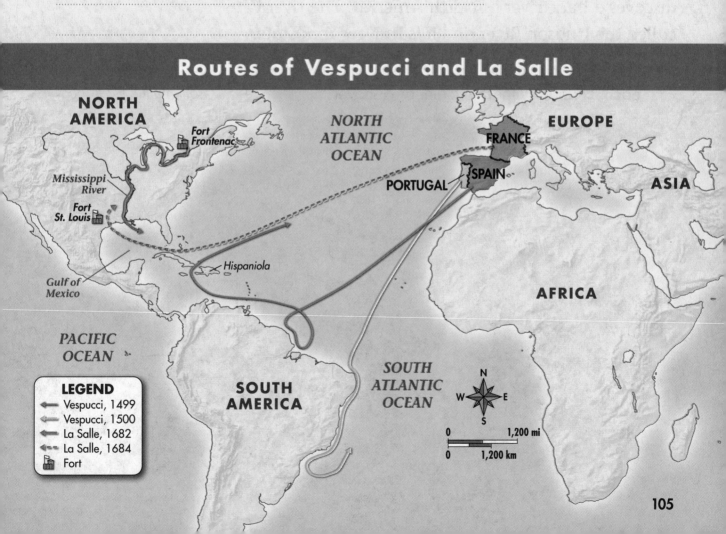

Routes of Vespucci and La Salle

NORTH AMERICA

Fort Frontenac

Mississippi River

Fort St. Louis

Gulf of Mexico

Hispaniola

PACIFIC OCEAN

SOUTH AMERICA

NORTH ATLANTIC OCEAN

SOUTH ATLANTIC OCEAN

PORTUGAL

SPAIN

FRANCE

EUROPE

ASIA

AFRICA

N
W   E
S

0   1,200 mi
0   1,200 km

LEGEND
- Vespucci, 1499
- Vespucci, 1500
- La Salle, 1682
- La Salle, 1684
- Fort

English Explorers

English explorers wanted to explore the Americas, too. In June 1497, John Cabot arrived on the coast of North America and went on shore. Cabot explored the coast before sailing back to England. He wanted to tell everyone about his discovery. Later, England claimed all of North America. The English believed that Cabot had been the first person to discover this land.

In 1580, Sir Francis Drake became the first English explorer to sail around the world. He claimed land near present-day San Francisco for England. When Drake finished his trip, he was honored by the queen.

Beginning in 1607, Henry Hudson sailed for England to search for the Northwest Passage to India. After many failed attempts to do so, he moved to Holland. In 1609, he sailed from Holland, again trying to find the Northwest Passage. He could not find it, but he did discover a huge river in North America. The river is called the Hudson River and it is in New York state.

3. **Identify** and underline the sentences that tell what each explorer helped to claim or discover.

Henry Hudson and his crew sail into the Hudson River.

4. ◉ **Sequence Analyze** the list of events. Then fill in the chart by sequencing the events.

Samuel de Champlain founds Quebec City.
Jean Nicolet explores Lake Michigan.
Henry Hudson discovers the Hudson River.

Date	Event

5. ❓ **Identify** one explorer from this lesson. **Explain** his contribution to shaping a community.

my Story Ideas

....

....

....

6. In this lesson you read about international explorer Christopher Columbus. **Compare** and **contrast** Columbus with a later, American explorer, Daniel Boone. **Describe** how each of them contributed to the expansion of existing communities or the creation of new communities.

....

....

....

Timelines

A timeline shows when events took place. A timeline can be divided into years, decades, or centuries. A decade is ten years, and a century is 100 years. The timeline below shows when some states became part of the United States. It is divided by 50 years, or five decades.

Events are placed on a timeline in the order in which they happened. The event that happened first, or earliest, is placed on the left part of the timeline. Which of the four states shown below became a state first? If you look toward the left, you see that Virginia was the first to become a state. As you read the timeline from left to right, you learn which events happened first, second, third, and then last. The last, or most recent, event is shown on the right.

States Become Part of the Country

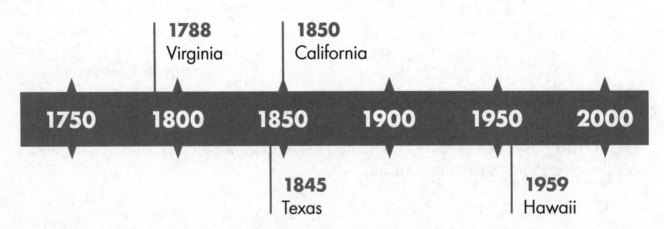

Look at the timeline. Which became a state first: California or Texas? If you read from left to right, you can see that Texas became a state before California. How many years apart did Texas and California become states? That's right! The answer is five years.

 **Try it!**

Complete the timeline. **Interpret** the timeline to answer the questions below.

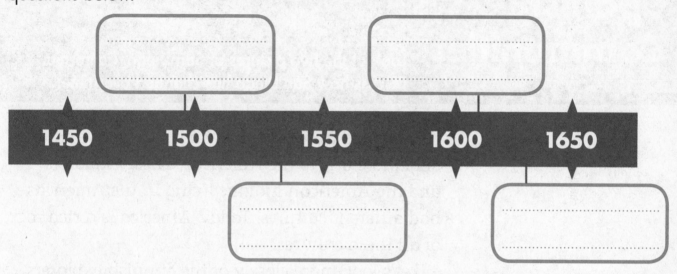

1450   1500   1550   1600   1650

1. Read the list of years and events below. Then fill in the timeline with each explorer's name to show when he traveled.

   1535 Jacques Cartier sailed the St. Lawrence River.

   1492 Christopher Columbus sailed to the Americas.

   1634 Jean Nicolet explored Lake Michigan.

   1609 Henry Hudson discovered the Hudson River.

2. **Identify** which explorer traveled first.

   ....

3. St. Augustine, Florida, was settled in 1565. **Explain** whether this happened before or after Jacques Cartier sailed the St. Lawrence River.

   ....

4. **Identify** the two explorers who traveled within three decades of each other.

   ....

Early Spanish Communities

Envision It!

Look at the two pictures of San Diego, California. Discuss how San Diego has changed over time.

Explorers from Portugal, Spain, France, and England came to the Americas. These explorers and the American Indians living in the Americas had different cultures. Today, America is a rich mix of all these cultures.

Let's look more closely at the Spanish explorers who brought their culture to America.

Spanish Exploration in Florida

Some explorers who sailed to the Americas wanted gold, gems, and riches. Other explorers wanted to be famous.

American Indians told a special **legend,** or a story from the past whose facts cannot be checked. The legend was about a magical spring whose water made people young again. Spanish explorer Juan Ponce de León wanted to find the spring. He wanted to find the Fountain of Youth.

In 1513, Ponce de León landed near present-day St. Augustine, Florida, during his search. He took control of the land for Spain. He named the land *La Florida*, which means "land of flowers."

Ponce de León

Vocabulary

legend	colonize
fort	mission
colony	citizen

Ponce de León and his men did not find the Fountain of Youth. Ponce de León was very disappointed and left Florida. He sailed to what is known today as Puerto Rico and then back to Spain.

Ponce de León sailed to the west coast of Florida in 1521. He brought with him about 200 settlers, 50 horses and other animals, as well as farm tools. When Ponce de León and his party landed, they went to battle with a group of American Indians. Ponce de León was wounded, and he died soon after.

Ponce de León was the first European to explore the area of Florida that is near St. Augustine. This led to others exploring the area after him.

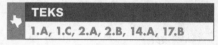

TEKS
1.A, 1.C, 2.A, 2.B, 14.A, 17.B

1. **Describe** how Ponce de León's landing affected American Indian communities.

....

....

....

....

Present-day Florida

Alabama · Georgia · Tallahassee ★ · Jacksonville • · St. Augustine • · Gulf of Mexico · Tampa • · Miami •

N W E S

LEGEND
★ Capital city
• City

0 — 140 mi
0 — 140 km

Spain and France Fight to Settle Florida

Spain and France both wanted to build a settlement in Florida. In 1564, the French set up a fort and a colony on the St. John's River. A **fort** is a strong building or area that can be defended against enemy attacks. A **colony** is a place ruled by another country. The French fort was named Fort Caroline.

Fort Caroline was close to where the Spaniards had first landed. The Spanish treasure ships sailed along the Florida coast past Fort Caroline on their way from South America to Spain. The French fort and settlement threatened the Spanish ships. King Philip II of Spain came up with a plan to keep his ships safe from enemy attacks. He sent Don Pedro Menéndez de Avilés [ah vee LAYS], a Spanish explorer, to set up and lead a Spanish colony in Florida. The king felt he could depend on Menéndez to protect the Spanish ships.

King Philip II of Spain wanted to protect Spanish treasure ships, like the one shown at left, that were threatened by Fort Caroline, shown below.

King Philip ordered Menéndez to explore and settle Florida. He also told Menéndez to drive out any settlers and pirates from other countries. A pirate is a person who robs ships or boats at sea.

Menéndez arrived in Florida in 1565. Menéndez, his soldiers, and the settlers built a fort for security. They named it Castillo de San Marcos. The area was protected from the ocean. It could be defended easily. Then Menéndez started a settlement. He called it St. Augustine.

Menéndez defeated the French at Fort Caroline. Then a hurricane off the Atlantic Ocean wrecked an entire French fleet of ships. As a result, Spain controlled the coast of Florida. More Spaniards came to settle in St. Augustine. It became the first permanent European settlement in North America.

Don Pedro
Menéndez de Avilés

2. ◉ **Sequence** **Review** the section. Then, list the sequence of events that led to the Spaniards settling St. Augustine.

....

....

....

....

....

....

St. Augustine is the oldest European city in the United States.

The Spanish Explore the Southwest

In the 1500s Spanish people already lived in New Spain, present-day Mexico. They heard another American Indian legend describing Seven Cities of Gold, one of them named Cibola. This city was supposed to be located to the north, in the present-day Southwest region of the United States.

Spanish explorer Francisco Vazques de Coronado influenced the history of the region through his explorations in search of gold. Cibola turned out to be an American Indian village. There was no gold in Cibola. However, the Zunis told Coronado to continue north to Quivira. Today, some people say that American Indians invented legends to make trouble for Spanish explorers. Coronado's expedition did not find gold in Quivira either, and he returned to New Spain in 1540, disappointed. All the same, even 60 years later, explorers like Juan de Oñate followed in Coronado's footsteps in search of Quivira gold.

Juan de Oñate

Oñate left New Spain in 1598 with an expedition of soldiers, colonists, children, and cattle. They crossed the Chihuahuan Desert. On the forty-fifth day, the expedition ran out of food and water. The travelers searched for plants to eat, but they found very little to eat or drink. Many people nearly died. Finally, they came to the Rio Grande, and their lives were saved.

After resting, hunting, and fishing for ten days, Oñate ordered a day of Thanksgiving. A member of the expedition described the celebration.

> We built a great bonfire and roasted the meat
> and fish, and then all sat down to a repast
> the like of which we had never enjoyed before.
> We were happy that our trials were over…

Some historians say that this feast was truly the first Thanksgiving. Every year in El Paso, Texas, people reenact this important event.

Spanish Settlements in the Southwest

After the day of Thanksgiving Oñate colonized New Mexico for Spain, and most of his expedition began to make homes. To **colonize** means to settle lands for another country. This was the first Spanish settlement in the Southwest. Oñate was famous for being a cruel leader. In fact, when Oñate returned from searching for gold in Quivara, most of his colony was gone. He was not the only Spaniard to settle the Southwest, though.

In present-day Texas, Spaniards started settlements called missions. A **mission** is a settlement that has a church where religion is taught. In 1691, present-day San Antonio was land where Papaya Indians lived. By 1718, the Mission San Antonio de Valero stood there. That mission later became known as the Alamo.

Texas missions taught American Indians Spanish culture.

3. **Describe** how Juan de Oñate contributed to the expansion of existing communities or the creation of new communities.

....

....

Spanish Settlements in California

After the Spaniards settled St. Augustine and the Southwest, they colonized other places. The Spaniards colonized parts of California. Here the Spaniards began towns called pueblos. They also built presidios, or forts. In California, just as in Florida and the Southwest, the Spaniards also set up missions.

The first missions in California were built in the 1760s. They were set up as places to teach the American Indians who lived there about Spanish culture and religion. Spain's king sent a religious leader named Junípero Serra to continue setting up missions. He and other leaders taught some of the American Indians how to read and write the Spanish language, and how to prepare Spanish foods.

The Spaniards built pueblos like this one in present-day California.

Spain Loses Power

The country of Spain sent money to support the missions. Then, in the early 1800s, Spain told the religious leaders to stop building missions in California. The last mission was built in 1823.

People moving to California at that time wanted the Mexican government to make the American Indians leave the missions. Mexico had control of California. So, in 1826, the head of government in California allowed many of these American Indians to leave and become Mexican citizens. A **citizen** is an official member of a community. When they left the missions, the American Indians needed new places to live and new jobs. Leaving the missions sometimes made their lives more difficult. However, many California Indians did not like how the missions affected their cultures.

4.  Sequence **Identify** and underline the sentences that tell when the first and last missions were built.

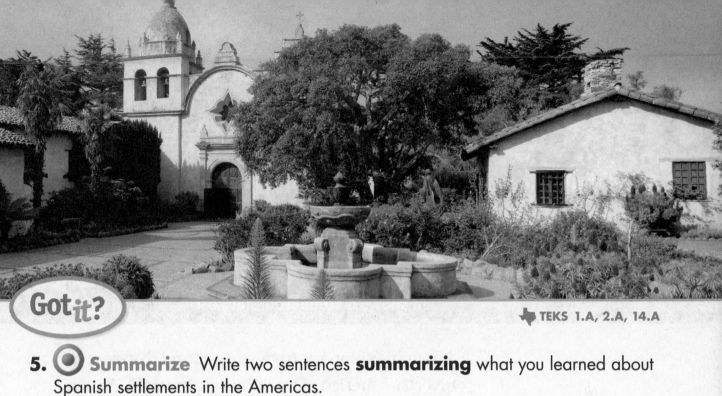

Got it?

5. ⊙ **Summarize** Write two sentences **summarizing** what you learned about Spanish settlements in the Americas.

....

....

....

....

6. ❓ **Identify** reasons the Spanish formed communities in the present-day United States.

my Story Ideas

....

....

....

7. In this lesson you read about Spanish explorers during the sixteenth and seventeenth centuries. **Compare** a Spanish explorer from long ago to the present-day Hispanic hero Ellen Ochoa. **Describe** how their ideas have changed communities in the past and the present.

....

....

Early French Communities

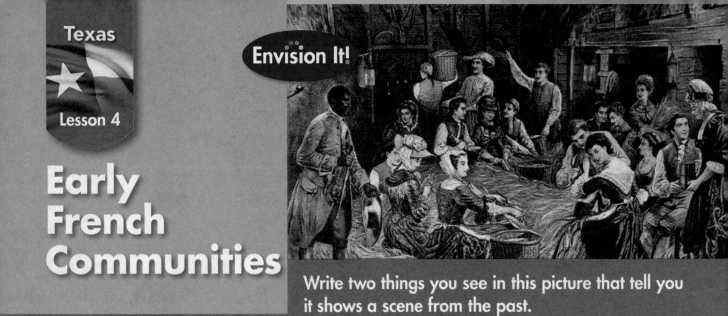

Envision It!

Write two things you see in this picture that tell you it shows a scene from the past.

French explorers traveled to many different parts of North America. The explorers brought French culture with them to the places they traveled. Many cities in North America founded by the French have kept parts of French culture.

The French Come to North America

In 1498, Vasco de Gama, an explorer from Portugal, found an all-water route to India. The French thought it might be faster to travel by inland waterways, so they explored rivers and streams.

In 1534, Jacques Cartier landed in Newfoundland. Then he explored the Gulf of St. Lawrence in present-day Canada. Cartier later sailed up the St. Lawrence River. He realized that it was not the direct route to Asia that he was looking for. Rough waters made traveling west too dangerous, so he returned home.

St. Louis, Missouri, is a city that was first settled by the French. In 1700, priests built a mission there. American Indians joined the priests, but the settlement did not last.

Newfoundland, Canada

LEGEND
— Present-day border

N W E S

0   300 mi
0   300 km

Quebec Churchill River Labrador

ATLANTIC OCEAN

Newfoundland

Gulf of St. Lawrence

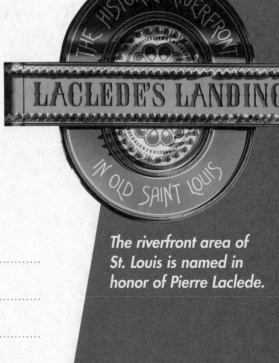

UNLOCK THE BIG ?

I will know about early French explorers and settlers in North America.

Vocabulary

expedition
territory

Around 1760, a Frenchman named Pierre Laclede traveled to the same place the mission had been set up in 1700. Here he set up a trading post where things such as fur could be traded for other items. Laclede wanted to buy fur from the American Indians. He named the area St. Louis for King Louis of France. Laclede said he wanted to set up "one of the finest cities in America." He did!

In time, France lost control of St. Louis. The city opened to new settlers and new businesses. However, French culture is still important in St. Louis today.

TEKS
1.A, 1.B, 2.A, 2.B, 3.C, 4.A, 4.B, 17.B

1. **Describe** how Laclede's ideas shaped Saint Louis.

....

....

....

....

....

The riverfront area of St. Louis is named in honor of Pierre Laclede.

PEARSON realize. Go online to access your interactive digital lesson.

119

Champlain Builds Quebec City

In 1608, Samuel de Champlain sailed from France to present-day Canada. He built a village near an area where an American Indian group called the Huron already lived. He became friends with the people of this nation.

Champlain called his village Quebec City. England and France fought over this village. They both wanted to take control because of its location. Quebec City was on two waterways, the St. Lawrence and the St. Charles rivers. Settlers could use these rivers for trade and for traveling from one place to another. In 1759, the English won a battle against the French. As a result, French rule in Canada ended.

Today, French culture is still strong in Quebec City. People speak French, and they celebrate French customs and traditions. Old Quebec is a popular place to visit. It is the part of the city on top of a hill. Le Chateau (sha TOH) Frontenac is in the center of Old Quebec. It was built in 1893 on a hilltop overlooking the St. Lawrence River. Standing there, you can see for miles.

Le Chateau Frontenac

2. **Explain** why the location of Quebec City was so important.

....

....

....

....

....

....

Exploring the Mississippi River

The French explored inland waterways instead of traveling along the coast. In 1672, a Frenchman named Louis Joliet was put in charge of an expedition down the Mississippi River. An **expedition** is a trip made for a special reason. Joliet and a priest named Father Marquette traveled from present-day Canada down the Mississippi River. They traveled to the places that we know today as Green Bay, Wisconsin, and Chicago, Illinois. They learned that the Mississippi River empties into the Gulf of Mexico.

Earlier in the 1600s, Robert de La Salle explored the Great Lakes, the Mississippi River, and more. He claimed the entire Mississippi region for France. In 1634, Jean Nicolet took seven American Indians with him in a large canoe and they went on an expedition to Lake Michigan. Nicolet also discovered what is now the state of Wisconsin.

Because of these explorers and others like them, the French began to gain power and control in North America. They claimed big parts of the continent for France.

3. ◎ Sequence **Identify** who explored the Mississippi River first: Louis Joliet or Robert de La Salle.

....

Joliet traveled by canoe through the wild rapids near Montreal, Canada.

121

French Lose Power in North America

Both the British and the French wanted to control the northern part of North America. As a result, the French and Indian War began. It lasted from 1754 to 1763. Some American Indians fought with the French against the British. The French lost the war and lost control of much of their land to the British.

In 1803, France continued to lose power in North America. The United States bought the Louisiana Territory from France. A **territory** is an area of land owned by a country either within or outside the country's borders. This is called the Louisiana Purchase. It stretched all the way from the Mississippi River to the Rocky Mountains and more than doubled the size of the United States.

A British soldier fighting in the French and Indian War

4. **Trace** the outline of the Louisiana Purchase. Then **draw** a dotted line around all of the states.

Louisiana Purchase

ROCKY MOUNTAINS

Louisiana Purchase

Mississippi River

Indiana Territory

Ohio

New Hampshire
Vermont

Mass.

New York

Rhode Island
Connecticut
New Jersey
Delaware
Maryland

Pennsylvania

Virginia

Kentucky

Tennessee

North Carolina

South Carolina

Unorganized Territory

Georgia

Mississippi Territory

ATLANTIC OCEAN

LEGEND
- State
- Territory
- Louisiana Purchase
- Disputed area

N
W   E
S

0   400 mi
0   400 km

Got it?

↟ TEKS 1.A, 2.A, 3.C, 17.B

5. ◉ **Sequence Identify** three main events of the lesson in order from first to last. For each event, **explain** why it was important.

[ ]

↓

[ ]

↓

[ ]

6. **?** **Describe** seventeenth-century exploration of the Mississippi River.

myStory Ideas

....

....

....

....

7. Research the Huguenots, another group of French immigrants who came to live in North America long ago. **Explain** to a partner why the Huguenots left France, and why they formed communities long ago in what is the present-day United States.

....

....

PEARSON
realize Go online to access your interactive digital lesson.

123

Early English Communities

Envision It!

You are traveling by ship from England to Virginia in 1607. Draw three things you bring with you.

The exploration of North America opened up new lands to settle. The Spaniards and French started new settlements here. Now the English came, too.

Roanoke Colony

In 1587, Sir Walter Raleigh sent English settlers to start a colony on Roanoke Island in present-day North Carolina. Raleigh put John White in charge of the settlers. When Roanoke Island needed supplies, White sailed back to England, and he did not come back to the colony until 1590.

When John White returned to the island, all 113 men, women, and children he had left there were gone. White found the word *CROATOAN* carved on a tree. Some people think White told the settlers to carve this word if they moved while he was gone.

The lost colony is still a mystery. Some scientists believe there was a **drought**, or not enough water at that time. Some historians think the settlers may have gone to live with American Indians, or that the settlers may have died from disease or hunger.

1. **Identify** and underline the clue that tells what might have happened to the settlers of Roanoke Colony.

Roanoke Colony

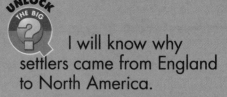

UNLOCK THE BIG ?

I will know why settlers came from England to North America.

Vocabulary
....

drought   Quaker
debt   pilgrim
interpreter

Jamestown

Around May 14, 1607, 105 English settlers arrived in what is now Virginia. Captain Christopher Newport brought them there on three ships: the *Godspeed*, the *Discovery*, and the *Susan Constant*. The settlers named their new colony Jamestown, and they named the nearby river after King James I.

Long before the English came, American Indians built villages and planted crops in Virginia. Soon after the English settlers arrived, the settlers ran out of food. While Captain John Smith, a colony leader, searched for more food, American Indians captured him and his group. They brought the group to their chief, Powhatan. One legend says Smith's life was saved by Powhatan's daughter, Pocahontas.

By the time Smith returned to Jamestown, only about 38 settlers were still alive. The rest had died of hunger and disease.

2. **Identify** things early communities needed to survive.

....

....

TEKS

1.A, 1.B, 1.C, 2.A

Pocahontas saves Captain John Smith.

England's Colonies

Everyone vanished at Roanoke Colony. Many died at Jamestown, yet the English settlers did not give up. In fact, they would go on to settle 13 colonies. By the 1660s, some settlers had moved south from Virginia. A colony was set up in present-day North and South Carolina. People called it Carolina.

The colonists who settled in the southern colonies brought African slaves with them. The enslaved Africans farmed the land.

In 1733, James Oglethorpe founded the Georgia colony. Oglethorpe set up this colony to help people who were in prison for not paying a debt. A **debt** is money that is owed to another person. People owing debts settled in Georgia. Oglethorpe wanted to give these people a chance to start a new life in his colony.

Mary Musgrove also played a key role in the founding of Georgia. Musgrove, a Creek American Indian, served as an interpreter for Oglethorpe. As an **interpreter,** she helped the English and American Indians speak with each other because she was able to speak both languages. She helped the American Indians and English get along and keep the peace.

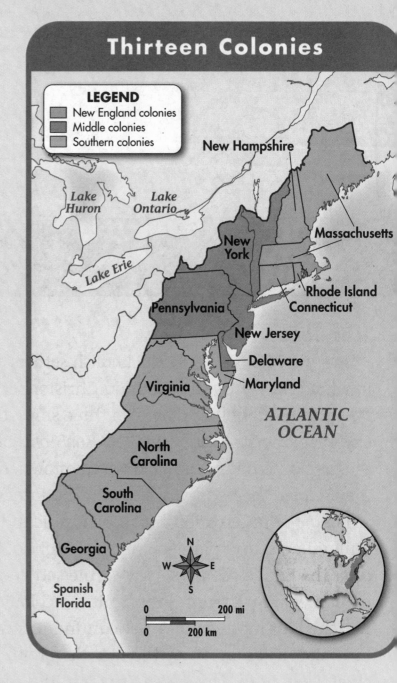

Thirteen Colonies

LEGEND
New England colonies
Middle colonies
Southern colonies

Lake Huron
Lake Ontario
Lake Erie

New Hampshire
Massachusetts
New York
Rhode Island
Connecticut
Pennsylvania
New Jersey
Delaware
Maryland
Virginia
North Carolina
South Carolina
Georgia
Spanish Florida

ATLANTIC OCEAN

N W E S

0   200 mi
0   200 km

3. **Identify** and circle the names of the southern colonies on the map.

Settling the Middle Colonies

New York, New Jersey, Pennsylvania, and Delaware are the middle colonies. Can you guess how they got this name? They are right between the southern colonies and the colonies to the north.

In 1664, Holland lost the land that would later become three of the middle colonies in a war against the English. The Duke of York got one part of the land. He named it New York, after himself. The duke gave the other part of his land to two friends. These other parts eventually became the colonies of New Jersey and Delaware. Pennsylvania, however, was started in a very different way.

William Penn started the colony of Pennsylvania as a "holy experiment." Penn was a Quaker. A **Quaker** is a follower of a religion that believes in peace and equal treatment for all people. Many people came to Penn's colony. People from Germany and Ireland were among the first settlers to come there for religious freedom.

Benjamin Franklin is one of the most famous people who lived in Philadelphia, Pennsylvania. He moved there because there were many more opportunities than in his home city of Boston, Massachusetts. Wherever Franklin went, he tried to make it a better place to live. He began Philadelphia's first fire department. Thanks to Franklin, Philadelphia became a safer city.

4. Choose one of the middle colonies, and **explain** how it was started.

....

....

....

A statue of William Penn

Benjamin Franklin was a firefighter in Philadelphia.

New England Colonies

Massachusetts, Connecticut, Rhode Island, and New Hampshire were called the New England colonies.

In 1620, William Bradford led a group of Pilgrims on board a ship called the *Mayflower*. A **pilgrim** is a person who travels for a religious reason. Sixty-six days later, they landed in Provincetown Harbor in present-day Massachusetts. They came to the colonies to be free to follow their religion.

First, the Pilgrims formed a community in Plymouth, Massachusetts. Then, they wrote a plan of government called the Mayflower Compact. It said the colonists themselves would make laws for the good of the community. Everyone agreed to obey these laws. This was the first time European colonists in America had made laws for themselves.

People act out the first Thanksgiving.

Bradford became the leader. He was a good leader. The Pilgrims and American Indians began trading food and other items. Squanto, an American Indian who spoke English, served as an interpreter. In 1621, the Pilgrims and the American Indians sat down to share in a harvest feast. Today, we mark this as the first Thanksgiving.

A woman named Anne Hutchinson did not follow the Pilgrims' beliefs. She began spreading her own beliefs. As a result, in 1634, she was forced to leave Massachusetts. She later founded Portsmouth, Rhode Island.

5. ◉ Sequence **Identify** and underline the first and second things the Pilgrims did when they came to America.

6. ⊙ **Main Idea and Details Review** the section. Then fill in the chart below with details that support the main idea. **Identify** the needs that cause people to form communities.

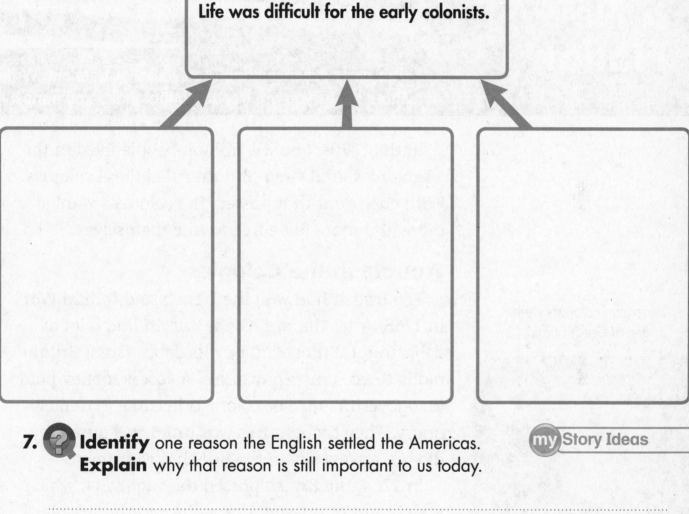

Life was difficult for the early colonists.

7. **Identify** one reason the English settled the Americas. **Explain** why that reason is still important to us today.

my Story Ideas

....

....

....

8. Describe how Benjamin Franklin changed his community by starting Philadelphia's first fire department.

....

....

....

Creating a New Nation

Envision It!

This early American flag is a symbol of freedom. Write three things you are free to do that make you happy.

In the 1770s, about 2 million people lived in the 13 colonies, and Great Britain ruled these colonies. With each year that passed, the colonists wanted more and more to be free to rule themselves.

Trouble in the Colonies

The British had won the French and Indian War in 1763. After the war, Great Britain had a lot of debt. To raise money to pay its debts, Great Britain made the colonists pay taxes. A **tax** is money paid to a government. The colonists became extremely angry. They thought this was unfair because they did not have a say in the British government.

In 1764, the British passed the Sugar Act, which taxed most of the sugar brought into the colonies. Then in 1765, Great Britain passed the Stamp Act. The Stamp Act taxed all printed items, such as newspapers and legal papers.

The colonists became more angry, saying, "No taxation without representation!" They would not pay taxes unless they had a say in the government.

The Stamp Act ended, but there were new taxes on paper, glass, and lead. Many colonists refused to buy these things, so the British lost a lot of money.

American colonists were angry at Great Britain.

UNLOCK THE BIG ?

I will know the causes and effects of the American Revolution.

Vocabulary

tax   independence

protest   revolution

legislature   constitution

patriot

In 1773, the British passed the Tea Act, which said the colonists could buy tea only from Great Britain. To **protest,** or complain, some colonists dressed as American Indians. They went on British ships in Boston Harbor, and they dumped all the tea overboard! This was called the Boston Tea Party. The British were angry, so they closed Boston Harbor and also took many powers away from the Massachusetts legislature. A **legislature** is a part of government that makes laws.

The problem was over money, power, and control. Who should rule America: Great Britain or the colonists?

TEKS

1.A, 1.B, 1.C, 2.A, 3.A, 3.C, 10.A, 17.B

1. **Explain** why the colonists dumped all of the tea overboard in Boston Harbor.

....

....

....

....

The Boston Tea Party

PEARSON **realize** Go online to access your interactive digital lesson.

131

American Patriots

Many American colonists known as Patriots grew more and more angry about British rule. A **patriot** is a person who loves and defends his or her country and upholds people's rights. The Patriots wanted the American colonies to be free.

The Patriots came from different backgrounds. Some were young, like Nathan Hale. Others were older, like Benjamin Franklin. Some were leaders, like Thomas Jefferson. Others were farmers, like Daniel Shays. They all worked hard to win **independence,** or freedom, for the colonies.

On April 18, 1775, a Patriot named Paul Revere rode from Boston to Lexington, Massachusetts, to warn colonial leaders Samuel Adams and John Hancock that British troops were coming to arrest them. Revere also wanted to stop the British from taking the colonists' weapons. He went to each house along his ride to warn everyone that the British were coming.

A war was about to begin. The War for Independence, or the war between the American colonies and the British, is also called the American Revolution. A **revolution** takes place when people want to take over the government that rules them and create a new one. The war started on April 19, 1775, in the towns of Lexington and Concord in Massachusetts.

Paul Revere's ride

2. Explain why people became Patriots.

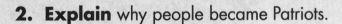

Freedom and Government

In the summer of 1776, Thomas Jefferson wrote the Declaration of Independence. It told the world why the colonies were breaking away from Great Britain. It explained what the new nation stood for.

The first part said that people have rights that the government must protect. The second part listed the complaints the colonists had against the British king. The third part said the colonies were now free and independent states and not part of Great Britain.

The American Revolution lasted eight years. It took America that long to win independence from Great Britain. Fifty-five people met in Philadelphia in May 1787 to write a new plan of government, the United States Constitution. A **constitution** is a written plan of government that explains the beliefs and laws of a country. George Washington, Benjamin Franklin, and James Madison were three Founding Fathers. They helped write the Declaration of Independence and the Constitution and helped the country grow.

On September 17, 1787, the members completed their work. They had written a new plan of government for the United States. The people, not a king, would rule the new, independent nation.

3. ◎ **Summarize** what was included in the three parts of the Declaration of Independence.

....

....

....

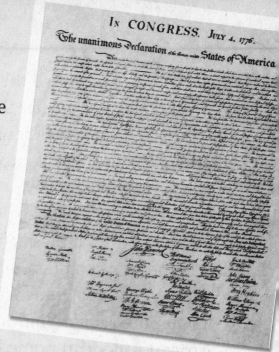

Declaration of Independence

Signing the Declaration of Independence

Washington, D.C.

George Washington led the colonial soldiers in the American Revolution. After the war, he wanted to go to his home at Mount Vernon, Virginia, and farm his land. Other leaders wanted Washington to lead the new government.

George Washington

On February 4, 1789, the people elected Washington our first president. Lawmakers decided to build the new capital at a place they called Federal City. Today, it is known as Washington, D.C.

One hundred square miles of land was set aside. An African American named Benjamin Banneker surveyed, or measured, the land to figure out its border. Banneker had taught himself to survey land by studying the stars in the night sky. He used stones to mark the land at each mile.

In the year 1791, a Frenchman named Pierre L'Enfant designed Washington, D.C. He chose the sites for the two most important buildings there: the Capitol and the White House. He also designed wide streets lined with trees. He set up spaces so that statues could be built to honor important people.

Washington, D.C., is named after George Washington. He is remembered as a great leader. A general summed up George Washington's life this way: ". . . first in war, first in peace, and first in the hearts of his countrymen."

4. **Identify** and underline the names of the people who helped create Washington, D.C.

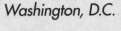

Washington, D.C.

5. ◉ Sequence **Analyze** the lesson. Then **sequence** the events below in the order of the year they happened.

> • The U.S. Constitution is completed.　• The French and Indian War ends.
>
> • Great Britain passes the Stamp Act.　• Paul Revere rides to Lexington.

1763 ....

....

1765 ....

....

1775 ....

....

1787 ....

....

6. **Explain** how the Founding Fathers helped build a new nation.

my Story Ideas

....

....

....

7. **Research** the Bill of Rights. **Explain** what religious freedom is, and why the Founding Fathers added it to the Constitution. **Identify** two groups that moved to the colonies for religious freedom.

....

....

Lesson 1 TEKS 4.B

America's First Peoples

1. Read the question carefully. Determine the best answer to the question from the four answer choices provided. Circle the best answer.

What is the reason the Iroquois settled in present-day New York State and Canada?

A to separate themselves from other groups

B to show they were strong leaders

C to use trees from the forests to build homes

D to look for beaver furs

Lesson 2 TEKS 1.A

Early Explorers

2. **Review** the lesson. Then fill in the chart with the correct information about each explorer.

Explorer	Country	Where They Explored
Christopher Columbus		
Samuel de Champlain		
Sir Francis Drake		

Lesson 3 ⬥ TEKS 2.A, 2.B

Early Spanish Communities

3. **Identify** the reasons Spaniards explored the Americas and built
pueblos and presidios.

....

....

....

....

4. **Identify** one way the Spaniards met their need to teach
American Indians about Spanish culture. Then, write the American
Indian point of view on the same subject.

....

....

....

....

....

....

Lesson 4 ⬥ TEKS 1.B

Early French Communities

5. **Identify** the Frenchmen who shaped Saint Louis and
Quebec City.

....

....

Lesson 5 ⭐ TEKS 1.C

Early English Communities

6. Describe how William Bradford contributed to the creation of a new community.

....

....

....

Lesson 6 ⭐ TEKS 3.C, 10.A, 17.B

Creating a New Nation

7. Identify the purposes of the Declaration of Independence and the U.S. Constitution.

....

....

....

....

....

8. ◎ Sequence **Number** the following events in order. Then write the year, or years, each event took place.

_____ The American Revolution began. _____

_____ The Boston Tea Party took place. _____

_____ George Washington became our first president. _____

_____ James Madison helped write the United States Constitution. _____

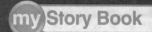

Go online to write and illustrate your own **myStory Book** using the **myStory Ideas** from this chapter.

How does our past affect our present?

TEKS
SS 3.A
ELA 17

In this chapter you have learned about how our history affects our life today. Explorers came from all over the world to America. We learned from these early explorers.

Think about your own life. **Write** about something you learned in your past that helps you today.

....

....

....

....

Now **draw** a picture showing something you learned when you were younger that you do or use today.

U.S. Government

Why do we have government?

Think about why leaders make rules. Then **write** about why rules are important.

....

....

....

....

....

....

....

....

Texas Essential Knowledge and Skills

1.A Describe how individuals, events, and ideas have changed communities, past and present.

2.A Identify reasons people have formed communities, including a need for security, religious freedom, law, and material well-being.

9.A Describe the basic structure of government in the local community, state, and nation.

9.B Identify local, state, and national government officials and explain how they are chosen.

9.C Identify services commonly provided by local, state, and national governments.

9.D Explain how local, state, and national government services are financed.

10.A Identify the purposes of the Declaration of Independence and the U.S. Constitution, including the Bill of Rights.

10.B Describe and explain the importance of the concept of "consent of the governed" as it relates to the functions of local, state, and national government.

17.A Research information, including historical and current events, and geographic data, about the community and world, using a variety of valid print, oral, visual, and Internet resources.

17.C Interpret oral, visual, and print material by identifying the main idea, distinguishing between fact and opinion, identifying cause and effect, and comparing and contrasting.

18.A Express ideas orally based on knowledge and experiences.

George Washington
America's First President

my Story Video

You may know of a story about George Washington when he was a child. In the story, his father gave him a hatchet. A hatchet is a small ax used to chop wood. One day, George chopped down a cherry tree with his hatchet. George's father saw the cherry tree on the ground. Shocked, he asked his son, "What did you do?"

"I cannot tell a lie, Pa," George said. "I cut the tree down with my hatchet." Even though George's father was unhappy that George cut down the tree, he was happy that his son was honest.

Today, we know that this story is not true. It was likely made up to show that George Washington was an honest person. However, there are stories about him that are true. These stories are based on facts. Here are some facts about Washington.

In 1732, Washington was born in Virginia. He lived with his family on a farm. In 1743, Washington went to live with family at Mount Vernon. Soon after, he worked as a surveyor. As a surveyor, he measured and charted land.

Washington worked as a surveyor.

141

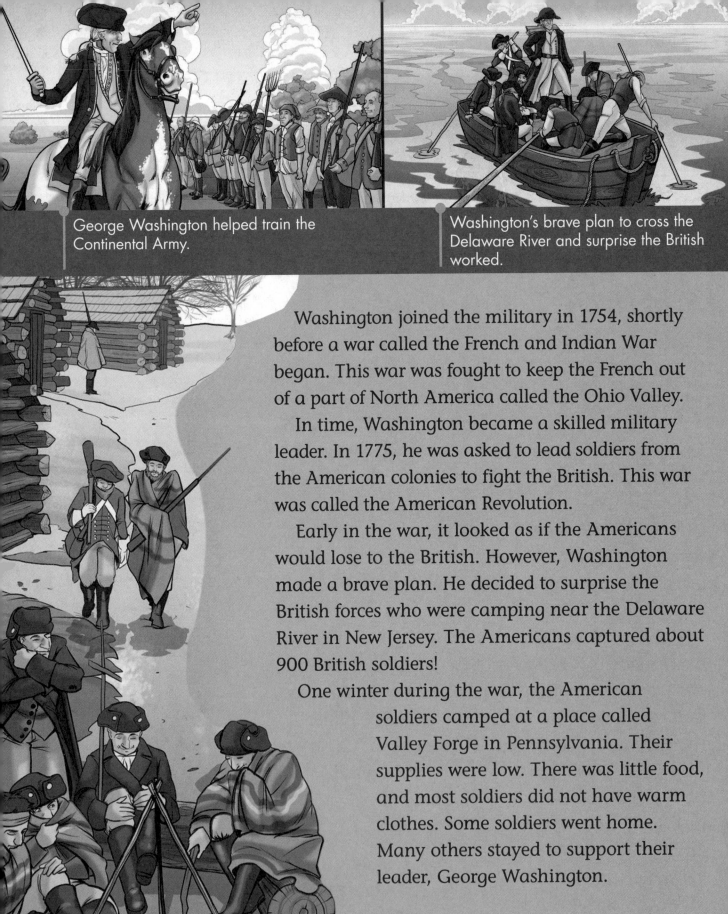

George Washington helped train the Continental Army.

Washington's brave plan to cross the Delaware River and surprise the British worked.

Washington joined the military in 1754, shortly before a war called the French and Indian War began. This war was fought to keep the French out of a part of North America called the Ohio Valley.

In time, Washington became a skilled military leader. In 1775, he was asked to lead soldiers from the American colonies to fight the British. This war was called the American Revolution.

Early in the war, it looked as if the Americans would lose to the British. However, Washington made a brave plan. He decided to surprise the British forces who were camping near the Delaware River in New Jersey. The Americans captured about 900 British soldiers!

One winter during the war, the American soldiers camped at a place called Valley Forge in Pennsylvania. Their supplies were low. There was little food, and most soldiers did not have warm clothes. Some soldiers went home. Many others stayed to support their leader, George Washington.

At Valley Forge, soldiers used whatever supplies that they could find.

Many Americans trusted Washington.

Washington and other leaders helped build a strong government.

The American Revolution ended in 1783. The American colonies won and were now free from Great Britain. The colonies became the United States of America. After the war, Washington planned to go home to Mount Vernon. However, he had become a well-known leader and had more work to do. In 1787, Washington traveled to a large meeting in Philadelphia called the Constitutional Convention. American leaders came together to write a plan for the new government. This plan became known as the United States Constitution.

In 1788, Washington was elected as the first president of the United States. He used the ideas and laws written in the Constitution to show what the job of the president should be. Today, presidents still do many of the same tasks that Washington did as president.

Washington died at Mount Vernon in 1799. The story of the cherry tree was not true. However, through his actions, we know that Washington was honest, brave, and loyal to his country.

Think About It Based on this story, how did Washington show he was loyal to his country? As you read the chapter ahead, think about what Washington's life shows you about supporting the government.

Our Constitutional Republic

Circle the pictures that show items that help keep people safe.

Think about some of the rules that you follow in your classroom. Some rules help keep order. For example, students should listen while others speak. Other rules keep everyone safe. During fire drills, it is important that everyone walk calmly and quietly. Students, teachers, and principals all make and follow rules to help schools run smoothly.

Why We Need Government

In communities all around the world, people set up governments. People need governments to make laws that keep order and help communities run smoothly. Just as there are classroom rules, there are laws that describe how citizens should behave. Some of these laws keep people safe. There are speed limits and traffic lights to help prevent automobile accidents. There are also laws that protect people's rights.

People also need governments to provide services that they cannot provide for themselves. Governments hire police officers and firefighters. Police officers make sure people follow laws. Like firefighters, they work to protect people and their property.

Firefighters protect people.

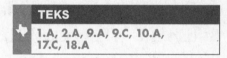

UNLOCK
THE BIG
?

I will know why we need government and what America's government is about.

Vocabulary

constitutional republic
represent
liberty

There are different forms, or types, of government in different communities around the world. The government of the United States is run by its citizens. It is a constitutional republic. In a **constitutional republic**, people are governed by the leaders they elect. These officials must follow the laws of the country.

In some governments around the world, the people do not have a say in who leads them. The country may be ruled by a king or queen whose father or mother was the king or queen before them. A king or queen may or may not allow people to vote for laws. A country may also be ruled by a single person or a small group who rule with complete power. In these countries, people have no say in who leads or in what the laws will be.

TEKS
1.A, 2.A, 9.A, 9.C, 10.A, 17.C, 18.A

1. **Identify** and underline the reasons people need government. Then **identify** the form of government of the United States.

Governments place signs near roads to remind drivers to drive carefully.

Freedom and Happiness

In the 1700s, King George III and the British government ruled the colonies in North America. Many people living in the colonies, including Patrick Henry, spoke out against British rule. Henry and other colonists wanted people to **represent**, or speak for, them in government. They also wanted a government that protected the rights of all of its people, not just those in Great Britain. The rights that colonists wanted included the right to live freely, the right to follow any religion, the right to vote, and the right to a fair trial.

The colonists wanted **liberty**, or freedom, from British rule. They asked Thomas Jefferson to write the Declaration of Independence. One purpose was to tell the rights people should have.

"We hold these truths to be self-evident [clear], that all men are created equal, that they are endowed [born with] by their Creator with certain unalienable [secure] Rights, that among these are Life, Liberty and the pursuit of Happiness."

— Declaration of Independence

Patrick Henry speaks out against British rule.

146

The Declaration of Independence had another purpose. Jefferson wrote that a government must protect citizens' rights. If a government took away these rights, the people could change the government or form a new one. The colonists did not have these rights when Great Britain ruled them. They fought a war against Great Britain to win these rights. This war was called the American Revolution. The Americans won the war in 1783.

2. ◉ **Cause and Effect** **Identify** the missing cause and effect. Then fill in the chart.

The American Revolution

Cause	Effect
	The colonists wrote the Declaration of Independence.
Colonists fought against Great Britain in the American Revolution.	

An Independence Day celebration

The States Come Together

Even before the American Revolution was over, the American colonies declared themselves states in a new nation. After the war, the states faced problems. People in the different states argued over money and land. In addition, the leaders could not set rules for trade between the states. The Americans needed a plan to bring the country together. As a result, many leaders gathered to write the United States Constitution.

Some of the laws in the Constitution are based on ideas used long ago by the government in Greece. These ideas include that a government gets its power from the people. In the United States, people vote for leaders to represent them. In Greece, however, each citizen voted only on issues.

Before the Constitution could become law, 9 of the 13 states had to sign it. In doing so, the states agreed that the Constitution was the highest law. Although each state had its own constitution and laws, state laws could not go against the United States Constitution.

The United States Constitution

Leaders met in Philadelphia to write the Constitution.

In 1788, New Hampshire was the ninth state to sign and agree to the United States Constitution. The United States Constitution then became the new plan of government.

3. ◉ **Summarize Write** a summary that **identifies** the purpose of the United States Constitution.

....

....

....

Got it?

🔻 TEKS 2.A, 10.A, 18.A

4. ◉ **Summarize Write** a summary that **explains** why people need government.

....

....

....

....

5. ❓ **Explain** why American leaders wrote the United States Constitution.

 my **Story Ideas**

....

....

....

6. In this lesson, you learned about the purpose of the Declaration of Independence. Not all colonists, however, agreed with the idea of breaking away from Great Britain. Assume the role of a colonist in favor of independence. **Prepare** a speech to **express** your ideas orally about the purpose of the Declaration of Independence and why it should be signed.

Summarize

When you summarize, you state the main idea and key details in your own words. You can identify a main idea for print material that you have read. You can also find a main idea in oral material, which is something you hear, or visual material, such as photographs. In print, oral, and visual material, the main idea is the most important idea. Details give you facts about the main idea.

To write a summary, first put the main idea in your own words. Then write one or two sentences that describe the details. Again, use your own words.

Read the passage. Notice the main idea and details. Then read the summary.

The American Flag

We have rules about how to display the American flag because it is important to show respect for it. One rule is that when the flag is hung on a wall, the blue part with the stars must be on the top left as you face the flag. Many people hang the flag on a wall when they hang it inside of a building. Another rule is that the flag should never touch the floor or the ground.

This sentence states the main idea.

These sentences are the key details.

Summary

There are rules about showing the American flag. The flag should be hung a certain way on a wall. It should also stay above the ground.

This sentence tells about the main idea in the writer's own words.

These sentences tell about the key details in the writer's own words.

Learning Objective

I will know how to summarize in my own words.

TEKS

SS 17.C Interpret oral, visual, and print material by identifying the main idea.

Read the passage aloud with a partner. Study the visuals.

> You may have heard the saying that signing a paper is "putting your John Hancock" on it. This saying dates back to 1776 when the Declaration of Independence was written. A group of leaders met in Philadelphia to decide what should be included in the Declaration. After Thomas Jefferson finished writing it, the leaders signed the document before sending it to the British king. John Hancock was one of the first people to sign it. He signed his name very large so that the king would be able to read it without his glasses! As a result, Hancock's signature became very well known. Now when people are asked to put their signature on something, the signature is known as their "John Hancock."

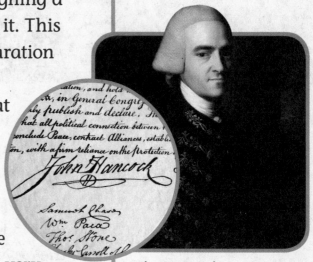

John Hancock

1. **Interpret** the material you read and heard and the visuals. Tell your partner the main idea.

   ....

2. **Identify** and underline the key details.

3. Write a summary that **identifies** the main idea and key details. Read your summary to a partner.

   ....

   ....

   ....

Branches of Government

Envision It!

Write who you think lives and works in the White House in Washington, D.C.

The writers of the U.S. Constitution wanted to make sure the power to rule the nation was divided equally. They organized the government into three parts, or branches. The **legislative** branch makes laws and raises and collects taxes to fund the government. The **executive** branch enforces, or carries out, the laws. The judges in the **judicial** branch make sure that laws are fair. Each branch has specific duties and responsibilities in our government. No one branch has more power than any other branch.

The Legislative Branch

The legislative branch is called **Congress.** Congress has two parts: the Senate and the House of Representatives.

The Senate is made up of two representatives from each state. A **representative** is a person chosen to speak for others. Citizens vote to choose these representatives. There are 100 senators. Senators are elected every six years, and they can be elected many times.

United States Capitol

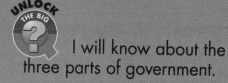

Vocabulary

legislative	representative
executive	bill
judicial	veto
Congress	Cabinet

There are 435 representatives in the House of Representatives. The number of representatives in the House depends on the number of people living in each state. The more people who live in a state, the more representatives the state has. Texas has 32 representatives. All representatives are elected every two years. Like senators, representatives speak for the people who vote for them.

The representatives in Congress raise and collect taxes. The money from taxes is used to fund, or pay for, the government. Congress also makes laws for the country. Some laws deal with safety, while other laws make sure that all people are treated fairly. All laws begin as ideas. Once an idea is written down for the government to decide on, it is called a **bill.** Before a bill can become a law, both parts of Congress must vote on it and approve it. The bill is then sent to the president to sign.

TEKS
9.A, 9.B, 9.D, 17.A

Congress meets in the U.S. Capitol.

1. Underline the sentences that **explain** how the national government is funded.

The Executive Branch

The executive branch carries out the laws. This branch is headed by the president of the United States. All the voters in the nation can elect the president. The president serves a term of four years and can only be elected for two terms. The president lives and works in the White House in Washington, D.C.

The president has more than one role in our government. One responsibility is to sign bills so they become laws. However, if the president does not agree with a bill, the president may **veto,** or reject, it. If a bill is vetoed, the only way it can become a law is if most of the members of Congress vote again to approve it.

The president is in charge of the United States military. This means the president is the commander-in-chief of members of the Army, the Navy, the Marines, and the Air Force. The president also represents our country to the rest of the world. As a world leader, the president meets with leaders from other countries to work together to solve problems.

Mount Rushmore is in South Dakota. It shows the faces of Presidents Washington, Jefferson, Roosevelt, and Lincoln.

The president also works with the Cabinet. The **Cabinet** is a group of advisors, or people who tell a leader what they think about a subject. Each advisor leads one of the 15 different departments, or groups, in the executive branch. These advisors help provide the president with information about important issues in the country. These issues may be about education, health care, or security. The president selects these advisors. However, the Senate must approve the president's choices.

The president's office in the White House is called the Oval Office.

2. ◉ **Summarize** Write a summary that **describes** the president's responsibilities.

....

....

....

....

The Judicial Branch

The judicial branch of the government is made up of courts. Judges in the courts make sure that laws are fair. They also decide the consequences, or the results, for people who break laws.

United States Supreme Court Building

The Supreme Court is the highest court in the United States. It has nine judges. Judges in the Supreme Court are called justices. The Supreme Court justices make sure the laws passed by Congress follow the U.S. Constitution. The justices also decide court cases between citizens of different states.

The president nominates, or chooses, the justices for the Supreme Court. However, the Senate must approve each choice. Supreme Court justices do not have a term limit. Once a person becomes a justice, he or she can serve for any amount of time.

The U.S. Constitution includes ways to make sure that the three branches of government work together. This system is called checks and balances. This means that each branch can check the actions of another. This helps make sure that the three branches share the power to rule. One branch does not have more power than the other branches.

The nine justices of the Supreme Court

3. Describe the roles of the justices who serve on the U.S. Supreme Court.

....

....

....

....

Got it?

🔸 TEKS 9.A, 17.A

4. ◎ **Main Idea and Details Analyze** what you have read in the lesson. Then **describe** the basic structure of government in the nation by filling in the chart.

```
                    ┌─────────────────────────────────┐
                    │    Branches of Government        │
                    └─────────────────────────────────┘
                         ↑          ↑          ↑
```

Legislative Branch	Executive Branch	Judicial Branch

5. ⑦ **Describe** why we have three branches of government.

my Story Ideas

....

....

....

6. Use the Internet and other reference materials to **identify** the people who represent you in the national government, and **explain** how they were chosen to represent you.

Levels of Government

Envision It!

Write why schools are important to a community.

There are three different levels of government in our country: local, state, and national. Each level provides services to citizens. Each level of government is given the right to govern by the people.

The Consent of the Governed

In the Declaration of Independence, Thomas Jefferson wrote that government gets its power from the "consent of the governed." That means that since the people set up the government, they give the government its power. It also means that the people have the power to change the government.

The United States is a constitutional republic. The people give the government power by voting for leaders. They elect officials to act for them, or govern. The U.S. Constitution describes the way officials are elected and what their duties are.

The U.S. Constitution is the highest law in the country. Sometimes, people want to change the Constitution. Changes to the Constitution are called amendments. Representatives in both parts of Congress vote on amendments. If Congress

The Declaration of Independence, 1776

We hold these truths to be self-evident, ... That to secure these rights, Governments are instituted among Men, deriving their just powers from the consent of the governed...

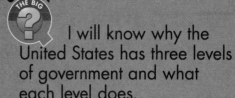

I will know why the United States has three levels of government and what each level does.

Vocabulary

mayor
council
governor
census

TEKS

9.A, 9.B, 9.C, 9.D, 10.B

approves the amendment, it goes to the states for approval. If 38 of the 50 states approve the amendment, the Constitution is changed.

Each state also has its own constitution. In most states, changes to state constitutions must also be approved by the people before they can be made. The current Texas Constitution was passed in 1876. Since then, voters have passed amendments to their constitution 474 times!

The people expect their elected officials to act on their behalf. If people are unhappy with their officials, they can act. They can share their opinions at town meetings. They can call or write to their officials to discuss issues facing their city, state, or even the country. They can also elect new officials in the next election.

Citizens can attend town meetings to tell their local government officials what they think.

1. **Explain** why "consent of the governed" is an important concept in the way local, state, and national governments work.

....

....

....

PEARSON realize Go online to access your interactive digital lesson.

159

Local Government

Cities and towns have local governments that serve their community. These governments can be organized in different ways. The way a city or town government is organized is described in the city or town charter. A charter is a legal document that describes what the powers of the local government are.

In some cities and towns, people elect a mayor or city manager as the head of the executive branch. A **mayor** is a leader of the community.

The people who make the rules and laws in a community are part of a city or town council. A **council** is a group that makes laws. Council members are often elected. These lawmakers make up the legislative branch. In some cities and towns, the council appoints someone as city manager to carry out the council's laws. Sometimes, the mayor of a city or town is chosen from the council.

The judicial branch is made up of a city's or town's courts. A judge decides what happens to people who do not follow laws. Sometimes a jury, or a group of citizens, decides if a person broke a law. Many local judges are appointed by the mayor or council of the city or town in which they serve. However, some local judges are elected.

San Antonio mayor Julian Castro reads to children. Castro is a leader in his community.

The local government provides many services that people in the community use every day. It is in charge of the police department and the fire department. The local government also provides schools, libraries, and parks. It makes sure that trash is collected. It may also cut down trees that have been damaged in storms. The local government takes care of roads. It paves roads so they are smooth, paints lines on roads, and puts up signs so the roads are safe for drivers.

Local governments provide schools for public education.

Where does the local government get the money to pay for all these services? Some money comes from the state government. Other services are paid for by the taxes that the local government collects. Local governments collect taxes on property, such as homes and businesses in the city or town. Some local governments can also charge sales tax on items you buy.

Local government also charges its citizens a fee to use some of its services. These fees help pay for the service. For example, many large cities provide buses for transporting people in the city. However, people must pay to ride the bus.

2. ◉ **Main Idea and Details** **Identify** and underline some of the services a local government provides.

3. **Explain** how local governments pay for services they provide.

....

....

....

State Government

Each state has a state government that runs it. The states also have constitutions. State constitutions describe the responsibilities of the governor, the legislature, and the courts. The **governor** is the head of a state's executive branch and is elected by the people in the state. The governor can appoint officials to help carry out laws.

Before he became president, George W. Bush was governor of Texas.

The state legislature makes laws for the state. Nearly all 50 states divide the legislative branch into the Senate and the House of Representatives. The people in each state elect the members of their state legislature. These lawmakers meet in the capitol in the state's capital city.

State governments also have courts in their judicial branch. Judges who work in state courts listen to issues that local courts could not solve. In some states, judges are elected by the people. In others, judges are appointed.

The state government provides services, too. It decides the rules for voting, such as if a person must show identification. State governments also work with local governments to keep up state highways. Some of these services are paid for with money from the national government. Others are paid for with taxes the state collects.

4. **Identify** and write the name of your governor and your state representatives. **Explain** how they are chosen.

Members of the Texas legislature meet in this building in the capital city of Austin.

....

....

162

National Government

The three branches of the national, or federal, government serve as a model for local and state governments. The president, members of Congress, and the Supreme Court justices share the responsibilities of running the country. The president and members of Congress are chosen by the people. The president appoints Supreme Court justices. The president also appoints people to the Cabinet to advise on issues.

The national government provides services that cities and states do not. Some of these services are paid for with taxes. Other services are funded by fees paid for by people who use the services. The national government prints paper money and makes coins. It runs the United States Postal Service. It is in charge of trade between states and between countries. The national government also manages the national parks.

Rangers teach about plants and animals in the national parks.

The national government serves the whole nation in other ways, too. Every ten years the national government takes a **census,** or a count of the population. This count helps the government decide how much money different communities need. The national government can also organize an army to protect the nation or its people. The government sometimes has soldiers help people and communities after harsh storms.

5. ◎ **Summarize** Write a summary that **identifies** the services provided by the national government.

....

....

Governments Work Together

Even though the local, state, and national governments all have their own responsibilities, they often work together. They work together to complete large projects such as building roads, bridges, and buildings. Local and state leaders may also ask the national government for help if there is a storm or disaster and they need resources to provide help to their citizens.

The three levels of government do similar kinds of work. They all collect taxes from citizens. This money is used to pay for the services the governments provide. The national government collects taxes on the money people earn from their jobs. Some states also collect this tax. Local governments collect taxes on items people buy and on homes and businesses they own. Local governments also rely on money from the state to fund services. States rely on money from the national government to fund services.

A local courtroom

The courts in all three levels also work together. If a local court does not resolve an issue, the case moves to a state court. Cases that are not resolved by state courts may then be decided by the United States Supreme Court justices.

6. **Explain** how each level of government pays for the services it provides.

....

....

....

....

7. ◉ **Main Idea and Details** **Identify** three services provided by each of the three levels of government.

Services Provided by Government

Local Government	State Government	National Government

8. ❓ **Explain** why people elect local, state, and national leaders.

my Story Ideas

....

....

....

....

9. In this lesson, you learned about the three levels of government. Research and **describe** the basic structure of government in your city or town and in the state of Texas. **Identify** your local leaders and your state representatives. **Explain** how your representatives are chosen.

....

....

....

Compare Viewpoints

When you compare viewpoints, you can learn different ideas about an issue. People use key phrases to show their point of view, such as *I think*, *I feel*, and *in my opinion*. Read each citizen's viewpoint on how to use empty land in a community. Then look at the diagram to see the similarities and differences in the viewpoints.

Viewpoint 1

I think the empty land should be used for a playground. We should build a slide, swings, and a sandbox. Then children will have a safe place to play. I feel this will help keep children in the community active and healthy.

Viewpoint 2

In my opinion, we should use the empty land for a farmers' market. I think a farmers' market will help children and adults in the community to be healthy. The market will also help the local farmers make money.

Viewpoint 1

- Give children a safe place to play
- Help keep children active

Both

Help keep children healthy

Viewpoint 2

- Help adults to be healthy
- Help local farmers make money

Compare the citizens' viewpoints about how to make a school less crowded. Then fill in the diagram to show the similarities and differences between the two viewpoints.

Viewpoint 1
Many new families have moved to our community. As a result, the school is very crowded because there are so many new students. I think we need to build a new school. It will cost money, but then classes will not be so crowded. Students will be able to have more time with their teachers.

Viewpoint 2
In my opinion, we should split the school schedule. Students in grades K–3 should go to school from 7:00 A.M. to 1:00 P.M. Students in grades 4–6 should go to school from 1:30 P.M. to 6:30 P.M. The school will be less crowded, and we will not have to pay to build a new school.

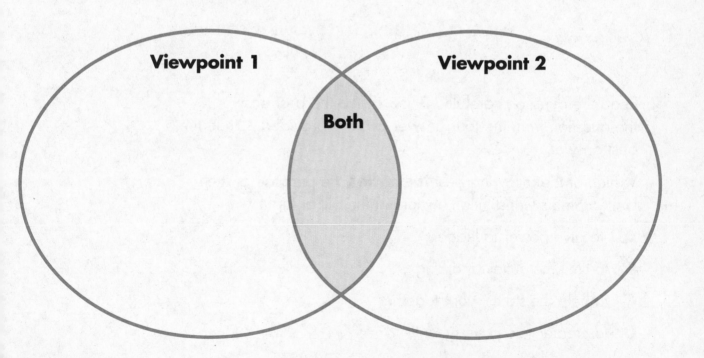

Viewpoint 1 — Both — Viewpoint 2

PEARSON realize Go online to access your interactive digital lesson.

167

Lesson 1  TEKS 9.C, 10.A

Our Constitutional Republic

1. **Identify** services that local governments provide to help keep people safe.

....

....

....

2. Underline the phrase that **describes** what liberty means.

   to pay taxes   to go to school

   to work   to live freely

3. ◉ **Summarize** **Identify** the purposes of the Declaration of Independence.

....

....

....

....

4. Read the question carefully. **Determine** the best answer to the question from the four answer choices provided. Circle the best answer.

   Which of the following best **identifies** the purpose of the United States Constitution, including the Bill of Rights?

   A   to give power to leaders

   B   to limit the duties of a king

   C   to help the states work together

   D   to create state governments

Branches of Government

5. Draw a line to match the branch of government to the phrase that **describes** its job.

executive branch   makes laws

legislative branch   makes sure laws are fair

judicial branch   carries out the laws

6. Identify the two parts of Congress.

....

....

7. Explain the different jobs the president has as the leader of the executive branch.

....

....

....

8. Explain how each branch of the national government is chosen.

....

....

....

9. Describe the system that makes sure the three branches of government work together.

....

....

....

Lesson 3   TEKS 9.B, 9.C, 10.B

Levels of Government

10. Read the question and **circle** the best answer.

Identify a service provided by the state government.

   F It prints money.

   G It manages national parks.

   H It decides the rules for voting.

   J It sets up the post office.

11. ◎ **Summarize Identify** an official at each level of government and **explain** how they are chosen.

....

....

....

....

12. Describe how the three levels of government work together to provide services.

....

....

13. Describe the concept of consent of the governed as it relates to how all levels of government function.

....

....

....

....

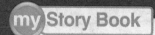

Go online to write and illustrate your own **myStory Book** using the **myStory Ideas** from this chapter.

 Why do we have government? ➥TEKS
ELA 17

The government keeps order, protects our communities, and provides us with many services. Each level of government, no matter what services it provides, works to help people.

Think about our government. **Explain** how your life might be different if our government were not a constitutional republic.

....

....

....

....

Now draw a picture to show something you are free to do because our government makes it possible.

PEARSON realize. Go online to access your interactive digital lesson.

171

Citizenship

How can I participate?

Describe some ways that people help others. Then write about a time when you did something to help someone else.

....

....

....

....

Texas Essential Knowledge and Skills

1.A Describe how individuals, events, and ideas have changed communities, past and present.

9.B Identify local, state, and national government officials and explain how they are chosen.

9.C Identify services commonly provided by local, state, and national governments.

10.A Identify the purposes of the Declaration of Independence and the U.S. Constitution, including the Bill of Rights.

11.A Identify characteristics of good citizenship, including truthfulness, justice, equality, respect for oneself and others, responsibility in daily life, and participation in government by educating oneself about the issues, respectfully holding public officials to their word, and voting.

11.B Identify historical figures such as Helen Keller and Clara Barton and contemporary figures such as Ruby Bridges and military and first responders who exemplify good citizenship.

11.C Identify and explain the importance of individual acts of civic responsibility, including obeying laws, serving the community, serving on a jury, and voting.

12.A Give examples of community changes that result from individual or group decisions.

12.B Identify examples of actions individuals and groups can take to improve the community.

12.C Identify examples of nonprofit and/or civic organizations such as the Red Cross and explain how they serve the common good.

17.C Interpret oral, visual, and print material by identifying the main idea, distinguishing between fact and opinion, identifying cause and effect, and comparing and contrasting.

17.E Interpret and create visuals, including graphs, charts, tables, timelines, illustrations, and maps.

19.A Use a problem-solving process to identify a problem, gather information, list and consider options, consider advantages and disadvantages, choose and implement a solution, and evaluate the effectiveness of the solution.

Volunteering
Mentor, Tutor, Friend

my Story Video

Alicia is a teen volunteer at the Boys and Girls Club in her neighborhood. A volunteer is a person who improves the community and helps others. Today, Alicia is taking a 9-year-old girl named Kareena on a tour of the club. Kareena spends most days just like any other 9-year-old girl. She goes to school, helps with chores at home, and wonders what she will be when she grows up. Kareena is curious about what Alicia does as a volunteer at the Boys and Girls Club.

"Hi Kareena, welcome to the Boys and Girls Club," says Alicia. "Let me show you around!" As Alicia and Kareena walk together through the club, Kareena is excited to see all of the great things it has: a game room, a study lounge, a computer room, an art room, and even a TV room. "Coming to a club like this would be fun," says Kareena. "Do you have checkers? I haven't played that since I was six!"

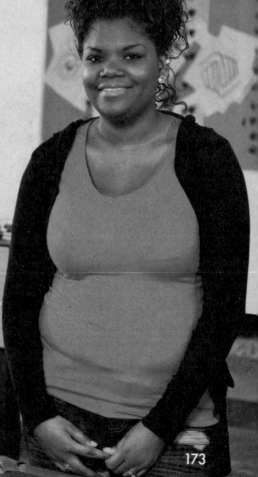

Alicia was eager to show Kareena the Boys and Girls Club.

173

Alicia enjoys working at the front desk where she greets children as they arrive at the club.

Alicia likes helping children with their homework.

Alicia helps Kareena work on the computer.

For the past year, Alicia has volunteered at the Boys and Girls Club five days a week. Her favorite job is working at the front desk. As children arrive at the club, she checks them in and helps them decide what to do first. She also likes to help the younger children with their homework. Sometimes she gets to be creative and decorate the bulletin boards. "Even playing a simple board game can be a lot of fun with these kids," Alicia tells us.

Alicia went to the Boys and Girls Club as she was growing up and realized how important the volunteers were. Having a teenage mentor at the club had a big impact on Alicia. A mentor is someone you can trust to be loyal and helpful to you. "I want to be a role model," Alicia says, "and I want to help my community the way it helped me." Alicia enjoyed going to the club as a child, so now she works hard as a volunteer so she can have an impact on someone else.

The staff at the Boys and Girls Club appreciates Alicia's help.

One of the most important skills that Alicia learns by volunteering is how to interact with children.

Volunteering is part of being a good citizen. As a volunteer, Alicia contributes to the club's success. "The teens that volunteer here get experience," she explains, "and in return the staff gets help with the hard work." The club staff, or the group of people that works there, is very small. They appreciate the volunteers' help, and so do the children.

While volunteering has given Alicia the chance to help others in the community, it also gives her a chance to grow in different ways. "Some of the skills I learn here, especially interacting with the kids, you can't find in a book."

As she gets ready for college, she realizes that her volunteer work is something great to include in her college admission applications. Alicia is even thinking further into her future. "Almost everyone in my family has served in the military," she tells us. "Someday, I'd like to serve my country, too, but not until after college." Volunteering can teach us skills we can use for the rest of our lives.

Think About It Based on this story, do you think you would like to volunteer when you are older? As you read the chapter ahead, think about what Alicia's story tells you about being a good citizen.

Alicia and Kareena had a great time playing basketball.

Good Citizens, Good Deeds

Envision It!

Mark an X in the boxes next to pictures that show children being helpful.

Good citizens help people in their community.

As a member of a community, a state, or a nation, you are a citizen. Good citizens have important characteristics. They show respect for others and themselves. They are truthful, just, and honest. They know that all people are equal, and they treat them equally.

Being a Good Citizen

How do you know when you are being a good citizen? You welcome the new family that moves in next door. You help carry a neighbor's groceries. A storm leaves branches all over the sidewalk. You pick them up. These are all actions of a good citizen. You are doing good deeds. A **deed** is an action. A good deed is an action that helps others.

Many citizens in communities do good deeds. When the fire department in a community needs a new fire truck, citizens sometimes raise money to buy one. When people are needed to read to children at the library, some citizens offer to spend their free time doing so. Often, citizens work together for the good of all the people who live in a community.

Vocabulary

deed
amendment
volunteer

People in the community notice how other citizens behave and what they do. Good citizens are role models in the community. This means they set good examples for others to follow.

TEKS
9.B, 9.C, 10.A, 11.A, 11.B, 11.C, 17.E

1. Identify and draw how you can be a good citizen.

This good citizen is using his free time to read to children at the library.

PEARSON
realize
Go online to access your interactive digital lesson.

177

Our Rights

Citizens of the United States have many rights. Some of these rights were part of the United States Constitution when it was first written. The Constitution is our country's plan of government.

Some people thought that the Constitution needed to include more basic rights of citizens. As a result, ten **amendments,** or changes, were added to the Constitution in 1791. These ten amendments are called the Bill of Rights. The Bill of Rights protects some basic rights of citizens.

The Bill of Rights gives people the right to practice the religion of their choice or no religion. It gives them the right to speak and write their opinions. Citizens also have the right to a fair, legal trial if charged with a crime. The Bill of Rights also gives people the freedom to gather in peaceful groups in public to speak about issues that concern them.

In the United States, one of the most important rights citizens have is the right to vote. Citizens vote to elect leaders. These leaders run our government. Citizens also vote on important issues, such as how the government should spend its money.

Bill of Rights

2. Look at the picture. **Identify** the civic responsibility the girl is performing and **explain** its importance to our government.

....

....

....

....

Good citizens vote on important issues, even at school!

Our Responsibilities

Voting is both a right and a responsibility of good citizens. A responsibility is a duty, or something that must be done. The study of the rights and duties of citizens is called civics. By voting in school elections, students help make decisions. When citizens are 18 years old, they can vote for community leaders, such as the mayor. They can also vote for state and national leaders, such as the governor or the president.

Good citizens have other responsibilities, too. For example, they should respect the rights and property of others. If you wait patiently at the water fountain, you are respecting the rights of others. If you give back a classmate's pencil that you borrowed, you are respecting the property of others.

Good citizens have a responsibility to their community. Some citizens are volunteers. A **volunteer** improves the community and helps others. Volunteers work for no pay. They can work in soup kitchens, they can collect clothing for the homeless, or they can bring meals to people who are too sick to leave their homes. Volunteers can help clean up parks and sidewalks. They help because it is something they want to do.

Some people volunteer to help people who need food.

3. **Identify** three ways to show good citizenship and serve the community.

....

....

Our Rules and Laws

We have rules at home and at school. Some families have a rule that everyone must make his or her own bed. That kind of rule helps keep things neat and clean. Schools often have a rule that says students must walk, not run, in the hallways. If students do not follow this rule, they could get hurt.

People follow community laws so that everyone stays safe.

We have laws in our communities. Governments make laws for the common good of all people. Some of those laws help keep us safe. For example, a community may have a law that says people must cross the street at a crosswalk. This community law makes crossing the street safe.

Rules and laws help us to know what to do. They help keep order. Suppose students in a classroom shouted out answers whenever they wanted. It would be difficult to get anything done. That is why there is a rule to raise your hand if you want to speak.

Some people choose not to follow rules or obey laws. They put their safety and the safety of others at risk. At times, people who disobey laws may have to pay a fine or even go to jail.

It is important for all citizens to follow rules and laws. Rules and laws help make our community, state, and nation a safe and orderly place to live.

Students raise their hands so everyone can take turns speaking in class.

4. ◉ **Summarize** **Describe** two rules or laws and **explain** how each helps people in a community.

....

....

....

....

⬇ TEKS 11.B, 11.C

5. ◉ **Fact and Opinion** Read each statement. **Identify** if it is a fact or an opinion. Then write "fact" or "opinion" next to each statement.

.... School hallways are safer when everyone walks.

.... I think there should be a rule that everyone in our class has to clean their desk before they go home.

.... Making your bed helps keep your room neat.

6. ❓ Think about a good deed you have done. **Analyze** what you learned from doing that good deed.

my Story Ideas

....

....

....

7. Research who first responders are, **identify** what they do for their communities, and **explain** why we call them heroes. **Analyze** ways to support first responders in the community. Then work with a group to put your plan into action.

....

....

....

Problem Solving

Conflict and Resolution

Sometimes when people do not agree, there is a conflict. A conflict is a strong disagreement, or problem. When there is a problem, it is important to find a resolution, or solution, that helps everyone get along. A solution is a way to solve a problem. You can solve a problem by cooperating, or working together.

Read the steps below. Then read the paragraph to see how one problem was solved.

Problem Solving Steps

Step 1 Identify the problem.

Step 2 Gather information.

Step 3 List the options.

Step 4 Think about the advantages of each option.

Step 5 Think about the disadvantages of each option.

Step 6 Choose a solution.

Step 7 Put the solution into action.

Step 8 Evaluate the solution you chose.

Problem Solving

Step 1

Step 7

Harry and Ann finished their animal drawings. Harry wanted to use cotton balls to make wool for his sheep. Ann wanted to use the same cotton balls to make tails for her rabbits. They realized that there was a problem. How could they resolve this problem? They used the problem solving steps to find a solution. Ann used three cotton balls for the rabbits' tails. Harry took the rest and spread them apart to make sheep wool.

TEKS

SS 19.A Use a problem-solving process to identify a problem, gather information, list and consider options, consider advantages and disadvantages, choose and implement a solution, and evaluate the effectiveness of the solution.

Read the paragraph. Then answer the questions.

Aiden and Maria share one classroom computer during the school day. Sometimes they both need to use the computer at the same time. Today they both need it to finish their projects that are due the next day. Aiden and Maria have a problem.

1. **Describe** the problem Aiden and Maria are having.

....

....

....

2. **Explain** what Aiden and Maria should do to solve the problem.

....

....

....

....

....

....

3. **Identify** a resolution to Aiden and Maria's conflict.

....

....

....

PEARSON realize. Go online to access your interactive digital lesson.

183

Taking Action for Our Rights

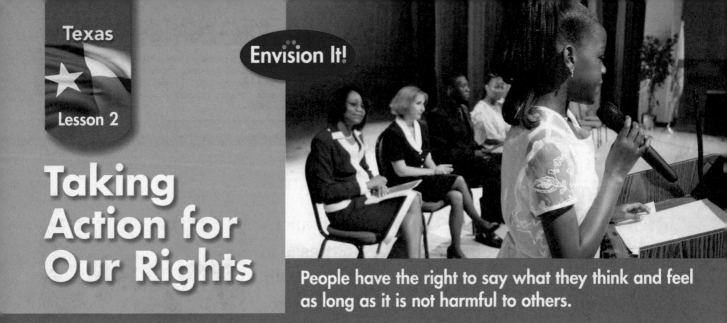

Envision It!

People have the right to say what they think and feel as long as it is not harmful to others.

Today, citizens have many rights and freedoms. But these rights and freedoms did not come easily. Throughout history, both famous leaders and ordinary people have worked hard to make sure everyone is treated equally.

Susan B. Anthony

Even after the Bill of Rights was added to the U.S. Constitution, women did not have the same rights as men. Susan B. Anthony wanted to change that. As a young adult, she went to meetings and gave speeches about treating people fairly.

In 1848, Elizabeth Cady Stanton, Lucretia Mott, and other women organized a **convention**, or a large meeting. They wanted to discuss women's rights. A large group of people met in Seneca Falls, New York. One right the women wanted was **suffrage**, or the right to vote. It was the first time that women gathered in public to demand the right to vote. The Seneca Falls Convention was the start of the suffrage movement.

Three years later, in 1851, Susan B. Anthony joined her friend Elizabeth Cady Stanton in the suffrage movement.

In 1880, Susan B. Anthony spoke at a suffrage meeting in Chicago, Illinois.

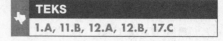

UNLOCK THE BIG ? I will know about people who fought for the rights and freedoms of our country's citizens.

Vocabulary

convention   segregate

suffrage   delegate

civil rights

Write what you think the student in the picture might be speaking about.

Susan B. Anthony and Elizabeth Cady Stanton worked to form the National American Woman Suffrage Association in 1869. Susan B. Anthony served as the president of this group for eight years.

In 1870, the Fifteenth Amendment to the United States Constitution was passed. It gave African American men the right to vote. Still, women could not vote. In 1872, Anthony voted in the election for United States president. This action was against the law, and she was arrested. She also had to pay $100 for breaking the law, but she refused to pay. She felt it was unfair.

After Anthony died in 1906, other women continued the fight. Finally, in 1920, the Nineteenth Amendment became law. Women had won the right to vote!

TEKS

1.A, 11.B, 12.A, 12.B, 17.C

Women voted for the first time in 1920.

1. ◉ **Fact and Opinion Identify** and write one fact about Susan B. Anthony.

....

....

....

....

Thurgood Marshall

Thurgood Marshall worked hard for civil rights. **Civil rights** are rights of all citizens to be treated equally under the law. Marshall believed that all citizens, not just some citizens, should have civil rights.

Thurgood Marshall

Marshall grew up in Baltimore, Maryland. He often debated at home with his father and brother. People who have different viewpoints often debate, or argue to convince others to agree with them. Marshall continued to debate in college and later became a lawyer. He began to argue in court to change unfair laws.

At this time, laws **segregated,** or separated, African American and white people in many places. These places included theaters, restaurants, and other public places. African American children and white children were segregated in colleges and schools, too. Marshall wanted to end segregation, especially in schools.

Reverend Oliver Brown, an African American, wanted his daughter, Linda, to attend a school for white students. The African American school was far from the Browns' home. Linda Brown had to cross a dangerous railroad track to get there. The white school was close to the Browns' home, but school leaders would not allow Linda to attend. Other African American families joined in the fight for civil rights.

Linda Brown's case was brought before the Supreme Court. Marshall argued this case, trying to convince the Supreme Court justices that school segregation was wrong. His debating skills helped him win the case. In 1954, all nine Supreme Court justices voted to end school segregation. This court case is known as *Brown* versus *Board of Education*.

Marshall continued to protect people's rights. In 1967, Marshall was chosen to be the first African American Supreme Court justice. He served on the Supreme Court for 24 years.

2. Create a banner that supports equal rights.

3. A mother and daughter sit on the steps of the Supreme Court after segregation is made illegal. **Identify** and circle the part of the photograph that shows a change in civil rights.

Nettie Hunt explains Brown v. Board of Education *to her daughter, Nickie.*

Eleanor Roosevelt

Eleanor Roosevelt worked hard to improve people's lives. Roosevelt was the First Lady, or the wife of the president. Her husband, Franklin D. Roosevelt, was president from 1933 to 1945. While she was the First Lady, Roosevelt traveled all over the world to visit schoolchildren, sick people in hospitals, coal miners, and even people in jail. She told her husband everything she learned about these people. She was aware that all people need basic human rights.

In 1945, Eleanor Roosevelt had the opportunity to work as a leader for human rights. She was chosen to be the American delegate to the United Nations (U.N.). A **delegate** is a person chosen to act for others. The U.N. is a world group that works for peace. While at the U.N., Roosevelt led a group that worked for human rights. The group wrote a bill of rights for all people. It recognized that all people in the world had human rights. They had the right to be treated equally under the law. They had the right to own property and the right to leave their country and then return.

Eleanor Roosevelt visited many children.

188

4. Identify some of the human rights that Eleanor Roosevelt worked for.

....

....

....

Got it?

TEKS 11.B, 12.A, 17.C

5. Fact and Opinion Read each statement. **Identify** if it is a fact or an opinion. Then write "fact" or "opinion" next to each statement.

.... Eleanor Roosevelt worked for human rights.

.... Thurgood Marshall was the best Supreme Court justice.

.... Susan B. Anthony was the most important woman in American history.

6. Identify one of the leaders you read about in this lesson. **Explain** why he or she is a good citizen.

my Story Ideas

....

....

....

7. Research the life of Helen Keller. Find out why she was a good citizen. Use the computer to create a piece of digital art that expresses her life. Share what you learned with the class.

Fact and Opinion

A fact is something that can be proved true or false. The sentence, "George Washington was the first president of the United States," is a fact. You can prove it by doing research. The sentence, "George Washington was a funny man," is an opinion. An opinion tells someone's feelings, beliefs, or ideas. An opinion cannot be proved true or false.

Read Caroline's letter aloud and look at the photo. Contrast the facts and opinions in the chart below.

Hi Grandma,

I just got your letter. Do you want to know what I learned in school today? Today we read about leaders. Thurgood Marshall was the greatest leader of all. He was a lawyer. He always argued for good reasons. Marshall worked to end school segregation. He also became the first African American Supreme Court justice. You should read about Thurgood Marshall, too!

Love,
Caroline

Thurgood Marshall

Facts	Opinions
• Marshall was a lawyer. • He worked to end school segregation. • He became the first African American Supreme Court justice. • He wore glasses.	• Marshall was the greatest leader of all. • He always argued for good reasons. • You should read about Thurgood Marshall, too! • He was handsome.

Learning Objective

I will know the difference between a fact and an opinion.

 TEKS

SS 17.C Interpret oral, visual, and print material by distinguishing between fact and opinion.
ELA 12 Students analyze, make inferences and draw conclusions about the author's purpose in historical and contemporary contexts and provide evidence from the text.

Take turns **reading aloud** the letter that Caroline's grandmother wrote to a partner. Fill in the chart with facts and opinions based on what you hear and see in the photo.

Hi Caroline,

I agree with you. I think that Thurgood Marshall was special. I read about leaders in the library today. I read about Eleanor Roosevelt. She was another great leader. She was the First Lady from 1933 to 1945. Her husband, Franklin Delano Roosevelt, was president at that time. Mrs. Roosevelt wanted equal rights for all people. I think we'll have a lot of fun learning about leaders when you visit.

With love,
Grandma

Eleanor Roosevelt

Facts	Opinions

PEARSON **realize** Go online to access your interactive digital lesson.

191

Taking Action for a Cause

Envision It!

ADOPT A PET

Look at the picture. Explain what the girl is doing at the animal shelter.

Many people in our country and all over the world give their support to different causes. A **cause** is something that people feel strongly about. Some people work for world peace, others work to protect Earth, and some groups raise money for research to help cure diseases. People and organizations join together to work for good causes.

Mary McLeod Bethune

Mary McLeod Bethune wanted to give African American girls a chance to go to school. She wanted to open a school in Daytona Beach, Florida. The only money she had was $1.50, yet Bethune would not give up on this important cause.

In 1904, Bethune opened her school. It was called the Daytona Normal and Industrial Institute. At her school, Bethune taught African American girls how to read and write. She used old boxes for desks, burned twigs for pencils, and mashed berries for ink. The girls also learned to cook, sew, and clean. Bethune wanted her students to be good citizens, so they worked in the community, too.

Mary McLeod Bethune with a group of students

Vocabulary

cause	strike
union	boycott
motto	

People from the community donated money to Bethune's cause. In 1923, Bethune's school was able to join with a school for boys called the Cookman Institute. The new school later became Bethune-Cookman College.

Next, Mary McLeod Bethune created an organization for African American women. The organization worked to get African American women better housing, better working conditions, and, of course, a better education. Bethune worked hard to make this organization successful.

In 1936, President Franklin D. Roosevelt asked Bethune to lead the National Youth Administration (NYA). It was a great honor for Bethune. The NYA helped young people find part-time jobs, and Bethune helped by providing job training.

Today, students still attend Bethune's school, now called Bethune-Cookman University. Mary McLeod Bethune is a role model for the students and everyone who has a good cause to support.

1.  **Fact and Opinion Identify** and underline three facts about Mary McLeod Bethune.

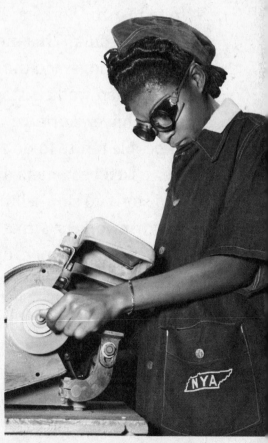

A National Youth Administration student

TEKS

1.A, 11.B, 12.A, 12.B, 12.C, 17.C

PEARSON **realize** Go online to access your interactive digital lesson.

193

César Chávez

César Chávez had been a farmworker as a child. He knew about their hard lives and that they were paid very little and worked long hours. Years later, he took up the cause to help farmworkers have better lives. Many kinds of workers have unions. A **union** is a group of workers who join together. The workers usually want better treatment and better pay. César Chávez felt farmworkers needed a union. In 1962, Chávez started the National Farm Workers Association (NFWA). Chávez was elected president of the NFWA. Later, the name was changed to United Farm Workers. The union's **motto,** or saying, was *Viva la Causa*. This means "Long Live the Cause."

César Chávez meets with farmworkers.

In 1965, Chávez led the union's first strike. A **strike** happens when workers stop working until things change. Chávez started a boycott. A **boycott** happens when people refuse to do something for a reason. Chávez asked customers to stop buying grapes. He wanted stores to stop selling grapes, too.

The farmworkers' strike went on for several years. Finally, the farm owners agreed to raise the workers' pay. The conflict was resolved peacefully.

People wore pins like this one to support the grape boycott.

2. Explain why Chávez wanted people to boycott grapes.

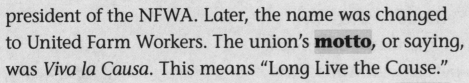

....

....

....

Clara Barton

In the mid-1800s, Clara Barton volunteered during the American Civil War by helping soldiers find lost baggage and by handing out medicine. The American Civil War was fought between the northern and southern states in our country. Barton also cared for wounded soldiers. She was often called "the angel of the battlefield."

Clara Barton

Later, while Barton was in Europe, a war broke out between France and Germany. Barton worked for the Red Cross in Europe, taking care of soldiers who were hurt. She wanted to start the Red Cross in the United States. Barton's wish came true in 1881.

Today, the American Red Cross continues working for Barton's cause by helping and caring for people all over the world. Red Cross workers arrive quickly to help people after dangerous storms, floods, or earthquakes. They provide food, shelter, clean water, and medicine. The Red Cross makes sure that there is a supply of blood ready for people who need it. The Red Cross also helps people stay in touch with family members in the United States military who are serving our country far from their homes.

3. ◉ **Main Idea and Details** **Identify** and write one detail that supports the following main idea: Clara Barton helped people.

Nonprofit and Civic Organizations

The work that Clara Barton did and the Red Cross continues to do is the work of nonprofit organizations. A nonprofit organization is not set up to earn income for the organization. Its purpose is to serve the common good. This means that nonprofit groups work to help others and to meet their needs.

Many of the needs that these groups provide are basic needs such as food, shelter, and clothing. A food bank is another example of a nonprofit organization. It takes food that is donated from people and businesses. The food bank gives the food to families in need. These families may be struggling to meet their basic needs.

Nonprofit organizations that operate within a community are called civic organizations. Civic organizations provide services to a community and help its residents meet their needs. The goal of a civic organization is to improve life for people in the community.

Volunteers sort food at a local food bank.

American Red Cross workers pack supplies.

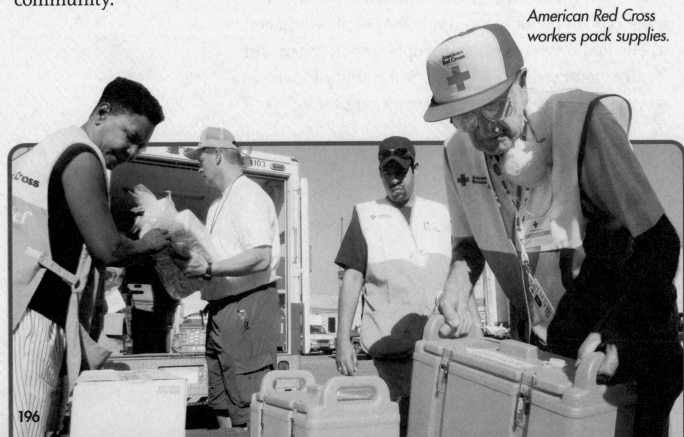

4. Explain how nonprofit and civic organizations such as the Red Cross serve the common good.

....

....

....

Got it?

🔹 TEKS 11.B, 12.A, 12.B, 17.C

5. ◎ **Fact and Opinion** Read each statement about César Chávez. **Decide** if it is a fact or an opinion. Then write "fact" or "opinion" next to each statement.

.... César Chávez started the first union for farmworkers.

.... César Chávez worked for the most important cause.

6. ❓ Think about the different examples in this lesson of good citizens working together. **Identify** ways people can make changes when they work together.

my Story Ideas

....

....

....

....

7. Research the life and work of Ruby Bridges. Write a paragraph to **explain** why she showed good citizenship.

....

....

....

....

Lesson 1 🏴 **TEKS 11.C, 17.E**

Good Citizens, Good Deeds

1. Identify three good deeds a citizen might do in the community.

....

....

....

....

2. Fill in the chart below. **Identify** two rights and two responsibilities of citizens.

Rights	Responsibilities

Taking Action for Our Rights

3. Draw a line to **match** each leader with the rights that he or she fought for.

Thurgood Marshall   women's right to vote

Eleanor Roosevelt   equal rights for all people

Susan B. Anthony   ending school segregation

4. ◉ **Fact and Opinion** Read the following statements about Susan B. Anthony. **Identify** each statement as a fact or opinion.

.... Susan B. Anthony is someone people should admire.

.... Susan B. Anthony worked with Elizabeth Cady Stanton.

5. Explain what Susan B. Anthony, Thurgood Marshall, and Eleanor Roosevelt had in common.

....

....

....

....

....

Lesson 3 ➡ TEKS 1.A, 12.B, 12.C

Taking Action for a Cause

6. Write a sentence that **describes** how Mary McLeod Bethune changed communities.

....

....

....

....

7. Read the question carefully. **Determine** the best answer to the question from the four answer choices provided. Circle the best answer.

Which of the following means that César Chávez wanted people to stop buying grapes?

A He joined the military.

B He picked crops as a child.

C He started a boycott.

D He formed a union.

8. Explain how the American Red Cross helps to serve the common good after dangerous storms and floods.

....

....

....

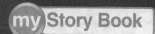

Go online to write and illustrate your own **myStory Book** using the **myStory Ideas** from this chapter.

 How can I participate?

TEKS
SS 11.C
ELA 17

In this chapter, you have learned about citizenship. You learned about ways you can participate in your school, in your community, and in your country.

Think about how you can help others in your community. Write about one way you can make a difference today.

....

....

....

....

Now draw a picture of something you can do when you get older to make a difference in your school or in your community.

A Growing Nation

How does life change throughout history?

Look at a picture of a classroom from the 1960s. **Describe** how your classroom looks like this classroom and how it looks different.

....

....

....

....

....

Texas Essential Knowledge and Skills

1.A Describe how individuals, events, and ideas have changed communities, past and present.

1.B Identify individuals, including Pierre-Charles L'Enfant, Benjamin Banneker, and Benjamin Franklin, who have helped to shape communities.

1.C Describe how individuals, including Daniel Boone, Christopher Columbus, the Founding Fathers, and Juan de Oñate, have contributed to the expansion of existing communities or to the creation of new communities.

2.A Identify reasons people have formed communities, including a need for security, religious freedom, law, and material well-being.

2.B Identify ways in which people in the local community and other communities meet their needs for government, education, communication, transportation, and recreation.

4.A Describe and explain variations in the physical environment, including climate, landforms, natural resources, and natural hazards.

8.E Identify individuals, past and present, including Henry Ford and other entrepreneurs in the community such as Mary Kay Ash, Wallace Amos, Milton Hershey, and Sam Walton, who have started new businesses.

14.A Identify and compare the heroic deeds of state and national heroes, including Hector P. Garcia and James A. Lovell, and other individuals such as Harriet Tubman, Juliette Gordon Low, Todd Beamer, Ellen Ochoa, John "Danny" Olivas, and other contemporary heroes.

16.A Identify scientists and inventors, including Jonas Salk, Maria Mitchell, and others who have discovered scientific breakthroughs or created or invented new technology such as Cyrus McCormick, Bill Gates, and Louis Pasteur.

16.B Identify the impact of scientific breakthroughs and new technology in computers, pasteurization, and medical vaccines on various communities.

17.B Sequence and categorize information.

17.C Interpret oral, visual, and print material by identifying the main idea, distinguishing between fact and opinion, identifying cause and effect, and comparing and contrasting.

17.D Use various parts of a source, including the table of contents, glossary, and index as well as keyword Internet searches, to locate information.

17.E Interpret and create visuals, including graphs, charts, tables, timelines, illustrations, and maps.

18.B Use technology to create written and visual material such as stories, poems, pictures, maps, and graphic organizers to express ideas.

Benjamin Franklin
A Man Who Changed History

my Story Video

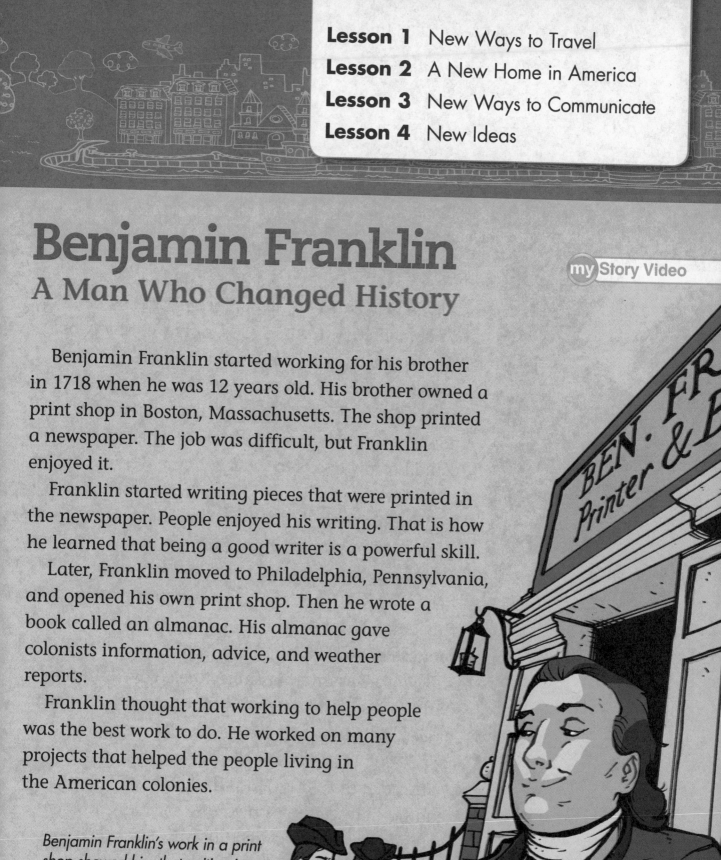

Benjamin Franklin started working for his brother in 1718 when he was 12 years old. His brother owned a print shop in Boston, Massachusetts. The shop printed a newspaper. The job was difficult, but Franklin enjoyed it.

Franklin started writing pieces that were printed in the newspaper. People enjoyed his writing. That is how he learned that being a good writer is a powerful skill.

Later, Franklin moved to Philadelphia, Pennsylvania, and opened his own print shop. Then he wrote a book called an almanac. His almanac gave colonists information, advice, and weather reports.

Franklin thought that working to help people was the best work to do. He worked on many projects that helped the people living in the American colonies.

Benjamin Franklin's work in a print shop showed him that writing is an important skill.

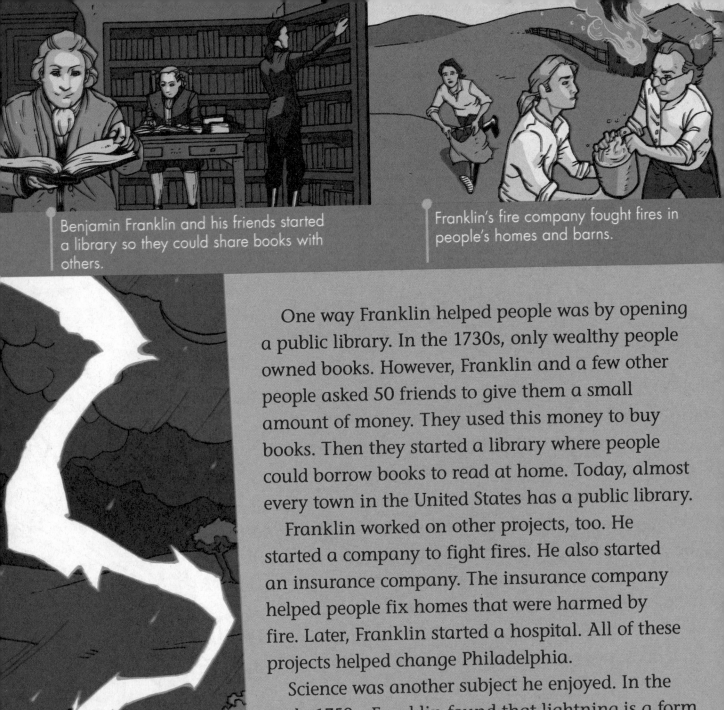

Benjamin Franklin and his friends started a library so they could share books with others.

Franklin's fire company fought fires in people's homes and barns.

One way Franklin helped people was by opening a public library. In the 1730s, only wealthy people owned books. However, Franklin and a few other people asked 50 friends to give them a small amount of money. They used this money to buy books. Then they started a library where people could borrow books to read at home. Today, almost every town in the United States has a public library.

Franklin worked on other projects, too. He started a company to fight fires. He also started an insurance company. The insurance company helped people fix homes that were harmed by fire. Later, Franklin started a hospital. All of these projects helped change Philadelphia.

Science was another subject he enjoyed. In the early 1750s, Franklin found that lightning is a form of electricity. He then created the lightning rod to help keep buildings safe during storms.

In the early 1780s, Franklin had trouble both reading and seeing far away. To solve his problem, he made eyeglasses called bifocals. Bifocals allow people to see both near and far.

Franklin's lightning rods give lightning a path to the ground, keeping buildings safe.

Franklin traveled to France. Many people were excited to meet him.

Franklin helped to write the Declaration of Independence in 1776.

Franklin's work helping people and the new items he created made him famous. Many people wanted to meet him. They painted pictures of him. They asked for his advice.

He traveled to Great Britain and France. When he was in Great Britain, Franklin tried to explain that the American colonists were very angry with the British. He wrote letters about the problems in the American colonies. But the British would not agree to change the laws that the colonists thought were unfair.

Finally, Franklin joined with other American colonial leaders. They all agreed that the colonies should be free from Great Britain. They also agreed that they needed to choose their own leaders. Franklin helped to write the Declaration of Independence. Later, he helped to write the United States Constitution.

During the 1800s, Franklin's work changed life in America in many ways. Even today, we can still see his ideas at work around us.

Think About It Based on this story, how did Benjamin Franklin change life in America? As you read the chapter ahead, think about how helping others has changed people's lives throughout history.

New Ways to Travel

☐   ☐

Mark an *X* under the kinds of transportation you have used to get from one place to another.

Boats helped Lewis and Clark explore the West.

How do you travel from one place to another? You probably walk or ride in a car or bus. Long ago, explorers and settlers traveled by boat and by foot as they tried to learn about new lands.

Travel by Trails and Rivers

When Europeans arrived in North America in the 1500s, they knew nothing about the land. However, American Indians knew the land well. They traveled by boat on rivers and by foot on trails they had made. They showed Europeans where to find what they needed. Later, explorers from Spain brought horses to North America. Horses made travel easier and faster.

As the country grew, many people wanted to explore the West. In 1803, President Thomas Jefferson hired Meriwether Lewis and William Clark to explore the land west of the Mississippi River. He asked them to learn about the American Indians and the land in the West.

Lewis and Clark traveled with about 48 other men. Sacagawea (sak uh juh WEE uh) was an American Indian who helped them understand the language of the American Indians they met.

UNLOCK THE BIG ?

I will know how new ways of traveling have changed people's lives.

Vocabulary

canal

wagon train

transcontinental

toll

It took two years for Lewis and Clark to finish their trip. The map below shows where they went.

Their stories made many people want to move west. People heard about the huge open spaces and the chance of getting land they could farm. Because of Lewis and Clark, many people traveled to the West and set up new communities.

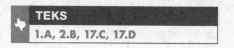
TEKS
1.A, 2.B, 17.C, 17.D

1. Use the map scale to **measure** the distance Lewis and Clark traveled on their route.

....

....

....

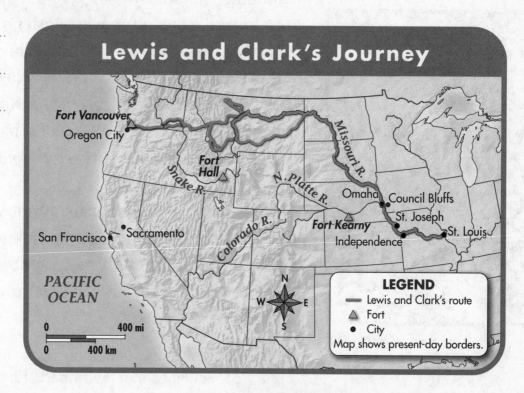

Lewis and Clark's Journey

Fort Vancouver
Oregon City
Fort Hall
Snake R.
Missouri R.
N. Platte R.
Omaha
Council Bluffs
St. Joseph
Fort Kearny
St. Louis
Independence
San Francisco
Sacramento
Colorado R.

PACIFIC OCEAN

0   400 mi
0   400 km

LEGEND
— Lewis and Clark's route
△ Fort
• City
Map shows present-day borders.

The Erie Canal improved transportation of goods and people.

Rivers and Canals

In the early 1800s, rivers were an important way to carry heavy goods. However, some rivers were too narrow or too fast for big boats. Sometimes a canal was built to let boats get through safely. A **canal** is a waterway that is dug by people.

In 1825, the Erie Canal helped connect the Great Lakes to New York City. Goods from what are now Wisconsin and Michigan were shipped over the Great Lakes. The goods were then carried down the Erie Canal to the Hudson River and then on to New York City. Soon, New York City became an important port. A port is a town or city that has a place for ships to land.

Wagon Trains

Another form of transportation in the early 1800s was the covered wagon. Many people traveled to the West in wagon trains. A **wagon train** is a group of covered wagons that travels together for safety.

To make traveling west easier, Congress built the National Road. Many families began their trip on this paved road. It started in Maryland and ended in Illinois. From the end of the National Road, people traveled to the Oregon Trail, which began in Independence, Missouri. They followed this trail to Oregon.

The trip to Oregon took about six months. People faced harsh weather, sickness, and steep mountains. Although more than 12,000 people went west in the 1840s, a safer and faster way to travel was needed.

People walked or rode in wagons to find a better life in the West.

2. **Identify** and underline ways in which people in communities met their needs for transportation.

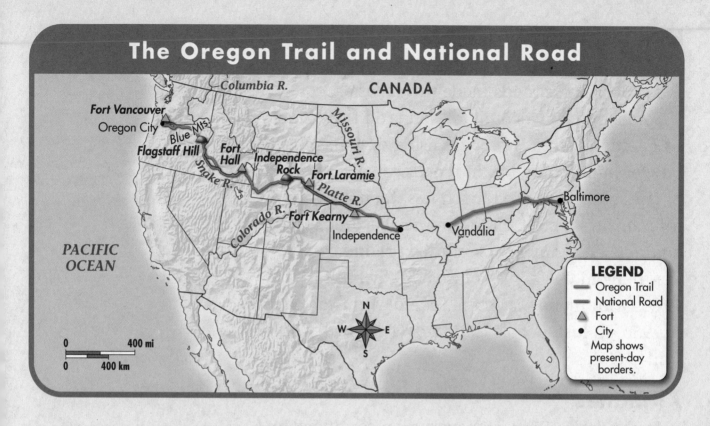

The Oregon Trail and National Road

Columbia R.

CANADA

Fort Vancouver
Oregon City
Blue Mts.
Flagstaff Hill
Fort Hall
Snake R.
Independence Rock
Missouri R.
Fort Laramie
Platte R.
Colorado R.
Fort Kearny
Independence
Baltimore
Vandalia

PACIFIC
OCEAN

N S E W

0   400 mi
0   400 km

LEGEND
— Oregon Trail
— National Road
△ Fort
• City
Map shows present-day borders.

Railroads Cross the Country

The first steam locomotive was built in 1804. Steam locomotives are trains that run with steam engines. As improvements were made over the next ten years, they became powerful and could go long distances. Soon, people began planning railroads.

In 1863, two companies began building a railroad line across America. One company began east of the Mississippi River and one near the West Coast. On May 10, 1869, the two lines met in Promontory, Utah. The new railroad was called the transcontinental railroad. **Transcontinental** means "across the continent."

Railroads were a big improvement over slow canal boats, muddy roads, and narrow trails. Now, people could travel quickly and safely from Omaha, Nebraska, to Sacramento, California.

A gold spike joined the eastern and western rail lines.

3. Underline the sentence that **identifies** what transcontinental means.

Highways Cross the Nation

Many new roads were built in the United States in the 1800s. These roads made travel easier.

Some landowners built toll roads on their land. A **toll** is money that is paid for using a road. Tolls helped pay for building and fixing roads.

The roads were used much less, though, after railroads were built. However, they became important again when many people started driving cars.

A huge highway system was finally built in the 1900s with money from the Federal-Aid Highway Act of 1956. At last, people could travel easily across the United States.

Airplanes

In the early 1900s, transportation continued to improve. Two brothers, Orville and Wilbur Wright, began building airplanes. On December 17, 1903, their first airplane flew. It stayed in the air for 12 seconds. Suddenly, people could fly!

The Wright brothers kept improving their design. The idea of traveling by airplane became popular.

Over the years, airplanes grew larger and more powerful. Today, jets carry people and items all over the world. A trip across the country, which once took months, now takes less than six hours.

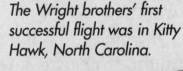

The Wright brothers' first successful flight was in Kitty Hawk, North Carolina.

4. ⊙ **Draw Conclusions Explain** how travel changed in the 1900s.

....

....

Got it?

TEKS 2.B, 17.C, 17.D

5. ⊙ **Draw Conclusions Analyze** each statement. Then write a conclusion you can draw about each statement.

Railroads were a big improvement over muddy roads.

....

....

Highways helped people travel across the United States.

....

....

6. ❓ **Explain** why wagon trains were the best way to travel across the country in the early 1800s.

my Story Ideas

....

....

....

7. Work in groups to **research** your assigned mode of transportation at the library. Use both print and digital sources. Use keyword searches and the table of contents, and the glossary or index of print materials to help you find information. Then **create** an advertisement for the mode of transportation as if it were brand new. Present your work to the class and participate in group discussions to identify the main idea as well as facts and opinions in other groups' advertisements.

....

....

Primary and Secondary Sources

Primary sources are documents, such as photographs, paintings, and maps, or artifacts from the time an event happened. Primary sources were written or used by someone who saw or lived through an event. Sometimes that person is called an "eyewitness."

Artifacts like compasses can be primary sources.

The primary sources on this page are from Lewis and Clark's journey. They used the compass to help them find their way. The journal entry was written by John Ordway, who traveled with Lewis and Clark.

Read the journal entry below. As you read, think about who created it and why. Also think about what it tells you about the past.

> one of the hunters...killed a panther on an island. It was 7 1/2 feet in length. it differs from these in the States. it is of a redish brown. and the first we have killed. passed very rapid water we have to double man the canoes and drag them over the Sholes and rapid places. we have to be in the water half of our time.
>
> August 3. 1805. John Ordway

Journals are primary sources, too.

What does Ordway's journal tell you about Lewis and Clark's journey? What did he see? How are the words and spellings in the journal different from the way people write today?

TEKS

SS 1.A Describe how individuals and events have changed communities, past and present.
ELA 22.A Use and understand the function of the following parts of speech in the context of reading and writing.
ELA 22.B Use the complete subject and the complete predicate in a sentence.
ELA 22.C Use complete simple and compound sentences with correct subject-verb agreement.

This passage from a textbook also tells about Lewis and Clark's journey. But it was written by someone who learned about the trip by reading other people's writings. It is a secondary source. In secondary sources, the author did not see or live through the events he or she describes.

This book is a secondary source.

The members of the Lewis and Clark expedition faced many dangers. The explorers followed rivers that were often very narrow or rapid.

They brought back examples of the plants and animals they found to show people what they found in the West.

Try it!

1. **Compare** the journal entry and the textbook.

   ....

   ....

   ....

   ....

2. Use the Internet to **research** more information about Lewis and Clark's journey. **Interpret** the information you find and determine whether it is from a primary source or a secondary source.

   ....

   ....

PEARSON realize | Go online to access your interactive digital lesson.

213

A New Home in America

List the items you would pack in your bag if you were moving to a new home.

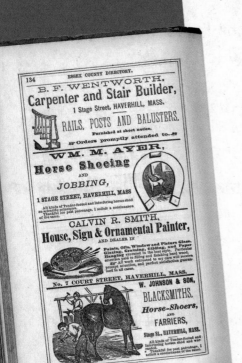

Many jobs were available in the United States.

People move to a new place for many reasons. Some need to find work. Some want religious freedom or a safe place to live. Some hope to earn more money. Some move to be closer to their family.

The Promise of America

People who move from one country to settle in a different country are called **immigrants**. Immigrants started coming to North America hundreds of years ago to start new lives.

Some of the first immigrants were people from Spain, France, and England. In the 1600s and 1700s, they crossed the Atlantic Ocean to come to North America. They settled in the Southeast, the Northeast, and even as far north as Canada.

In 1783, the United States won its freedom from Great Britain. At that time, the nation was made up of 13 states, and all of the states were located in the East.

The West was a huge open land with many rivers and mountains. The soil was rich for farming, and gold could be found in the streams and rocks. While people were looking for gold, they also found other minerals, such as silver. People found many ways to earn money in the West.

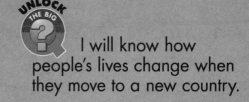

UNLOCK THE BIG ?

I will know how people's lives change when they move to a new country.

Vocabulary

immigrant   gold rush
frontier   exclusion
homestead

In the mid-1800s, thousands of immigrants from Europe and Asia came to the United States. Most settled in cities along the East and West coasts where there were many jobs and places to live. Other immigrants bought or rented land to farm.

Since the first Europeans arrived in North America, immigrants have had high hopes for their new home. They brought the skills and energy needed to make the country even greater.

One immigrant, John Roebling (ROH blihng), came from Germany to the United States in 1831. He built many bridges. One of his best-known bridges is the Brooklyn Bridge in New York City.

Most European immigrants sailed across the Atlantic Ocean and into New York Harbor. One of the first things they saw there was the Statue of Liberty. Even today, it welcomes immigrants.

TEKS
1.A, 1.B, 1.C, 2.A, 4.A

The Statue of Liberty holds a lamp to welcome people to the United States.

1. ◎ **Cause and Effect Describe** two causes of immigrants settling in the West.

....

....

....

Americans Move West

As more immigrants came and cities became crowded, many people looked for more land in the American frontier. A **frontier** is a region that forms the edge of a settled area. People crossed steep mountains and wide rivers. The search for more land was dangerous. An explorer named Daniel Boone helped make this search easier.

The Cumberland Gap trail had been used by American Indians for many years. It ran through the Cumberland Mountains. The map below shows the Cumberland Gap trail today.

In 1775, Boone worked with 28 men to widen the Cumberland Gap trail and add new paths. This new road was called the Wilderness Road. Wagons could now travel through the mountains. As a result, thousands of settlers and explorers traveled west, beyond the Appalachian Mountains. In 1805, Zebulon Pike (ZEB yuh lun pyk) explored the Mississippi River. Davy Crockett began exploring present-day Tennessee in 1813.

Daniel Boone helped new settlers travel to the American frontier.

2. **Describe** how Daniel Boone contributed to the changing of communities by widening the Cumberland Gap trail.

....

....

....

....

....

Cumberland Gap Trail Today

Kentucky

Cumberland Mountains

Ewing

Virginia

0   2 mi

0   2 km

Middlesboro

Town of Cumberland Gap

Tennessee

LEGEND
■ Cumberland Gap National Historical Park
▪▪▪ Cumberland Gap trail
• City/Town

The Homestead Act

The number of settlers moving west grew after 1862. In that year, the United States government passed the Homestead Act. A **homestead** is an area of land that includes a house and its buildings.

The Homestead Act made it possible for many Americans to get 160 acres of land for very little money. The act helped people settle the land in the West. It also helped the country add new states.

To be a homesteader, a person had to agree to build a house and live on the land for five years. After that, the person would own the land. Thousands of families traveled west to find a new home. By the 1900s, there were 600,000 homesteaders in the West.

Many homesteaders were immigrants. Others had been slaves in the South. By moving west, people could start new lives. They could farm and feed their families. They could start new communities and enjoy their religious freedom.

Life for the homesteaders in the West was difficult, though. They built homes using any materials they could find. They carried water in buckets. They grew all of their food. Neighbors were far from each other, so it was difficult to get help. Many people returned home because life on the frontier was so harsh.

Families could buy land to start a new life in the West.

3. **Draw Conclusions Identify** one detail that supports the conclusion that homesteaders started communities to fulfill a need for material well-being.

....

....

....

Immigrants From Asia

In 1848, gold was discovered in California. During the **gold rush**, thousands of people came from around the world to search for gold. Some of these people formed communities to meet their need for financial well-being.

Many immigrants came from China during the gold rush. At first, Americans welcomed them. However, some Americans thought that Chinese immigrants were taking too many jobs. In 1882, the United States government passed the Chinese Exclusion Act. **Exclusion** means "keeping people out of a place." This act stopped immigration from China for ten years.

In the 1880s, Japan started allowing workers to move to the United States. Many Japanese immigrants lived in California and in Hawaii, which was not yet a state. Most worked on farms or fished. Some owned small businesses.

Chinese immigrants needed special documents to work in the United States.

4. Use the scale. **Measure** the distance immigrants from China traveled to reach the continental United States.

Immigration from China and Japan, 1848–1900

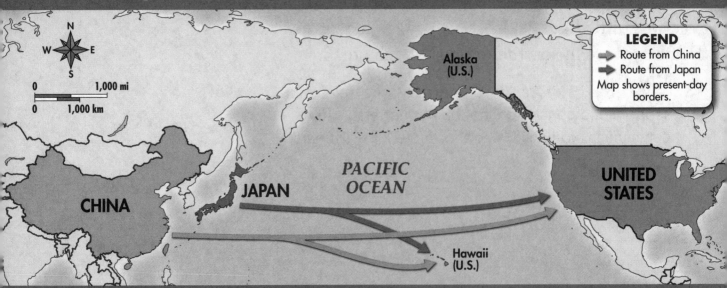

5.  **Draw Conclusions Analyze** the lesson and draw a conclusion about how each of these events changed communities in the United States.

Wilderness Road: ....

....

Homestead Act of 1862: ....

....

Gold Rush: ....

....

Chinese Exclusion Act of 1882: ....

....

6. **Describe** what you think it was like to cross the Atlantic Ocean by ship in the 1800s.

my Story Ideas

....

....

....

....

7. In a small group, **research** immigration to the United States from one country, such as Italy or Korea. Gather facts about reasons people relocated to the United States. Create a visual display such as a map or a graph that shows where immigrants settled in the United States. Identify reasons immigrants formed communities in the United States. Consider the possibilities that there were legal, religious, and safety concerns, as well as the need for material well-being.

....

....

....

New Ways to Communicate

Envision It!

1800s

Circle the items in each picture that help people communicate.

The Pony Express promised to deliver mail quickly and safely across the United States.

To learn about the world around us, we look and listen. We also use tools, such as telephones, radios, televisions, and computers. These tools help people communicate. When people **communicate**, they pass their thoughts or information to others.

The Pony Express

In the early 1800s, the only way to travel across the country was on horseback or by wagon train. Sending letters took anywhere from three weeks to two months.

As the country grew, the mail service had to improve. In 1860, a group of people had an idea. They set up the Pony Express. The Pony Express was a mail system that carried letters between St. Joseph, Missouri, and Sacramento, California. The map shows the route the mail traveled.

Young men carried mail bags on horseback for 75 to 100 miles. Riders changed horses every ten miles at relay stations.

At the end of their part of the trip, riders waited at their last station for another rider coming from the opposite direction. Then they would pick up that rider's mail bag and ride home.

1950s

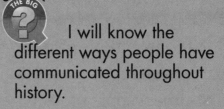
UNLOCK THE BIG ?

I will know the different ways people have communicated throughout history.

Vocabulary

communicate · · · telegraph

invention · · · technology

patent

Pony Express riders rode through heavy snow and rain. They also kept away from American Indians, who did not want them on their land.

The Pony Express improved how people communicated. Now mail could reach the West Coast in only ten days. The Pony Express lasted only 18 months, as new systems began making communication even faster and easier.

> **TEKS**
> 1.A, 2.B, 3.A, 16.A, 16.B, 17.E

1. **Interpret** the map. Circle places where Pony Express riders may have stopped to change horses.

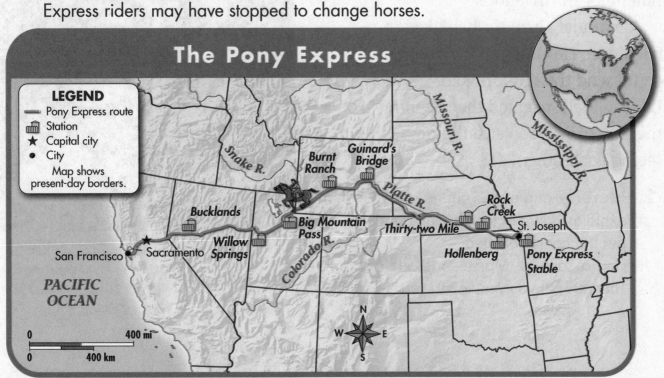

The Pony Express

LEGEND
— Pony Express route
🏛 Station
★ Capital city
● City
Map shows present-day borders.

Snake R.

Burnt Ranch

Guinard's Bridge

Missouri R.

Mississippi R.

Platte R.

Bucklands

Big Mountain Pass

Rock Creek

Willow Springs

Thirty-two Mile

St. Joseph

San Francisco

Sacramento

Colorado R.

Hollenberg

Pony Express Stable

PACIFIC OCEAN

0   400 mi
0   400 km

N W E S

Telegraphs and Telephones

New inventions also improved communication. An **invention** is something that is made for the first time. People protect their inventions by getting patents on them. A **patent** gives a person the right to be the only one making or selling an invention.

In 1832, Samuel Morse began work to develop a telegraph. A **telegraph** is a machine that sends and receives signals through a thin wire. Six years later, he invented the Morse code. Look at the image of the Morse code on the right. The Morse code uses dots and dashes to represent letters and numbers. Telegraphs used Morse code to deliver messages almost instantly.

In 1844, the first telegraph message was sent between two cities. It was not until 1854, however, that Morse was given a patent for his invention.

Alexander Graham Bell liked the telegraph. He wondered, though, if he could send the human voice through wires. In 1876, Bell invented the telephone. For the first time, people could talk without seeing each other.

2. **Identify** and underline the sentence that explains how the telephone changed how people communicated.
Find a copy of Morse code on the Internet. Then create your name in Morse code.

This is how Alexander Graham Bell's name would be sent in Morse code.

Alexander Graham Bell makes the first telephone call from New York City to Chicago, Illinois.

Radio and Television

The telegraph and the telephone helped people communicate over long distances. However, these inventions used wires that were strung between buildings or cities. In 1896, Italian inventor Guglielmo Marconi (goo LYEL moh mahr KOH nee) found a way to send messages without wires.

Marconi patented a way for radio signals to travel through the air. People could now send and receive messages without telegraph wires.

In 1901, he received the first radio message sent across the Atlantic Ocean. Suddenly, people around the world could communicate instantly.

Many inventions were created by one person. However, some were developed by many people. The television was one of these inventions. The idea for the television is based on the work of Morse, Bell, Marconi, and many other scientists. Each one created parts of the new machine.

Although the creation of today's televisions took many years, most of the work was done in the 1920s and 1930s. In 1939, the television was introduced to a large audience at the World's Fair in New York. By the late 1940s, many Americans owned a television. These televisions showed black-and-white pictures. Since then, many scientists have improved the television.

Today, almost every home in the United States has at least one television. In addition, people can watch television through their computers and other communication tools.

3. ◉ **Sequence** Look at the pictures of communication tools. **Sequence** them 1–4 in the order they were invented.

Communication Tools

☐ Radio

☐ Telephone

☐ Television

☐ Telegraph

Communication Today

In the last 20 years, communication has changed even more. Satellites quickly send and receive signals for radios, televisions, cellular phones, and computers.

Computer technology has also improved communication. **Technology** is the scientific knowledge about how things work. When Bill Gates was young, computers were huge machines. No one had a computer at home. He helped to make personal computers possible. Today, people write e-mail messages that travel around the world in just a few seconds. They send photos and videos on cellular phones and computers. In the future, there will be new ways of communicating quickly.

4. ● **Draw Conclusions** **Identify** and underline one impact of computers on your community. With a partner, **predict** and **discuss** how communication will change in the future.

Satellites send and receive signals to make communication faster.

5. ⊙ **Draw Conclusions Analyze** the lesson. Write a conclusion you can draw about how each invention has changed communities.

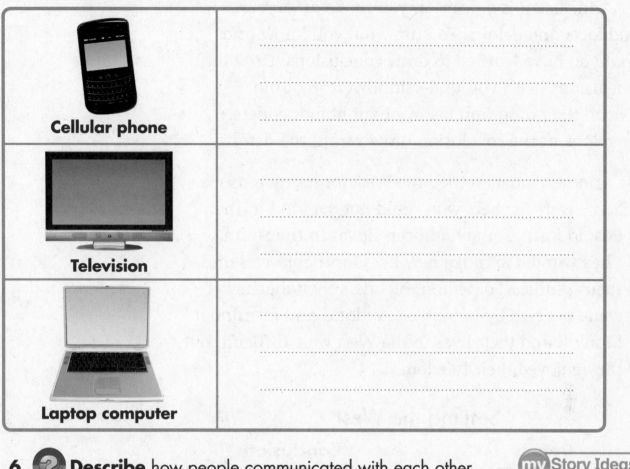

Cellular phone	
Television	
Laptop computer	

6. **Describe** how people communicated with each other before the invention of the telephone and how the telephone made communication easier.

7. **Research** the accomplishments of Maria Mitchell and Bill Gates. In a digital Venn diagram, **compare** and **contrast** the impact of their work.

Draw Conclusions

A conclusion is a decision you make after you read facts and details. You use what you know and what you have learned to draw conclusions. Drawing conclusions helps you understand your reading.

Read the paragraph below about homesteaders. Then look at the conclusion drawn from the details.

Homesteaders settled the West for many reasons. Some were farmers who could not get land in the East to farm. Some had been slaves in the South. They wanted to make new lives for themselves and their families. Some homesteaders thought they could get rich by buying cheap land and farming it. Many found their lives in the West were difficult, but they enjoyed their freedom.

Settling the West

Details	Conclusion
1. Farmers had no land in the East. 2. People who had been enslaved wanted to start new lives. 3. People wanted to get rich.	People became homesteaders in the West because they wanted a better life.

Homesteaders hoped for a better life.

TEKS

SS 2.B Identify ways in which people in other communities meet their needs for communication.
ELA 15 Locate and use specific information in graphic features of text.

Analyze the passage about the Pony Express. Then fill in the chart.

A Pony Express rider is on his way to deliver mail.

The Pony Express was created during the Civil War to help people find out what was happening around the country. Before the Pony Express, the mail had been carried by stagecoach and by boat.

Pony Express riders risked their lives to deliver the mail. They rode as fast as they could, and they did not rest very often.

Mail delivery was much faster with the Pony Express, but it was not safe enough or fast enough. The Pony Express went out of business after the telegraph was invented.

Analyze the passage, then fill in the chart with two more details about the Pony Express riders. Then write a conclusion you can draw from the details.

The Pony Express Riders

Details	Conclusion
1. Riders risked their lives.	
2.	
3.	

New Ideas

Light

Washing machine

Envision It!

Circle the inventions that help you to keep clean.

Throughout history, new ideas have changed people's lives. Some kinds of ideas involve making new things, such as cars. Others involve creating new ways to live. Both kinds of ideas can change communities.

In the late 1800s and early 1900s, more people began to work to give all Americans equal rights. When people have **equal rights**, they have the same rights as others.

Women wanted the right to vote. African Americans wanted their children to have the right to go to the same schools as white children. Workers wanted rules to keep them safe. Many Americans worked to turn these ideas into laws.

Education and New Inventions

In the early 1900s, many schools were segregated. White and African American students went to separate schools. Sometimes no schools were available for African American children.

Some people thought this was wrong. They wanted all children to have equal educations. In 1904, Mary McLeod Bethune opened a school for African American girls in Florida.

Mary McLeod Bethune helped African American girls get an education.

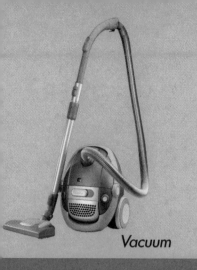

Vacuum

Refrigerator

UNLOCK
THE BIG
?

I will know how new ideas and machines changed people's lives throughout history.

Vocabulary

equal rights
assembly line
vaccine
activist

In 1954, the United States Supreme Court ruled that school segregation was against the law. Now all children could have equal educations.

In the 1900s, the lives of Americans changed in other ways, too. One big change was caused by the invention of the first practical, or useful, light bulb. In 1879, Thomas Edison had invented a light bulb that was cheap and reliable. It provided light without needing to light a fire or a candle.

It took years for electrical wires to be put in and power stations to be built. However, by the 1900s, factories and offices could stay open at night. People could walk safely on well-lit streets, too.

Today, inventions are still changing people's lives. Cameras and computers have changed the way people communicate, shop for goods, and gather information about the world.

TEKS

8.E, 14.A, 16.A, 16.B, 17.B, 17.D, 18.B

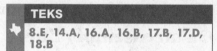

A camera from 2010

A camera from the early 1900s

1. **Main Idea and Details** **Describe** two ways that people's lives changed in the 1900s.

....

....

New Machines and New Businesses

In 1831, Cyrus Hall McCormick invented a machine that cut grain. It was called a reaper. Before, people cut crops by hand. The reaper made cutting grain faster and easier. Today, machines help farmers use more land and grow more crops.

One of the most important inventions of the late 1800s was the automobile, or car. In 1903, Henry Ford opened a business that built and sold cars. At that time, most people could not afford a car.

Ford wanted to build a car that everyone could afford. This led him to invent the assembly line. On an **assembly line,** each worker does only one part of a job. Ford's assembly line idea was used in factories around the world.

Assembly lines helped Ford make a car called the Model T. The Model T cost less than other cars. Now, millions of people could afford to buy cars. People like Ford who start new businesses have shaped communities in the past. They continue to do so today.

Mary Kay Ash started a business selling cosmetics. Wallace Amos started a business selling cookies. New businesses provide new jobs. They provide new products for people to buy.

2. **Identify** and underline the sentence that tells the type of new business that Henry Ford started in the early twentieth century.

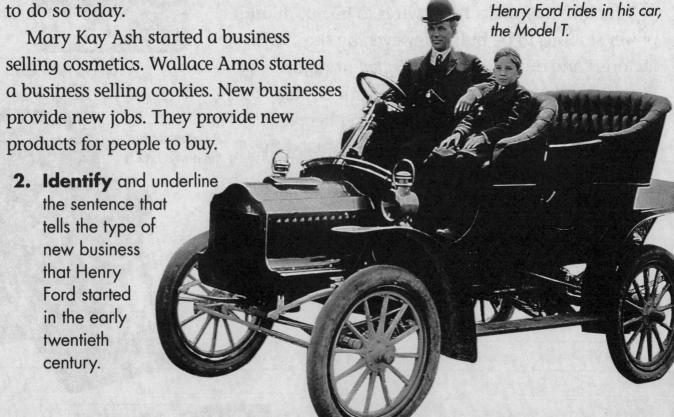

Henry Ford rides in his car, the Model T.

New Ideas in Medicine

In the 1700s, a disease called smallpox killed millions of people. No one knew what caused it. There was no cure.

Then in 1796, Edward Jenner found a way to protect people from this terrible disease. He gave them a vaccine made from a very weak virus. A **vaccine** helps people's bodies fight off disease. Jenner's vaccine helped people fight off smallpox.

Polio was another terrible disease. In the 1950s, a Jewish American doctor named Jonas Salk used Jenner's ideas to invent a vaccine against polio. Salk gave people a dead form of the polio virus. Salk's vaccine helped people's bodies learn how to fight off the polio virus. The vaccine saved the lives of many people.

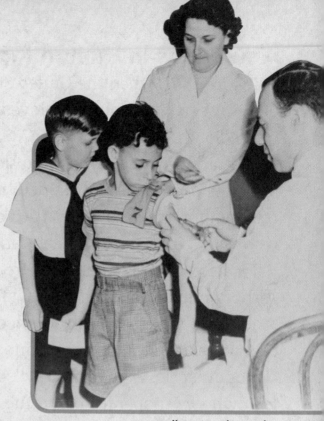

Dr. Salk gives the polio vaccine to a child in 1954.

Louis Pasteur (LOO ee pas TOOR) discovered that many diseases are caused by germs. Pasteur thought that people would not get sick if germs did not enter their bodies. In the 1860s, he invented a way to kill germs by heating foods and cooling them quickly. This process is called pasteurization. Today, most of the milk we drink is pasteurized.

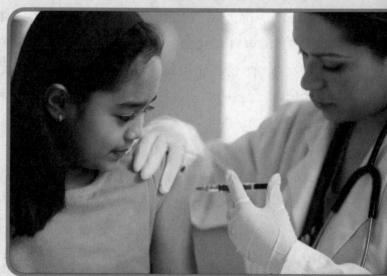

People today get many vaccines to help them stay healthy.

3. ◎ **Main Idea and Details Identify** the impact of pasteurization on communities.

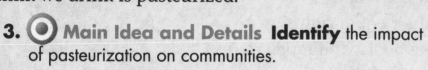

New Ideas in Human Rights

Before 1861, when the United States Civil War began, there were many enslaved African Americans in the South. One reason the Civil War was fought was that many people believed slavery was wrong.

Before and after the war, activists worked to win freedom for enslaved people. An **activist** is someone who works hard to make a change happen.

Frederick Douglass escaped from slavery in 1838. Although it was against the law for enslaved people to learn to read, Douglass learned how to read and write. He soon became famous for speaking out against slavery. Douglass also printed his own newspaper to spread the word that African Americans should be free.

Frederick Douglass

Another activist was Harriet Tubman. She escaped from slavery in 1849. For the next ten years, she kept returning to the South to help enslaved people escape. By 1860, she had freed more than 300 slaves. She risked her own freedom and her life to help others escape from slavery.

Harriet Tubman

After the Civil War ended in 1865, enslaved African Americans were finally free. However, African Americans still did not have the same rights as others. It would take many years and the work of many activists to make this happen.

In the 1950s and 1960s, Martin Luther King Jr. became a leader in the fight for equal rights for African Americans. He wrote books and made many speeches. He led thousands of people in a march on Washington, D.C., where he delivered his famous "I Have a Dream" speech.

Martin Luther King Jr.

Many Americans have worked for equal rights. Some have used their power in government to make changes. In 1964, President Lyndon B. Johnson helped pass a law that made it illegal to treat people differently in the workplace. The lives of many people changed as a result of all of these activists' work.

4. ◉ **Draw Conclusions** **Analyze** the details you have read to write a conclusion about equal rights activists.

....

....

TEKS 14.A, 16.A, 17.B, 17.D, 18.B

5. ◉ **Draw Conclusions** **Analyze** the following sentence. Then write a conclusion you can draw from it.

For ten years, Harriet Tubman kept returning to the South to help enslaved people escape to freedom.

....

....

6. Think about someone in the early 1900s who is driving a Model T Ford to a friend's house. **Describe** how that trip might be different from a trip you take in a car today.

my **Story Ideas**

....

....

7. Using a computer, **create** a chart with these three columns: Inventors/Inventions, Medicine, and Human Rights. For each column, choose one person from this book. Write their name and two details about their work. Then do keyword Internet searches to locate information about another person to add to each column.

....

Lesson 1 🔸 TEKS 1.A

New Ways to Travel

1. **Describe** how the National Road led to more people settling the West.

   ....

   ....

2. **Describe** how the transcontinental railroad changed the United States.

   ....

   ....

Lesson 2 🔸 TEKS 1.C, 4.A

A New Home in America

3. **Describe** and **explain** some of the landforms and natural resources that attracted early immigrants to the United States.

   ....

   ....

   ....

   ....

   ....

4. **Identify** the different types of jobs that Japanese immigrants did after they arrived in the United States.

   ....

   ....

New Ways to Communicate

5. 🎯 **Draw Conclusions** **Analyze** the details. Then fill in the chart with a conclusion you can draw from the details.

Details   **Conclusion**

1. The invention of the telegraph allowed people to send messages almost instantly.

2. The invention of the radio allowed people to send messages to many people at one time without wires.

3. People can now use computers to send e-mail messages instantly.

6. **Identify** ways in which these inventions changed the way people communicated with one another.

   a. Telephone ....

   ....

   b. Television ....

   ....

   c. Personal computer ....

   ....

Lesson 4 ⬥ TEKS 8.E, 14.A, 16.A, 16.B, 17.B

New Ideas

7. Draw a line to **identify** the scientist, inventor, or entrepreneur that matches each invention or business. Then **categorize** each item. Write *science, technology,* or *business* on the line.

Jonas Salk   way to kill germs ....

Henry Ford   cookies   ....

Mary Kay Ash   reaper   ....

Louis Pasteur   assembly line   ....

Wallace Amos   cosmetics   ....

Cyrus McCormick   polio vaccine   ....

8. Compare the heroic deeds of Harriet Tubman with the heroic deeds of Frederick Douglass.

....

....

....

....

....

9. Identify the impact of Edward Jenner's vaccine on communities.

....

....

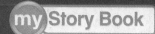
Go online to write and illustrate your own **myStory Book** using the **myStory Ideas** from this chapter.

How does life change throughout history?

TEKS
SS 2.B
ELA 17

Life has changed in many ways over time. Inventions and new ideas in transportation, communication, medicine, and technology have made our lives easier.

Think about how travel and communication have changed over the years. **Write** about the different ways you have traveled or communicated.

....

....

....

....

Now **draw** a picture that shows the way you travel or communicate most often.

PEARSON realize. Go online to access your interactive digital lesson.

237

Working in Our Communities

my Story Spark

How do people get what they need?

Think about the choices people make when they buy things. Then **write** about a choice you made when you bought something.

....

....

....

....

....

....

....

Texas Essential Knowledge and Skills

6.A Identify ways of earning, spending, saving, and donating money.

6.B Create a simple budget that allocates money for spending, saving, and donating.

7.A Define and identify examples of scarcity.

7.B Explain the impact of scarcity on the production, distribution, and consumption of goods and services.

7.C Explain the concept of a free market as it relates to the U.S. free enterprise system.

8.A Identify examples of how a simple business operates.

8.B Explain how supply and demand affect the price of a good or service.

8.C Explain how the cost of production and selling price affect profits.

8.D Explain how government regulations and taxes impact consumer costs.

17.C Interpret oral, visual, and print material by identifying the main idea, distinguishing between fact and opinion, identifying cause and effect, and comparing and contrasting.

17.E Interpret and create visuals, including graphs, charts, tables, timelines, illustrations, and maps.

17.F Use appropriate mathematical skills to interpret social studies information such as maps and graphs.

18.A Express ideas orally based on knowledge and experiences.

19.B Use a decision-making process to identify a situation that requires a decision, gather information, identify options, predict consequences, and take action to implement a decision.

Farmers Market
Meet Me at Third and Fairfax

my Story Video

Sloan's eyes light up when he sees Kip's Toyland. "This is the best place on Earth!" he declares. Today, Sloan is visiting Farmers Market at Third and Fairfax in Los Angeles, California. This historic market has been providing goods and services to local customers since 1934. Goods are things that people make or grow and then sell. A service is work that one person does for another.

Sloan was so excited when he arrived at Farmers Market that he did not know what he wanted to see first!

"No toys today, Sloan," says his mom. "We have other things we need to buy." As they head off to explore the market, Sloan notices all of the colorful displays. There is a variety of T-shirts and sweatshirts hanging in one store window, and there is bright, shiny jewelry on display in another window. Looking inside one of the children's stores, Sloan smiles as he finds a play area right in the middle of the store! He stops walking as he takes a moment to enjoy the smell of all the delicious food. "Mmm, I smell Chinese food," he says. "Maybe that's what I'll have for lunch!"

Welcome to Farmers Market

There is a wide variety of fruits and vegetables available at Farmers Market.

The butcher shop has many different kinds of meats to choose from.

People shop for things they need at the market. Many different people provide goods here at Farmers Market. Local farmers bring their fruits and vegetables so they can sell them directly to the people at the market. This is one of the reasons Sloan and his mom love coming to Farmers Market. Shoppers can be sure that the food they are buying is as fresh as it can be.

Sloan could not resist stopping to look at all of the delicious baked goods!

Sloan makes his way to the nearest vegetable stand. "There it is...broccoli. My favorite!" he tells us. Next to this vegetable stand is a butcher shop. "I really like chicken," Sloan says. There is a shop for just about every type of food you can think of, whether you are looking for meats, cheeses, or even fresh peanut butter. There is also a fish monger, or someone who sells fish and seafood, and several bakeries. If your dog needs a treat, there is even a bakery for him or her!

In the early 1930s, gas stations in the Farmers Market area had clear globes on top so you could see the color of the gas!

At the chocolate factory, Sloan watched as people made different chocolate treats.

People can also buy things they want at Farmers Market. There are toy stores, a hat shop, a spice store, and even a chocolate factory. Sloan sees a lot of things he wants, but he decides to ask his mom if she can buy only one of these things for him. "Okay, Sloan, you can have a baseball cap," she tells him. "I'll take that one," Sloan tells the storekeeper. "This is my favorite team. Thank you!"

Sloan proudly shows the souvenir penny he made.

Farmers Market is right in the middle of a big city. People who live nearby come here to shop, eat, and enjoy street musicians. It is a bustling, busy place. There are plenty of small souvenir stores here, too. A souvenir is something that serves as a reminder. "I had a great time at the market today," Sloan says. "I know I didn't need this souvenir penny, but isn't it neat?" People often buy souvenirs here to remember their trip to Farmers Market. If you could choose a souvenir, what would you choose?

Think About It Based on this story, do you think Farmers Market is a good place for people to find what they need and want? As you read the chapter ahead, think about what this story tells you about how people in communities work together to meet their needs and wants.

PEARSON realize. Go online to access your interactive digital lesson.

241

Meeting Our Needs and Wants

Envision It!

Circle two things that would help you do your work at school.

Have you ever said, "I really need that toy"? Do you really need it, or do you just want it? There is a difference between needing and wanting.

Needs and Wants

Needs are things you must have to live. Healthful food, water, clothing, and shelter are all needs. You need them to survive.

Wants are things you would like to have but do not need. You can live without them. Basketballs, special sneakers, and board games are wants.

Some things are wants for some people and needs for others. Some people want a boat so they can water ski. Others need a boat for transportation.

People earn money to buy the things they need and want. Most people earn money by working at jobs. They can also sell things they no longer want to make money.

1. **Identify** a way you could earn money.

....

....

Clothing and healthful foods are needs.

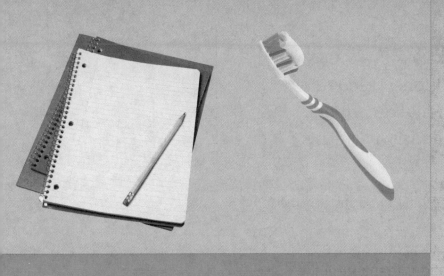

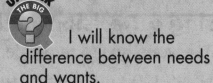
Vocabulary

needs   opportunity
wants   cost
scarcity   value
abundance

Enough or Too Much?

When there is **scarcity**, there is not enough of something to meet people's needs and wants. For example, if it does not rain for a long time, there may be a scarcity of water. Flowers may not bloom, and water levels may become low.

When there is scarcity, people must make choices about how to use what they have. If there is not enough water, people might decide not to water their lawns. This will make more water available for washing and drinking.

If there is an **abundance**, there is a lot of something. For example, if it rains for a long time, there might be an abundance of water. When there is an abundance of something, there is enough to meet people's needs and wants.

2. ◉ **Compare and Contrast Define** the words *scarcity* and *abundance* to explain the difference between them.

....

....

TEKS
6.A, 7.A, 17.C, 19.B

Little rain might lead to a scarcity of water.

Using a Decision-Making Process

Everyone has to make decisions. Using a decision-making process can make it easier to make choices. To make a decision, use the following steps.

1. Identify the decision that has to be made and all possible choices.
2. Gather information about all the choices.
3. Think about the information. Identify all the possible good outcomes and bad outcomes for each choice. Make a list of the outcomes to complete this step.
4. Make your choice.
5. Act on your decision.

3. Discuss with a partner how you would **use** a decision-making process to make a choice.

Scarcity, Value, and Choice

People have to make difficult decisions when there is scarcity. They must decide how to divide what they have so that everyone's needs will be met. They must find a way to make choices that are fair to everyone.

Some communities deal with scarcity by exchanging products with one another. For example, people in one community may have a lot of vegetables. People in another community may have an abundance of dairy products. These communities might exchange their extra products so that everyone has what they need.

When you exchange something with someone else, you give up one thing to get another thing.

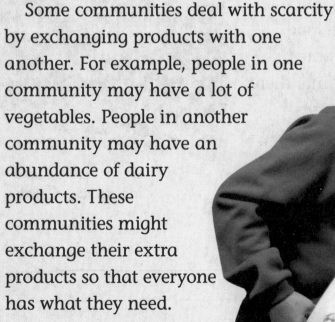

244

When there is a scarcity of money, people have to make careful choices about how they will spend what they have. Sometimes when you make a choice, you have to give something up. An item's **opportunity cost** is the value of the thing you give up when you choose one thing over another. An item's **value** is what it is worth to a person.

People do not always place a higher value on things that cost more. Even if an item costs more, it might not have a high value to someone who does not want or need it.

People usually compare things before they decide what to buy.

Suppose a family decides to move to a larger apartment. They find two apartments that everyone likes. Both are similar in size, and they cost the same amount of money to rent. The first apartment is close to the children's school and to the parents' jobs. However, it is far away from the community center and the grocery store. The second apartment is farther away from their school and jobs. However, it is closer to the community center and grocery store.

The family has to decide which they value more. This family chooses the first apartment. They decide that it is more important to be closer to their school and jobs. They spend more time either going to school or working. Therefore, the first apartment has more value to them.

4. Identify and underline the sentence that tells why the family chose the first apartment.

Choices in Communities

People living in communities around the world make choices every day. That is because no one can have everything. People have to decide what has value to them.

Often, people in a community work together to make choices. In this way, most people's needs can be met.

For example, imagine that two communities have a scarcity of money. People living in both communities decide that they can save money by working together. The communities decide to have one police department for both communities instead of one for each. This plan helps everyone stay safe and saves money.

World communities can help each other make choices, too. For example, one country might have a scarcity of water and another might have an abundance. People from both countries could meet and decide how much water they have together. Then they could make a plan to share their water. This plan makes sure everyone has enough.

People around the world make choices when they spend money.

5. Suppose your community's playground has a scarcity of baseball supplies. **Describe** a way you can work with others to get the supplies people want.

....

....

....

6. ◉ **Main Idea and Details** Suppose you are going camping. **Identify** your needs and wants. Tell whether each item is a need or a want.

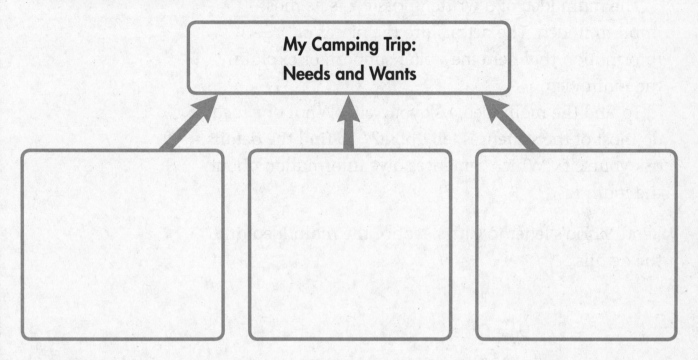

My Camping Trip:
Needs and Wants

7. ❓ **Describe** a time you had to decide between getting something you needed and something you wanted. **Explain** why you made your decision.

my Story Ideas

....

....

....

....

8. In this lesson, you learned about scarcity. **Identify** products and resources that are becoming scarce. **Create** a collage showing these products and resources. **Identify** which of these resources are needs and which are wants. **Explain** how to conserve scarce resources that help meet our needs.

....

....

PEARSON
realize Go online to access your interactive digital lesson.

247

Main Idea and Details

The main idea of a written passage is its most important idea. The details are the pieces of information that help the writer support, or explain, the main idea.

To find the main idea, ask yourself, "What one idea do most of the sentences tell about?" To find the details, ask yourself, "Which sentences give information about the main idea?"

Read Maria's letter to Chris. Notice the main idea and the details.

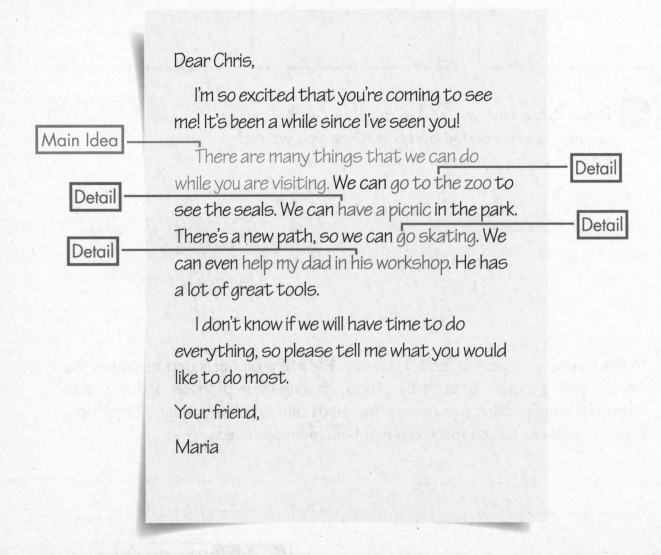

Dear Chris,

I'm so excited that you're coming to see me! It's been a while since I've seen you!

There are many things that we can do while you are visiting. We can go to the zoo to see the seals. We can have a picnic in the park. There's a new path, so we can go skating. We can even help my dad in his workshop. He has a lot of great tools.

I don't know if we will have time to do everything, so please tell me what you would like to do most.

Your friend,

Maria

Main Idea — Detail
Detail — Detail
Detail

I will know how to find the main idea and details in a written passage.

◆ TEKS

SS 17.C Interpret print material by identifying the main idea.

ELA 13.A Identify the details or facts that support the main idea.

 **Try** *it!*

Read Chris's letter to Maria. Then **answer** the question.

> Dear Maria,
>
> Wow! It's hard to choose from so many great ideas.
>
> I think I would like to go to the zoo with you. I'd love to see the seals. Mom says your zoo has a lot of them. I'd also like to see the pandas. We don't have pandas in our zoo. Maybe we can have a picnic there, too. I'm sure they have picnic tables.
>
> I can't wait to see you again!
>
> Your friend,
> Chris

Identify the main idea and details from Chris's letter to Maria. Then fill in the chart.

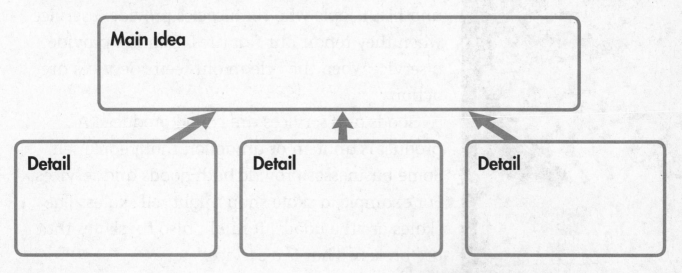

Main Idea

Detail	Detail	Detail

Producers and Consumers

Write a caption that describes what is happening in the picture.

Farms grow goods, such as oranges, for sale.

Your community has many businesses, both large and small. Some businesses make things, such as sneakers or computers. Other businesses sell these things. Some businesses do things for people, such as repair cars or clean clothes.

All businesses try to provide what people need or want. Let's look at how some businesses work.

Goods and Services

Goods are things that people make or grow and then sell. Sneakers and computers are examples of goods that are made. Oranges and other crops are goods that are grown.

A **service** is work that one person does for another. People who fix bicycles provide a service when they repair our flat tires. Dentists provide a service when they clean our teeth. Services are actions.

Goods and services are called products. A product is an item or an action that people sell. Some businesses provide both goods and services. For example, a skate shop might sell skates. The skates are the goods. It might also fix skates that are broken. That is a service.

UNLOCK
THE BIG
?

I will know the difference between goods and services and between producers and consumers.

Vocabulary

goods

service

producer

consumer

human resource

capital resource

profit

What are some goods and services that are available in your community? You might have a grocery store on your block that sells fruits, vegetables, bread, and milk. These foods are the store's goods.

Hair salons often sell both goods and services. Many salons sell goods, such as shampoo and hairbrushes. They also sell haircuts. Because it is an action, cutting hair is a service.

1. ◉ **Main Idea and Details** **Identify** three goods and three services.

Goods	Services

TEKS
7.B, 8.C, 8.D

A hair salon offers services such as haircutting.

PEARSON
realize. Go online to access your interactive digital lesson.

251

Producers and Consumers

Few people can make all of the products and services they need and want. Instead, most people buy goods and services from other people or from stores and businesses.

A person who makes a product or provides a service is called a **producer.** If you have ever made something, such as a birthday card, you have been a producer.

When people spend money to buy things they need or want, they are called **consumers.** If you have ever bought something, such as an apple, you have been a consumer. Consumers buy goods and services. The study of how goods and services are produced, distributed, and consumed is called economics.

Producers and consumers need each other. Producers need consumers to buy the goods they create and the services they offer. Consumers need producers to offer the goods and services that consumers cannot provide for themselves.

People can also be both producers and consumers. The man in the picture who is making a chair is a producer. He is making a product that someone else will buy. He is a consumer, too. That is because he bought the wood and tools from someone who produced them.

2. **Analyze** the picture. Circle the producer.

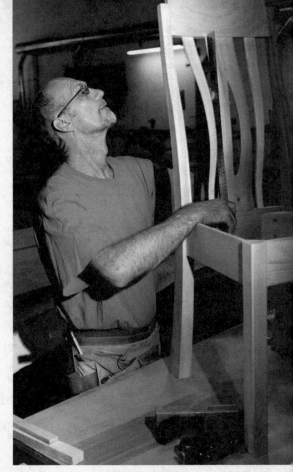

This producer is making a wooden chair.

Consumers buy goods from people, not just from stores.

Resources All Around Us

All businesses rely on resources. A **human resource** is a person who makes products or provides services. Human resources can also be called producers.

Natural resources are useful materials that come from Earth. Many kinds of natural resources are needed to make goods. Water, soil, and wood are all natural resources.

Capital resources are the things needed to produce goods and services. Computers, tools, and money are all capital resources.

Businesses try to use their resources wisely. When they do, they might make a profit. A **profit** is the money that businesses have left after their production costs are paid.

What are production costs? Businesses pay their workers, or human resources, money for doing their jobs. Some businesses buy goods to make the products they sell. Businesses also pay for the heat and water they use and for capital resources.

A business's profits depend on two things. The first is keeping their production costs low. The other is how much money they sell their product for. Say it costs a toy company $10.50 to make a toy. The company sells the toy for $15. That means they make a profit of $4.50 for each toy they sell.

This doctor and nurse are human resources.

3. **Explain** how production costs and selling price affect a company's profit.

....

....

....

Changing Roles

Suppose you are making lemonade on a hot day. You are a producer because you are making something. The good you are making is lemonade.

You are a consumer, too. That is because you had to buy things to make the lemonade. You probably bought lemons, sugar, and cups.

Producers and consumers can change roles. For example, bicycle factories are producers because they make bicycles that people buy.

However, they are consumers, too. That is because they probably buy some of the things they use to make bicycles. They may not make the tires or the paint they use. Instead, they may buy these things from tire stores and paint stores. That makes them consumers of tires and paint.

The factories use these items to make bicycles that they sell to consumers. Consumers pay money for the bicycles. The bicycle factory can then use this money to make more bicycles. Producers and consumers often change roles in the process of buying and selling products.

People can be both producers and consumers.

4. Write one sentence that **describes** a time when you were a producer. Write one sentence that **describes** a time when you were a consumer.

....

....

....

....

Government and Consumer Costs

The government affects how much consumers pay for a product. One way the government impacts consumer costs is by regulating businesses. Regulations are rules. These rules are designed to protect consumers. For example, there are rules that make sure the food and drinks we consume are safe. Other rules are designed to protect the environment. They keep businesses from polluting the environment too much.

Sometimes it costs money for businesses to follow government regulations. They may have to pay for machines to cut down on pollution. This cost becomes part of a business's production costs. If a business has higher production costs, they might raise the price of their product to make a better profit.

Another way government impacts consumer costs is with taxes. Sales taxes are taxes a person pays when they buy an item. State and local governments charge sales taxes. You pay sales tax in addition to the cost of the item. The more expensive the item is, the more you pay in sales tax.

Government regulations and taxes can affect the price consumers pay for a product.

5. **Explain** how the government's regulations and taxes can affect the cost of a toy you want to buy.

....

....

....

....

Scarcity and Production, Distribution, and Consumption

Scarcity means there is not enough of a product or service for everyone. When something is scarce, choices have to be made about how to use it.

Businesses cannot make every good or provide every service that consumers want. Sometimes resources are scarce. There might not be enough natural or human resources to make goods or provide services. So, businesses have to make decisions on how to best use the resources they have. When a business cannot make enough goods or provide enough services to meet consumers' needs, this leads to scarcity.

Scarcity can impact how goods and services are distributed and used. When a good is scarce, consumers have to make choices. A scarce product or service can cost more to buy because there are higher production costs or because businesses need to charge a higher selling price to make a profit. Consumers need to decide if they want to pay more for scarce goods and services.

Suppose wheat becomes scarce. Flour is made from wheat, so it becomes scarce, too. Bakeries and other food businesses will have to make decisions. They may not be able to make as much of their product or as many different products. Consumers may have fewer products to spend their money on.

If there is a scarcity of wheat, there can be a scarcity of products made of flour.

6. **Explain** how a scarcity of natural resources might affect consumers.

....

....

....

 TEKS 7.B

7. ◎ **Main Idea and Details Explain** what producers and consumers are. Then **explain** how scarcity affects them.

a. Producers are

....

....

b. Consumers are

....

....

c. How are producers and consumers affected by scarcity?

....

....

....

8. ❓ **Identify** a service that you can perform for someone in your family or in your neighborhood.

my Story Ideas

....

....

9. In this lesson, you learned how businesses provide goods and services that consumers want and need. **Identify** a business in your community. What good or service does it provide? **Explain** the impact on your community if this business began to slow down production and its product or service became scarce.

....

....

....

Exchanging Goods and Services

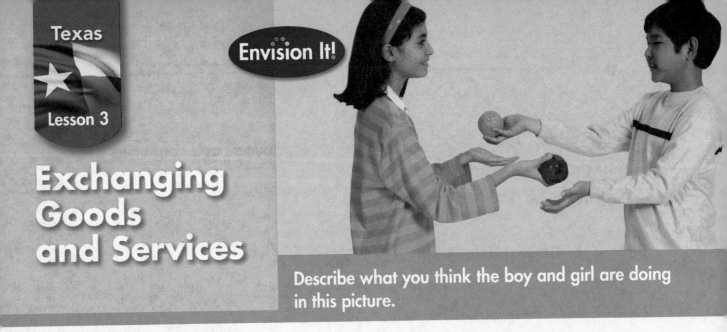

Envision It!

Describe what you think the boy and girl are doing in this picture.

Fruits, like these mangoes, are goods you can buy.

Have you ever wondered how fruit gets to a store? The farmer who grew the fruit probably met with a worker from the store. The store worker, or the buyer, looked at the fruit. The farmer, or the seller, talked about why the fruit was worth buying.

Then the buyer and the seller talked about the price. When they agreed, they made a deal. The store worker gave money to the farmer in exchange for the fruit. Finally, the fruit was delivered to the store. That is how fruit gets to a store.

Trade and Barter

Communities in the United States and around the world depend on each other for many things. One thing they need to do is trade with each other. When people **trade,** they use money to buy and sell goods and services. However, when they **barter,** they do not use money. Instead, one person gives a good or a service to another in exchange for a different good or service.

People have been trading and bartering goods for thousands of years. People in one place often make just a few goods. Then they barter their goods with people who have goods they need.

UNLOCK THE BIG ?

I will know different ways people trade goods and services and the effects of supply and demand.

Vocabulary

trade	import
barter	export
supply	free enterprise
demand	system

Bartering can be useful when people from different cultures meet. When Europeans came to the Americas, for example, they could not use money from their home countries. So they bartered with American Indians to get things they needed.

Europeans gave the American Indians tools and animals, such as axes and horses. In return, the American Indians gave the Europeans food, such as corn and potatoes, and furs that the Europeans used to stay warm.

Today, people usually use money to get the goods and services they need. Money makes trading goods and services easier. That is because money has a value that everyone agrees on. Money is very light, so it is portable, or easy to carry. It can also be divided into smaller units. If you buy something that costs 50 cents with a one-dollar bill, the seller can give you 50 cents in change. Money is also durable, which means it can last a long time.

1. **◎ Compare and Contrast** Underline the text that **explains** how trading and bartering are different.

TEKS
7.C, 8.A, 8.B, 17.C, 18.A

At first, people bartered for goods.

PEARSON realize — Go online to access your interactive digital lesson.

259

Supply and Demand

The amount of goods or services that people can sell is called the **supply.** The amount of goods or services that people want and can buy is called the **demand.**

In most cases, if the supply of something goes up, the price goes down. Suppose a store owner has too many sweaters. The owner may lower the price, and more shoppers might buy them.

What affects the supply of sweaters? If there are fewer sheep, there might not be much wool to make sweaters. If there is a storm, trucks might not be able to bring the sweaters to a store.

What happens if the supply goes down? The price might go up. Some people might decide to pay a higher price because they really want a sweater.

What affects the demand for sweaters? If the weather is warm, people might not want them. If few people buy sweaters, the price might go down.

Transportation is a service. Around holidays, such as Thanksgiving, many people travel great distances to be with family and friends. The demand for airline and train tickets goes up. The price of these tickets usually goes up, too.

Prices often depend on the size of the supply. If there is too much of something, prices often go down.

2. ◉ **Cause and Effect Identify** a good or service you use. **Explain** what might cause the supply of that good or service to go down.

....

....

....

....

Moving Goods Around the World

Today, people around the world buy and sell goods and services to one another. Trade between countries is called international trade.

People and countries import products from other countries. To **import** means to bring products and resources into one country from another. People and countries also export products to other countries. To **export** means to send products and resources from one country to another.

Today, international trade can be done easily. That is because goods can move from one country to another in only a few days.

Packing goods into big containers like these makes it easy to ship goods around the world quickly.

Fruit spoils very fast. However, airplanes, trains, ships, and trucks can bring fruit to stores quickly. This means people can buy fresh fruit that is grown far away but still tastes good. As people keep buying fruit, the supply goes down. But that amount can rise again quickly. That is because trucks and ships can bring more fruit to the store.

Communication also helps people today to trade quickly. People use the Internet and telephones to communicate instantly. They order products online or by phone. In this way, transportation and communication together help the supply of products to rise quickly.

3. Explain what helps the supply of products to rise quickly today.

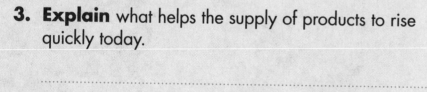

Free Enterprise System

In the United States, people and companies do business in a free enterprise system. A **free enterprise system** is an economy in which the people and private businesses decide what goods to make and buy and what work to do. The government does not make these decisions. A free enterprise system is also known as a free market system or capitalism.

In a free market, people and private businesses control supply and demand. Farmers in a free market decide which crops to plant. Factories decide which goods to make. Store owners decide which products to sell. People decide which goods and services they want to buy. If there is scarcity, people and businesses decide how to use the resources available, not the government.

Some countries do not have a free enterprise system. In these countries, the government controls what is bought and sold. In those countries, it is government that controls supply and demand. The people and private businesses have no control over supply and demand.

In a free enterprise system, farmers decide what crops to grow.

4. Look at the photo. **Identify** and circle examples of a free enterprise system.

5. **Explain** the role of a free market in a free enterprise system.

....

....

....

....

6. ◉ **Main Idea and Details** **Review** the lesson. Then fill in the chart with details that support the main idea.

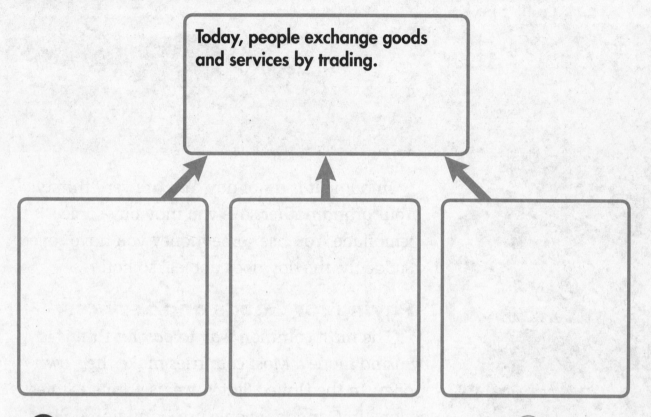

Today, people exchange goods and services by trading.

7. **Describe** a time when you exchanged a good or a service **my Story Ideas** with a friend or a family member.

....

....

8. Think about a good or service you use. **Explain** how supply and demand could affect the price of this good or service. Use your own knowledge of the good or service and what you learned about how supply and demand affect prices. **Present** your explanation orally to a small group.

Spending and Saving

Envision It!

Write what you think the girl might be saving her money to buy.

People in the United States, Japan, and Mexico use different forms of money. In Japan, people use yen.

Imagine it is a hot day. You are very thirsty! Your grandmother says you may buy some lemonade. You use some money you have saved. Suddenly, the day does not feel so hot!

Paying for Goods and Services

The most common way to pay for things is by using money. Most countries make their own money. In the United States, we use United States dollars. In Canada, people use Canadian dollars. In Mexico, people use pesos. People in the islands of the Caribbean use various forms of money. Some, like people in Jamaica, use dollars. In Haiti, people use gourdes. In Aruba, people use florin.

Instead of using money, people can also pay for things by bartering, or exchanging one thing for another. For example, you might give your cousin your granola bar in exchange for his apple.

Credit is another way to pay for things. **Credit** is a promise to pay for something. A **credit card** lets the cardholder buy things and pay for them later. The cardholder pays the credit card company every month until all of the money is paid back.

UNLOCK THE BIG ?

I will know different ways people pay for goods and services and how they save money.

Vocabulary

credit	interest
credit card	deposit
savings	loan
bank	budget

Savings

The money a person earns but does not spend is called that person's **savings.** For example, suppose you walk a neighbor's dog for a week. You earn $5, but you buy a comic book for $2. If you subtract $2 from $5, you have $3 left. Your leftover $3 is money you can save to use later.

People usually save money over a period of weeks, months, or even years. In this way, they can plan to buy something that they need or want. You can save money for small things, such as a basketball or a special jacket. You can also save for more expensive things, like a summer vacation or a college education. It takes longer to save for something that costs a lot of money than for something that only costs a few dollars.

1. Identify two ways people can pay for things they want and need.

....

....

TEKS
6.A, 6.B, 17.C

Doing small jobs for your neighbors can help you save money.

People can save money by putting it into a bank.

Savings Accounts in Banks

You can save money at home in a small jar or container. You can also save outside your home at a bank. A **bank** is a business that keeps, exchanges, and lends money to people.

A bank is a good place to save money because banks give you a bonus for saving. This bonus is called interest. **Interest** is the money a bank gives you for letting it hold your money. The bank gives you money while you save, and interest makes your savings grow.

Here is how a bank works. The money you put in the bank is called a **deposit.** The banker counts the money you deposit and records the amount in a little book or on a small piece of paper. Some banks also let you check your deposits online.

You might deposit your money by handing it to a banker or by using a cash machine. Either way, banks help you save. They keep your money safe, and they give you interest for saving.

2. ◉ **Main Idea and Details** **Review** the section. Then fill in the chart with details that support the main idea.

A bank is a good place to save money.

266

Borrowing Money

Sometimes people have to buy something, but they do not have enough money saved to pay for it. In these cases, they might need to borrow money from a person or from a bank.

When banks lend money, the money is called a **loan.** Where do banks get the money to lend to people? Banks lend the money that other people are saving. That is why banks pay interest. They pay people who save in exchange for using their money.

A loan is not a gift. People must pay it back. They have to pay a fee to borrow the money. That fee is also called interest. Read the chart below to see the steps involved in getting a loan.

How to Get a Loan

1. A person talks to a loan officer at the bank.

2. The bank decides how much money it will lend.

3. The bank makes sure the person is able to pay back the loan.

4. The person signs papers that tell how much the bank is lending and when the loan must be paid back.

5. The person gets the money. Soon, he or she starts paying back the loan and the interest.

3. Underline the sentence that **explains** where banks get the money they lend to people.

267

Making Budgets

Making a budget is a good way to help you save and spend your money. A **budget** is a plan that shows your income, expenses, donations, and savings. Your income is the money you earn. Your expenses are what you spend. Donations are money or goods you give to charities, or groups that help others. You can donate in different ways. You can give money you saved to a charity you support. Some people have fundraisers to raise money to give to charity. You can also give goods you buy to help a charity, such as canned goods to a food bank.

A budget helps you keep track of your money. You can also use a budget to save for special items. For example, Sue wants to buy a backpack that costs $25. She needs $10 to buy her mother a birthday gift. Sue also wants to give $10 to her local animal shelter to help them buy food for rescued animals. She earns $18 each week delivering newspapers.

Sue makes a budget to figure out how long she will have to work in order to save enough money to buy the backpack and the gift and donate to the animal shelter. After four weeks, she has enough money.

Communities have budgets just like people do. The mayor of a city might make a budget that helps the community buy new police cars. The school board might make a budget that helps it buy new books. They must all plan how to use the money they get from taxes to buy what the community needs and wants.

	MY BUDGET			
Week	Income	Expenses	Donations	Savings
1	$18	$6	$3	$9
2	$18	$7	$3	$8
3	$18	$8	$2	$8
4	$18	$6	$2	$10

Budgets help people plan how to use their money.

4. Underline the sentences that **explain** why budgets are important.

5. ◉ **Main Idea and Details Review** the lesson. **Identify** information about how people pay for things.

Ways to Pay for Things	How It Works	Why It Is Useful
Money		
Barter		
Credit		
Loan		

6. 🔑 **Identify** two ways you can save money.

my Story Ideas

....

....

....

7. In this lesson, you learned about budgets. **Research** how to create a budget. Then **create** a simple budget that includes how you will spend, save, and donate money. Include a plan on how you will earn money.

....

Line Graphs

Graphs show information in pictures. A line graph shows how something changes over time. Follow the steps below to create and interpret a line graph. Software can also be used to create line graphs.

1. Read the title at the top of the graph to learn what the graph shows. Then look at the numbers along the left side of the graph. In the graph below, they tell how many skateboards were sold. Look at the words along the bottom of the graph. In this graph, they tell in which month the total was calculated.

2. When you create a line graph, you place a dot on a line to show an amount at a certain point in time. To interpret a line graph, put your finger on the second dot from the left. Move your finger to the left on the light blue line until you reach a number. The number is 10. Move your finger back to the dot. Now move your finger down on the light blue line until you reach a month. The month is April. This dot shows that 10 skateboards were sold by the end of April.

3. Each dot shows the total number of skateboards that were sold. When you create a graph, connect the dots with a line. Follow the line to see how the number of skateboards sold changed over time.

TEKS

SS 17.E Interpret and create visuals, including graphs.

SS 17.F Use appropriate math skills to interpret social studies information such as maps and graphs.

ELA 15.B Locate and use specific information in graphic features of text.

Read and **interpret** the line graph below. Then **answer** the questions.

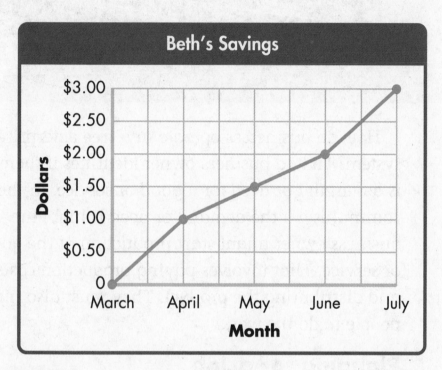

Beth's Savings

1. **Identify** how much money Beth had in March. **Identify** how much money Beth saved by July.

2. In April, Beth had $1.00. Look at how much money Beth had in May. Then **identify** how much money Beth saved between April and May.

3. **Explain** what this line graph shows.

4. Beth donates money to a local food bank. She donated $4 in March, $5 in May, and $8 in July. **Create** a line graph showing how much money Beth donated.

PEARSON
realize Go online to access your
interactive digital lesson.

271

Many Different Jobs

Envision It!

Draw some tools you could use to build a bridge like this one.

How do businesses operate in a free enterprise system? First, a business owner identifies if there is a demand or need for a good or service in the community. If the demand or need is high, the business owner might start production of the good or service. That involves paying production costs and distributing the product. They must also hire people to do the work.

Planning for a Job

People in a town have been talking about how difficult it is to get across a river. They have to walk or drive a long way to reach the bridge. They ask the local government to build a new bridge, and the government agrees. However, the workers cannot just start building. First, they need to think about the whole project.

They must ask many questions, including *Where should the bridge be built? What type of bridge will be best? How much will the bridge cost? What are the laws about bridges?* Once they have answers to these questions, they can create a plan.

Careful planning makes a project successful.

Vocabulary

specialization
division of labor
interdependence

Once they have a plan, the workers must gather the resources they need to complete the job. They need human resources, including people who can plan and build the bridge. They also need people who can measure distances, work with special tools, and use heavy machines.

TEKS
8.A, 17.C

They need natural resources, too, such as soil and wood. Most importantly, they need open land on both sides of the river so they can build roads that lead on and off the bridge.

In addition, they need capital resources, such as tools, machines, and money. The money is needed to pay the workers and to buy tools, machines, and other supplies.

1. ◉ **Sequence Identify** three steps involved in planning for a job.

....

....

....

Some projects need natural resources, such as this wood.

Special Skills and Jobs

Projects, like building a bridge, can include many different kinds of jobs. One person might draw the plans for the project, while another might figure out how much it will cost. A third person might get the tools and machines.

When each person has a special skill and does one job or one part of a project, it is called **specialization.** Specialization leads to a division of labor.

When there is a **division of labor,** a project is divided, or broken down, into smaller jobs. Each person then works on his or her own job, and together they get the project done.

Drawing plans for a job is a kind of specialization.

With specialization and division of labor, people do not have to learn every skill needed to complete a job. Instead, they can learn to do one job well. This saves time and money during a project. It also helps a project run smoothly.

Think about how many people it takes to produce the food we eat. Farmers grow crops. They specialize in keeping soil and plants healthy. Factory workers put soup, tuna, and other foods in cans. They specialize in keeping food safe and making it available to many people. Both the farmers and the factory workers have an important role in producing the food we eat.

2. ◉ **Main Idea and Details Explain** why specialization and division of labor are important to a project.

....

....

....

274

Jobs Help the World

Specialization and division of labor help people in communities around the world. That is because people can sell their products and skills to others who need them. Writing, welding, and teaching are skills. Growing food and fixing things are also skills.

People in different countries often develop skills that are important where they live. For example, people who live in places that have many trees might learn to work with wood. People who live in places that have a lot of water might learn to build boats. The people who work with wood sell it to the people who build boats. When these people trade with each other, they all get what they need.

This is why buyers and sellers around the world exchange goods and services. They depend on each other. When people depend on each other to get the things they need and want, it is called **interdependence.**

Trade is not the only way people around the world are interdependent. People attend schools in different countries. They also work in different countries. As they live and work together, people around the world learn from one another. They also better understand others' ideas.

3. Explain one way people around the world are interdependent.

....

....

Teaching is a specialized job.

Welding is a specialized job, too.

Jobs Today and Long Ago

Just as communities change over time, so do the ways people do their jobs. Long ago, farmers grew all of the food their families ate. They did their work by hand. They bartered for goods they could not make or grow. They grew as much food as they could.

Today, farmers still grow as much food as they can. However, they grow much more than farmers did long ago. That is because many specialize. They also use science to test their soil and add exactly what each crop needs. Machines, such as the harvester shown below, help them work more land.

Many people today have other types of specialized jobs. Some run businesses. Some learn a craft, like carpentry. Others learn to operate special machines.

You have a job, too. Your job is to be a student. You are learning many subjects. You are learning how to work with others and solve problems. You are doing projects in groups. All of these skills will help you become a successful student.

Some of the work that farmers once did by hand is now done by machines.

4. ◉ **Compare and Contrast Compare and contrast** farming long ago and today.

Farming Long Ago

Both

Farming Today

Got it?

🔶 TEKS 8.A, 17.C

5. ◉ **Main Idea and Details Explain** what specialization means. Then **identify** how two people in your school specialize in their work.

a. Specialization means

....

b. Two people in my school who specialize are

....

....

6. ❓ **Describe** how you use division of labor at home.   my Story Ideas

....

....

7. You've learned about production costs and selling prices. **Research** and **identify** how specialization can affect production costs and selling prices.

....

....

....

Lesson 1 TEKS 19.B

Meeting Our Needs and Wants

1. Read the list of items below. **Identify** and circle the items that are needs. **Identify** and underline the items that are wants.

shelter	food	movie ticket
basketball	game	clothing

2. **Describe** a decision-making process you might use to make a choice between buying two items.

....

....

....

....

Lesson 2 TEKS 8.C

Producers and Consumers

3. **Identify** resources that businesses use to produce goods.

....

....

4. **Explain** how government regulations impact consumer costs.

....

....

....

Exchanging Goods and Services

5. Read the question carefully. **Determine** the best answer to the question from the four answer choices provided. Circle the best answer.

What usually happens when the supply of something goes down?

A The price goes down.

B The price goes up.

C The price stays the same.

D The price keeps changing.

6. ◉ **Main Idea and Details** **Identify** two details that support the main idea.

Main Idea: The United States has a free enterprise system.

Details:

....

....

Spending and Saving

7. **Identify** ways people can spend, donate, and save money. Then **describe** how they can make spending, donating, and saving easier.

....

....

....

Lesson 5 TEKS 8.A

Many Different Jobs

8. Identify how a business that makes toys could use specialization to operate.

....

....

....

....

....

9. Draw a picture to **describe** how you and a partner could clean up your classroom by using division of labor.

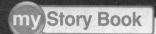

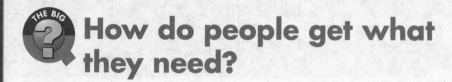

How do people get what they need?

TEKS
SS 6.A, 7.B
ELA 17

Everyone has needs and wants. People often need to buy things to meet these needs and wants. Before they buy something, they have to make choices. They often have to work with others to get what they need.

Think about a time you bought a good or a service. **Describe** what you bought and how you made your choice.

....

....

Describe how people work together as producers to make something your community needs. Draw a picture to show how they work together.

PEARSON realize Go online to access your interactive digital lesson.

281

Celebrating Our Communities

my Story Spark

THE BIG

?

How is culture shared?

Describe what you like to eat, what you like to wear, and what you like to do in your community.

....

....

....

....

....

....

....

Texas Essential Knowledge and Skills

2.A Identify reasons people have formed communities, including a need for security, religious freedom, law, and material well-being.

4.B Identify and compare how people in different communities adapt to or modify the physical environment in which they live such as deserts, mountains, wetlands, and plains.

4.E Identify and compare the human characteristics of various regions.

13.A Explain the significance of various ethnic and/or cultural celebrations in the local community and other communities.

13.B Compare ethnic and/or cultural celebrations in the local community with other communities.

15.A Identify various individual writers and artists such as Kadir Nelson, Tomie dePaola, and Phillis Wheatley and their stories, poems, statues, and paintings and other examples of cultural heritage from various communities.

15.B Explain the significance of various individual writers and artists such as Carmen Lomas Garza, Laura Ingalls Wilder, and Bill Martin Jr. and their stories, poems, statues, and paintings and other examples of cultural heritage to various communities.

17.A Research information, including historical and current events, and geographic data, about the community and world, using a variety of valid print, oral, visual, and Internet resources.

17.C Interpret oral, visual, and print material by identifying the main idea, distinguishing between fact and opinion, identifying cause and effect, and comparing and contrasting.

17.D Use various parts of a source, including the table of contents, glossary, and index as well as keyword Internet searches, to locate information.

Joseph Bruchac
Storyteller

my Story Video

When Joseph Bruchac was a boy, he lived with his grandparents in the mountains of New York. His grandmother had a lot of books all over the house. His grandfather was an Abenaki [ab uh NAK ee] American Indian. He taught Bruchac how to explore the woods and how to fish. Bruchac's grandfather never got angry with Joseph when he made a mistake. Instead, his grandfather would talk to him and help him learn from his mistakes. Later, Bruchac learned that this way of teaching was an important part of the Abenaki way of life.

Joseph Bruchac named one of his books Bowman's Store, after his grandparents' store.

Bruchac's grandparents owned a local store called Bowman's. Bruchac helped his grandparents in the store whenever he could. In winter, he sat by the wood stove and listened as farmers and other customers told stories. Bruchac grew to love books and storytelling. He also loved to write his own stories. As a child, he wrote poems.

Joseph Bruchac and Chinua Achebe talked of writing about their cultures.

Bruchac listened to others tell stories about the Abenaki.

When Bruchac was older, he met a writer from Nigeria, a country in Africa, named Chinua Achebe [CHIN wah ah CHAY bay]. Achebe told Bruchac that he had become a writer so he could tell the story of his people, the Igbo. Achebe had read stories about the Igbo that were written by people who did not understand Igbo culture. Achebe wanted to tell the world about his culture from the point of view of his people.

Bruchac understood Achebe's feelings. He heard stories about his own people, the Abenaki, when he visited Abenaki friends and family. Bruchac began to record the stories that were important to him and to the Abenaki culture.

Stories and storytelling are important parts of the Abenaki way of life. Stories are told not just to entertain people, but to teach them. Listeners learn that it is important to treat others kindly, to care for plants and animals, and to share.

Joseph Bruchac brings Abenaki stories and songs to schoolchildren.

Bruchac works as a writer. He has written books for both children and adults.

Bruchac and his family sing songs and tell stories of the Abenaki.

Stories are also used to teach children how to behave. The Abenaki people do not speak harshly to their children. Instead, if a child misbehaves, the child is told a story to show them the correct way to act. Some stories involve a raccoon that is known to misbehave. Others are about a wise leader. To the Abenaki people, telling stories is the best way to teach. Bruchac explains it this way:

> *"A story stays in a child's heart and helps that child grow up straight and strong."*

Today, Bruchac lives in the same house in New York in which he grew up. He has written more than 70 books, and he travels around the world as a storyteller. Bruchac also plays music. He, his sister, and his two sons formed a music group called the Dawnland Singers. Together, they play music and tell stories of the Abenaki people.

Think About It Based on this story, why do you think the Abenaki use storytelling as a way to teach others about their culture? As you read the chapter ahead, think about why it was important to Joseph Bruchac to share his culture.

People and Cultures

Compare the American Indian village above with the European city on the right.

Today, the United States is a nation of many different cultures. Culture includes the language people speak, the religion they follow, the holidays they celebrate, the clothing they wear, and the foods they eat. People who share a similar culture often live near each other in a **cultural region**. There are many different cultural regions in the United States.

Cultural Regions

Every cultural region is shaped by the people who first settled there. For example, American Indian groups lived in North America and South America long ago. Then in the 1400s and 1500s, European explorers from Spain, France, and England arrived. They brought their own cultures to the lands they explored. Their cultures were very different from the cultures of the American Indians they met.

Settlements in North America, 1700–1750

0   800 mi
0   800 km

St. Lawrence River
New France
Nez Percé
Mandan
Iroquois
Miami
Pomo Shosone
Pawnee
New Spain Hopi
Louisiana
Navajo
Comanche
Rio Grande
Calusa
Gulf of Mexico
ATLANTIC OCEAN
Caribbean Sea
Mississippi River
Thirteen Colonies

N E S W

LEGEND
- English
- French
- Spanish
- *Hopi* American Indian group

UNLOCK THE BIG ? I will know how culture is shaped by people and climate.

Vocabulary

cultural region
recreation

Circle the homes in both places. Discuss how they are different.

Soon, more Europeans came to settle the new lands the explorers had found. The map shows where in North America the Europeans settled. The European settlers and the American Indians often lived near one another. Both groups learned about each other's cultural heritage. For example, in Jamestown, Virginia, the American Indians taught English settlers new ways to plant crops. The English settlers taught the American Indians to use the tools that the settlers had brought with them.

Many places throughout North America and South America were once settled by Europeans hundreds of years ago. These places have kept some of the culture that the Europeans brought.

TEKS
4.B, 4.E, 15.A, 15.B

1. **Identify** an example of American Indians sharing their cultural heritage with English settlers in Jamestown, Virginia. **Explain** its significance.

....

....

....

The Spanish brought building styles, such as these in Toledo, Spain, with them from Europe.

People often use the Caribbean Sea for fishing. Fish are a valuable natural resource in the Caribbean.

Cultures in Warm and Cold Climates

Did you know that climate shapes a cultural region? Climate affects the type of shelters people build, their forms of recreation, the foods they eat, and the clothing they wear. **Recreation** is a way of enjoying yourself.

People who live in regions with warm climates, such as tropical Central America, often build shelters that help them to stay cool. They may build houses in shaded areas or with powerful air conditioners. In a cold climate region, people's homes are built to hold in the heat. They may also have large windows to let in sunlight.

Climate also affects recreation. People who live in warm climates near water can swim, fish, or go boating many months of the year. In cold climates, the water may be frozen for many months.

Fishing in cold climates is not always easy. These children are ice fishing on a frozen lake in Vermont.

What you eat for dinner tonight may also depend on climate. For example, if you live near rich soil in a temperate climate, you might be able to grow your own vegetables and fruits. If you live near the coast, you might eat some fresh fish. Today, foods from all over the world can be brought to an area by planes, ships, or trucks. However, many people still eat the foods that can be grown or found in their own region.

Climate also helps people choose what kind of clothing to wear. In the warm climates of the southeastern United States, people wear light clothing. These may include shorts and short-sleeved shirts, and hats to protect their skin from the sun. People also wear sandals to help their feet stay cool.

In cold climates, such as in parts of Canada, people need to stay warm. They wear layers of clothes under heavy coats. They wear gloves on their hands and thick hats to keep their heads warm. Places in cold climates are often wet with snow. People wear boots that keep their feet warm and dry.

2. Identify two ways people adapt to a cold climate.

....

....

In Mexico, people make and sell clothing to wear in the warm climate there.

Climates and World Cultures

The climates in Tibet and Egypt affect the cultural heritage of their people. Tibet is a cultural region in Asia. Egypt is a country in Africa. The climate of Tibet is mostly cold and can be dry. In Egypt, the climate is warm and dry. In fact, Egypt receives less rain than any country in the world!

The people in Tibet live on a plateau. One of the mountains surrounding the plateau is Mount Everest, the tallest mountain in the world! Grasslands cover much of the plateau. Many people in Tibet raise animals, including sheep and yaks. They use the animals in many different ways. They eat cheese and butter made from the milk these animals produce. In some places, people live in tents made from the thick hair of yaks. The yaks' thick hair helps keep the tents warm inside.

In Egypt, most people live near the Nile River so they can get water for drinking, bathing, and watering crops. Since much of the land is desert, those who do not live near the river often still rely on it for water. These people may farm by bringing water in from the Nile River or raise animals such as goats, sheep, or camels. Many people build homes with bricks made from the nearby resources of mud and straw. On hot nights, people sleep on the flat rooftops to stay cool.

Tibet

Egypt

3. 🎯 **Compare and Contrast** **Explain** one way the cultures in Tibet and Egypt are the same and one way the cultures are different.

....

....

....

....

Got it?

🚩 TEKS 4.B, 4.E

4. 🎯 **Compare and Contrast** **Categorize** the clothing, recreation, and shelter that can be found in regions with warm climates and regions with cold climates.

	Warm Climate Region	**Cold Climate Region**
Clothing		
Recreation		
Shelter		

5. ❓ **Write** whether you live in a cold climate or a warm climate. Then **describe** what you like about how the climate affects your way of life.

my Story Ideas

....

....

6. Do **research** to learn about how people adapt to their environment. Choose two environments: plains, mountains, wetlands, or deserts. **Compare** how the people in each environment change the environment to get food, shelter, and clothes, or for recreation. Make a poster to compare the cultures in each environment.

....

Compare and Contrast

When you compare two things, you tell how they are alike. When you contrast two things, you tell how they are different. Writers use words as clues to show what is alike and what is different. Words and phrases such as *both, like, similar to,* or *in common* show things that are alike. Words such as *yet, different, but,* and *however* show things that are different.

You can use a diagram to help you compare and contrast information that you read or hear. Read the paragraph below about Jenn and Owen. Then read the diagram to see what is alike and what is different about them.

> Jenn lives in Florida. Owen lives in Alaska. They both live in the United States, but the climate in each state is very different. Jenn lives in a warm climate. She can wear shorts nearly all year. Owen, however, lives in a cold climate. He wears heavy clothes that keep him warm.

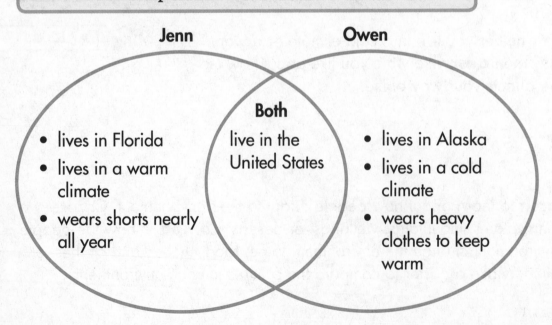

Jenn

- lives in Florida
- lives in a warm climate
- wears shorts nearly all year

Both

live in the United States

Owen

- lives in Alaska
- lives in a cold climate
- wears heavy clothes to keep warm

Learning Objective

I will know how to compare and contrast.

TEKS

17.C Interpret oral material by comparing and contrasting.

Work with a partner. Take turns reading aloud about the storms that Jenn and Owen have experienced. **Analyze** what you read. Then fill in the diagram with similarities and differences.

Jenn and Owen have experienced strong storms where they live. In Florida, there are hurricanes. Hurricanes have strong winds and lots of rain. When a hurricane is coming, schools are often closed. People put shutters on the windows to prevent them from breaking. They also stay home until the hurricane is over.

In Alaska, however, there are blizzards. During a blizzard, there are strong winds and long periods of snowfall. Schools are closed. Before a storm hits, Owen and his family make sure they have lots of wood for the fireplace. Like Jenn, Owen stays home with his family until the storm passes. Blizzards are similar to hurricanes since both storms can cause trees and power lines to fall.

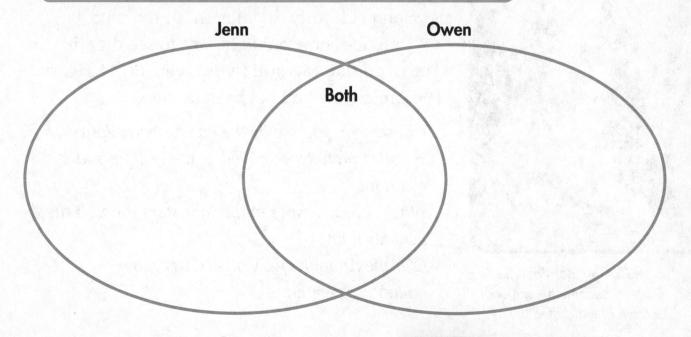

Jenn   Owen

Both

Culture Through the Arts

Envision It!

Describe what you see in this painting that shows farm life long ago.

You can learn many things about a culture from the art that people create. Most people think of the **arts** as paintings and sculptures, but the arts can also include songs, poems, stories, and dances.

Songs, Poems, and Culture

People write songs and poetry for many reasons. Some are about experiences, thoughts, a place, or people. Others tell about important events.

Our national **anthem**, "The Star-Spangled Banner," was a poem that Francis Scott Key wrote about a battle in the War of 1812. An anthem is a song of loyalty to a nation. In the song, Key describes how proud he was to see that the American flag was still flying over Fort McHenry. The Americans had not been defeated.

Oh, say can you see by the dawn's early light
What so proudly we hailed at the twilight's last gleaming?
Whose broad stripes and bright stars through the perilous fight,
O'er the ramparts we watched were so gallantly streaming?

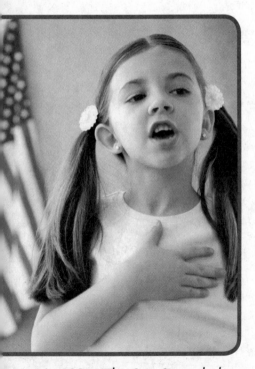

In 1931, "The Star-Spangled Banner" became the national anthem of the United States.

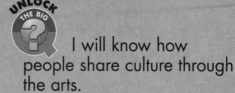

UNLOCK THE BIG ?
I will know how people share culture through the arts.

Vocabulary

arts
anthem
cultural heritage
legend

Phillis Wheatley was a young girl who was taken from her homeland in Africa and brought to Boston when she was eight years old. She was sold to the Wheatley family who chose to educate her instead of making her a servant.

Phillis wrote poems about many different subjects. Many of her poems were about her Christian faith, slavery, and famous people in her time. Wheatley also wrote about current events. At the outbreak of the American Revolution, Wheatley wrote the poem "To His Excellency General Washington."

TEKS
15.A, 15.B

Proceed, great chief, with virtue on thy side,
Thy ev'ry action let the Goddess guide.
A crown, a mansion, and a throne that shine,
With gold unfading, WASHINGTON! Be thine.

1. Write a poem **describing** a current event in the United States.

Phillis Wheatley published her first poem when she was just 12 years old.

....

....

....

....

Stories and Culture

People all over the world tell stories to share their history, their ideas, and what is important to them. Some stories are written, while others are spoken. Some stories celebrate the cultural heritage of different groups. **Cultural heritage** describes the traditions, customs, and artifacts of a cultural group. Some examples of cultural heritage are stories, dance, art, and buildings.

De Smet, South Dakota, is one community that celebrates Laura Ingalls Wilder.

Laura Ingalls Wilder was an author who wrote about her family and life during the pioneer days. The *Little House Books* show the harsh conditions that people who settled on the frontier dealt with. Today, the town where Wilder was born hosts a festival that celebrates Wilder and her family.

Bill Martin Jr. was an author who wrote hundreds of children's books. Martin did not learn how to read until he was in college. Many of his books help to teach children. For example, *Chicka, Chicka, Boom, Boom* teaches the alphabet.

Tomie dePaola is an author and an artist. His stories and pictures often show dePaola's cultural heritage. He is half Italian and half Irish. He has written stories about lives and **legends** from his culture. A legend is a traditional, fictional story. In *Patrick: Patron Saint of Ireland*, dePaola retells the legend of St. Patrick making the snakes leave Ireland.

Tomie dePaola writes many stories that celebrate his cultural heritage.

2. **Explain** why the work of Tomie dePaola is significant to the Irish and Italian communities.

....

....

....

Sculptures, Painting, and Culture

Looking at art is another way to learn about different cultures. Some artists use natural resources that are important to their culture to create works of art. In the mountains of South Dakota, artists and workers are carving a sculpture of the Lakota leader Crazy Horse into the rock. Sculptor Korczak Ziolkowski designed this memorial and also assisted with Mount Rushmore.

Crazy Horse Memorial

Some artists show details of their culture in paintings. Carmen Lomas Garza is a Chicana native artist who was born in South Texas. Garza creates paintings and other works of art that celebrate the Mexican American culture and experience and illustrate daily life.

Kadir Nelson is an American artist. Some of his paintings are of historical figures. He has painted images of Nelson Mandela, Frederick Douglass, and Dr. Martin Luther King Jr. In 2008, Nelson published his first children's book, called *We Are the Ship: The Story of Negro League Baseball*.

3. ◎ **Draw Conclusions Explain** why the paintings of Kadir Nelson are significant to both the African American and international communities.

Kadir Nelson shows an illustration he created for a children's book.

....

....

....

Dance and Culture

Dance is an important part of a group's culture. Long ago in Hawaii, a dance called the hula was performed for chiefs, kings, or queens. In a hula dance, the dancers used smooth and flowing movements of their arms and hips. The dancers wore costumes made from local resources that were important to the people. For example, the flowers on the island were made into necklaces called leis. Today, the hula is performed for all people.

Hula dancers

In areas near the Appalachian Mountains in the eastern part of the United States, people do folk dances. Folk dances are dances that have been passed down from one generation to another. Square dancing is a type of folk dance. Dancers stand in a "square." Each side of the square is made up of two people. They listen to a singer who calls out the instructions for each movement. For example, the singer may tell the dancers to move in a circle. There are a variety of movements. The square dancers often do not know what movement they will perform next!

In ballet, dancers make smooth movements. They may jump, spin, or dance on their toes. Many ballet dancers wear costumes and pointed shoes. Russian ballet dancers are well known throughout the world. In France and Russia, ballet dancing was first performed only for kings and queens. Today, however, people all over the world can see a ballet performance.

Ballet dancers

4. ⊙ **Compare and Contrast Analyze** the section.
Fill in the diagram to compare the hula dance and ballet.

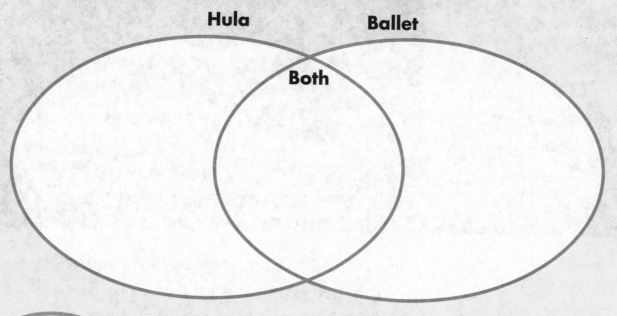

Hula   **Ballet**

Both

Got it?

⬇ TEKS 15.A, 15.B

5. ⊙ **Compare and Contrast** Identify at least two authors and artists described in this lesson. Then **explain** how there work is alike and why their work is significant to different cultures and communities.

....

....

....

6. ❓ **Describe** some of the arts you can find in your community.   my Story Ideas
Explain what they tell about your community's culture.

....

....

....

7. Go on the Internet and **research** a legend from an American Indian tribe in Texas. Then **create** a work of art that illustrates the legend and explains its significance to the culture you chose. **Present** your artwork to the class.

....

PEARSON
realize   Go online to access your
interactive digital lesson.   299

Cultural Celebrations

Envision It!

Think about a festival or celebration that you have been to. Draw an activity that you did there.

Families and communities celebrate many different holidays and special traditions. These celebrations help people remember important people or events, and are part of a cultural heritage.

Culture Through Traditions

People often have traditions that they follow on holidays. People in a culture learn these traditions from older family members or from people in their community. The traditions are part of the holiday each year.

An Independence Day celebration

Traditions can include eating a certain food, such as turkey on Thanksgiving. Other traditions include certain activities, such as watching fireworks on Independence Day. On some holidays, there is a tradition to wear a certain color. On St. Patrick's Day, many people wear the color green.

UNLOCK THE BIG ?

I will know how people share their culture through celebrations.

Vocabulary

landmark
harvest

Days to Honor Leaders

Some celebrations honor people. Martin Luther King Jr. was an important leader. He worked to get African Americans the same civil rights as other Americans. He wanted to bring about change peacefully, without force. People celebrate his life on Martin Luther King Jr. Day, a national holiday in January. Many schools and offices close. It is a day for service to others. People have also created statues to honor King.

King followed the ideas of Mohandas Gandhi from India. Gandhi believed that people should not use violence. He worked for change in his home country of India. He used peaceful ways and did not harm people. People in India celebrate Gandhi's birthday on October 2. On that day, people do not go to school or work. Instead, families do special works of service for others.

1. ◎ **Compare and Contrast** Underline sentences that **compare** how Martin Luther King Jr. Day and Gandhi's birthday are celebrated.

TEKS
13.A, 13.B, 15.A, 15.B

This statue of Martin Luther King Jr. is in Texas.

PEARSON realize · Go online to access your interactive digital lesson.

301

Celebrating Freedom

Around the world people celebrate their freedom in different ways. People in the United States celebrate Independence Day on the Fourth of July. Many Americans celebrate this holiday with their family and their friends. They hold parades, fly flags, picnic, and watch fireworks.

Many symbols and landmarks of the United States are part of Independence Day celebrations. A **landmark** is a building or other structure that is important to a culture. People gather at landmarks such as the Liberty Bell in Philadelphia.

In India, people celebrate their independence from British rule on August 15. People fly colorful kites and watch the raising of the Indian flag. The prime minister, or government leader, of India speaks about India's accomplishments each year.

On May 5, people in both Mexico and the United States celebrate Mexico's victory against French troops. The victory was a step forward on Mexico's path to freedom. This holiday is called Cinco de Mayo, which means "Fifth of May." On Cinco de Mayo, people typically watch parades, listen to music, and do or watch dances.

Colorful dresses and Mexican foods are part of many Cinco de Mayo celebrations.

2. ◉ **Compare and Contrast Compare** India's independence celebration with the United States'.

....

....

....

....

Ethnic Celebrations

Ethnic celebrations celebrate cultures. They celebrate important events and traditions.

Juneteenth is an ethnic celebration. It celebrates an important event. June 19, 1865, is the day that African Americans in Galveston, Texas, learned that slavery had ended. It was a day of great joy. Today, Juneteenth is a holiday in 29 states. Communities celebrate with parades, music, and speeches. Families celebrate with reunions and picnics.

In Austin, Texas, people celebrate Juneteenth with a parade.

In New York City, Puerto Rican Day is celebrated with a big parade. This day celebrates Puerto Rican traditions. People of Puerto Rican descent express pride by waving Puerto Rican flags. Puerto Rican music rings through the streets. People dance and enjoy traditional Puerto Rican foods.

Irish traditions are celebrated in many communities across the country. For example, in Dallas, the North Texas Irish Festival is held every year. This festival has storytelling, dancing, music, and more. Ethnic celebrations provide everyone opportunities to learn about different cultures.

3. Describe an ethnic celebration in your local community. **Compare** it with others.

....

....

....

Harvest Celebrations

People in many different cultures celebrate a large harvest. A **harvest** is the crops gathered at the end of the growing season. In the United States, festivals to celebrate corn harvests, cranberry harvests, and even strawberry harvests are part of the cultural heritage of some communities.

In Japan, a celebration is held in the hopes of a good harvest of rice. During the celebration, rice seedlings are planted in the fields. Throughout the day, people sing and dance to celebrate. Later in the year, another celebration is held to give thanks for the rice harvest.

Some holidays began as harvest celebrations but are now celebrated for other reasons. The first Thanksgiving was a harvest celebration. Settlers from England called Pilgrims gathered with American Indians to celebrate their harvest and to give thanks. Today, Thanksgiving is in November. Families and friends gather to eat a special meal and celebrate what they are thankful for.

In Japan, people plant rice at a harvest celebration.

Kwanzaa is a celebration that was based on a harvest festival held in some countries in Africa. In the United States and in some countries in Central America, African Americans celebrate Kwanzaa to honor important values.

During Kwanzaa, families light candles and share their values.

4. **Identify** and underline the harvest celebrations that take place in the United States.

Got it?

TEKS 13.A, 13.B, 15.A, 15.B

5. **Compare and Contrast Compare** two independence celebrations you read about.

....

....

....

....

6. **Write** about a cultural celebration that you share with your community. **Explain** its significance.

my Story Ideas

....

....

7. Do **research** to learn about an ethnic celebration that takes place in your community. Learn about what makes the celebration special. Do people eat special foods? Are there special decorations, activities, or dances? Choose something from the celebration that you can make. Then **present** what you made to your class, and discuss how it is part of the local ethnic celebration.

....

Our Nation's Diversity

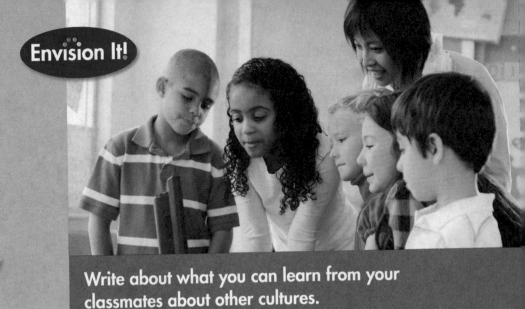

Envision It!

Write about what you can learn from your classmates about other cultures.

People from all over the world have come to live in the United States. Some have come for material well-being. Others have come in search of religious freedom. Because so many people have come to live in the United States, you can find diversity in each region. If there is **diversity**, that means there are many differences among people. There is diversity at work, in schools, and in communities. This diversity allows people in each region to build friendships with people from other cultures.

Susan From Seattle, Washington

Susan lives with her family in Seattle, Washington, in the West region of the United States. Susan's **ancestors**, or relatives who lived long ago, came to Seattle from the country of Japan. They came to the United States in the 1800s in search of gold. Susan lives in downtown Seattle. She lives in the urban area many people call the International District.

There are people from all over the world living in Seattle.

UNLOCK THE BIG ? I will know how people share and express their culture.

Vocabulary

diversity

ancestor

powwow

In the International District, there are people from all over the world, including Japan and China. Near her home, Susan shops with her mother for rice and spices from Asia that they use to make traditional Japanese meals. Many of these meals include rice and vegetables.

When Susan is at home, she speaks Japanese with her parents and her grandmother. At school, Susan speaks English like the rest of her classmates. Susan enjoys playing with friends and taking care of her family's garden. One of her favorite places to visit is the Japanese Garden in Seattle. It reminds her of all the cherry trees she saw on her last visit to Japan. In Japan, people celebrate when the cherry trees bloom.

TEKS
2.A, 13.A, 13.B, 15.A, 15.B

1. **Identify** an example of something Susan does to show, or demonstrate, her Japanese cultural heritage at home.

....

....

....

Susan reads in the garden.

Charlie From Comanche Nation

Charlie lives in the Southwest region of the United States. Charlie's family are Comanche American Indians. His ancestors have lived on the same land for hundreds of years. Today, some land in Oklahoma is reserved for the Comanches. This means it will always belong to the Comanches.

Charlie and his family attend gatherings called **powwows.** At the powwows, Charlie and his family sing and dance. They meet with other American Indians to celebrate their cultures.

Manuel From Chicago, Illinois

Manuel is from Chicago, Illinois. Chicago is a city in the Midwest region of the United States. Manuel lives in a part of Chicago where many people from Mexico, Central America, and South America have settled. In Manuel's neighborhood, most people speak Spanish at home.

Manuel's family came from Mexico to Chicago three years ago. They came to start a better life. Today, Manuel has many relatives in his neighborhood. Each Sunday, they go to a Catholic church because religion is an important part of their culture.

2. ◎ **Main Idea and Details**
Identify and underline characteristics of Manuel's and Charlie's cultural heritage.

Charlie and his family enjoy going to powwows.

Manuel speaks Spanish with his family, but at school he speaks English.

Sam From Long Island, New York

Sam lives on a farm on Long Island in the Northeast region of the United States. Sam's ancestors came from Italy. They traveled by ship and arrived at Ellis Island in the 1880s. Ellis Island was a center where newcomers came before they could enter the United States. His ancestors moved to Long Island to be farmers. Today, Sam lives on the same farm where his ancestors lived.

Since Sam was first learning to speak, his parents taught him to speak Italian. They want him to be able to speak to their relatives who still live in Italy. They also sing many Italian songs that his parents learned when they were young.

Sam helps his father sell their crops at the local farmers' market.

Eating together is important to Sam's family. On the weekends, they gather in the middle of the day to eat a large meal. Sam's grandmother cooks many different Italian foods. Sam's favorite is ravioli! Sam loves to help his grandmother make and arrange the noodles.

3. ◉ **Compare and Contrast Explain** how Sam's and Charlie's cultures are similar and different.

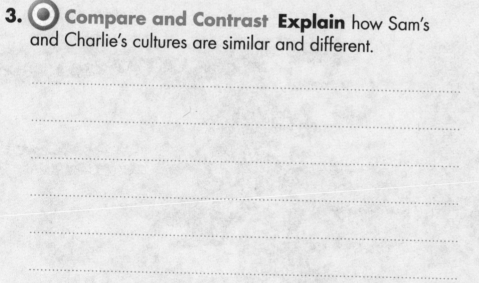

Abby From Atlanta, Georgia

Abby lives in Atlanta in the Southeast region of the United States. Atlanta is the largest city in Georgia. It is also a city with great diversity.

Abby is African American. Her ancestors were brought to Georgia from West Africa. They were forced to work on large farms called plantations with no pay. After the American Civil War, her ancestors were set free and they began to farm their own land.

Today, Abby's father works in the public library. He helps people learn about the history of the city and the history of African Americans. When Abby's father was young, his family began to celebrate Kwanzaa. Today, Abby's family has continued this tradition. During Kwanzaa, Abby likes to discuss the seven symbols and values that are part of the celebration.

4. **Compare** Abby's celebration of Kwanzaa with Charlie's celebration at a powwow. How are they the same?

....

....

....

Abby likes to read different types of books at the library.

Got it?

5. ◉ **Compare and Contrast Analyze** the information in this lesson about Manuel and Susan. Fill in the diagram to compare and contrast their cultures.

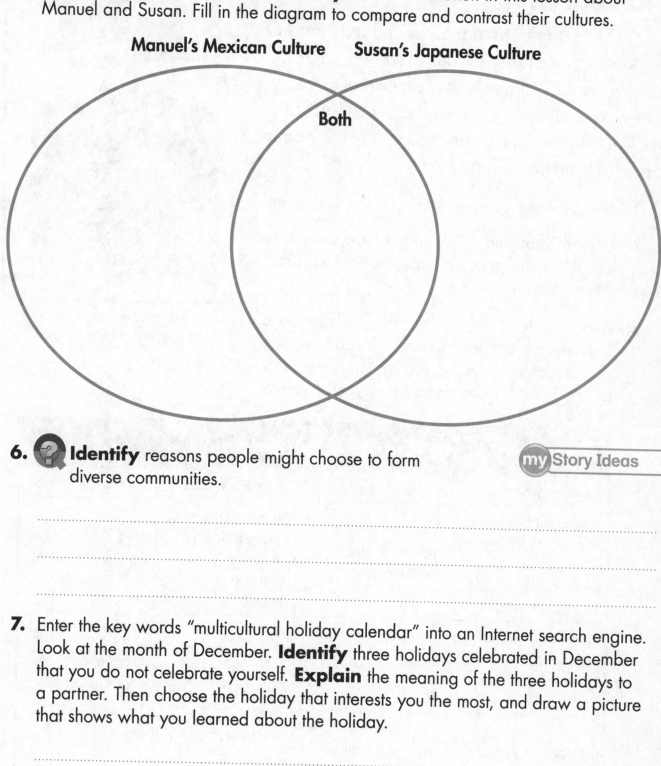

Manuel's Mexican Culture   Susan's Japanese Culture

Both

6. ❓ **Identify** reasons people might choose to form diverse communities.

my Story Ideas

....

....

....

7. Enter the key words "multicultural holiday calendar" into an Internet search engine. Look at the month of December. **Identify** three holidays celebrated in December that you do not celebrate yourself. **Explain** the meaning of the three holidays to a partner. Then choose the holiday that interests you the most, and draw a picture that shows what you learned about the holiday.

....

....

Research

When you research a topic, you learn more about it. For example, you can do research to learn about historical, or past, events in your own community, or anywhere in the world.

Follow these suggestions as you think about researching past events.

1. Narrow the topic, or choose just one past event.

2. Decide what kind of information you want to find out about the event, such as *where* it took place or *who* was involved.

3. Choose at least two sources that you can use to find the information you need. You can use print, oral, visual, and Internet sources. Look at the table below to learn more about each type of source.

This student is using a print source to research a topic.

Sources of Information			
Print Sources	**Oral Sources**	**Visual Sources**	**Internet Sources**
nonfiction books, atlases, newspapers, almanacs, encyclopedias, and magazine articles	experts and witnesses	photographs, maps, paintings, drawings, artifacts, and statues	valid Web sites ending with .gov, .edu, or .org
To locate information, use the table of contents, the glossary, and the index.			To locate information, use a keyword search.
Find print sources in your classroom or library.	Find oral sources on television or on the radio. Interview an expert.	Find visual sources in museums, books, or online.	

Learning Objective

I will know how to research a topic.

 TEKS

SS 17.A Research information about the community and world using a variety of resources.
SS 17.D Use various parts of a source to locate information.
ELA 25.B Generate a plan for gathering information about the research question.

Suppose you are researching historical events. **Answer** the questions below about how you would do your research.

Topic: Historical Events from the Community or World

1. First, you need to narrow the topic. **Write** one past event you would like to research.

   ....

2. **Explain** what kind of information you want to find about the event.

   ....

   ....

3. **List** examples of print, oral, and Internet sources you could use to learn about the topic.

   ....

   ....

   ....

4. **Describe** a visual source that could give you information about your event.

   ....

   ....

5. Use a keyword Internet search to find information **describing** the event you chose. **Write** one fact that you find.

   ....

   ....

 **Lesson 1** 🔹 TEKS 4.B, 4.E

People and Cultures

1. **Identify** and circle the picture that shows what a person might use for recreation in a cold climate.

Watering can   Surfboard   Sled

2. **Identify** and **contrast** things you could find in a home in a hot region and a home in a cold region.

....

....

....

Lesson 2 🔹 TEKS 15.A, 15.B

Culture Through the Arts

3. **Identify** the culture represented in the artwork of Carmen Lomas Garza.

....

4. **Compare and Contrast** **Compare** the books of Laura Ingalls Wilder and Bill Martin Jr.

....

....

....

....

Cultural Celebrations

5. Identify an example of a tradition that is part of America's cultural heritage.

....

....

6. Explain the significance of Martin Luther King Jr. Day.

....

....

....

7. ◉ Compare and Contrast Fill in the diagram with details that **compare** independence celebrations and harvest celebrations.

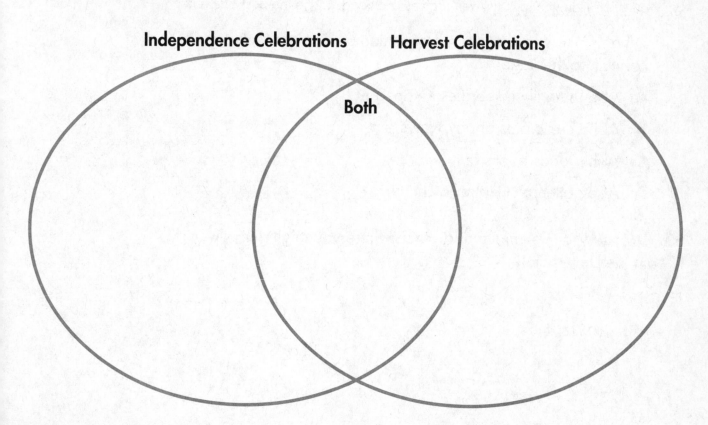

Independence Celebrations   Harvest Celebrations

Both

Lesson 4 ✦ **TEKS 2.A, 13.A, 15.A, 15.B**

Our Nation's Diversity

8. **Identify** reasons people have moved from around the world to the United States to form communities.

....

....

....

....

9. **Explain** the significance of a powwow.

....

....

10. Read the question carefully. **Determine** the best answer to the question from the four answer choices provided. Circle the best answer.

What is one way that Abby from Atlanta, Georgia, celebrates her cultural heritage?

A Abby's family celebrates Kwanzaa.

B Abby celebrates at powwows.

C Abby reads books at the library.

D Abby attends a Catholic church.

11. **Identify** one example of a place where you might find diversity in the United States.

....

....

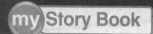

Go online to write and illustrate your own **myStory Book** using the **myStory Ideas** from this chapter.

How is culture shared?

TEKS
ELA 17

The United States is a nation of great diversity. People across the nation celebrate and share their culture in many different ways.

Write three ways that people share their culture with others.

....

....

....

....

....

Draw a picture that shows what you like most about your culture.

Atlas

The United States of America, Political

Washington
★Olympia

★Salem

Oregon

Montana
★Helena

Boise★
Idaho

Wyoming

North Dakota
★Bismarck

South Dakota
Pierre★

Carson City★
Sacramento★

Nevada

California

Salt Lake City★
Utah

Cheyenne
★

Denver★
Colorado

Nebraska

Lincoln★

Topeka★
Kansas

Arizona

Phoenix★

Santa Fe
★

New Mexico

Oklahoma

Oklahoma City★

Texas

Austin★

Alaska

Juneau★

Honolulu
★

Hawaii

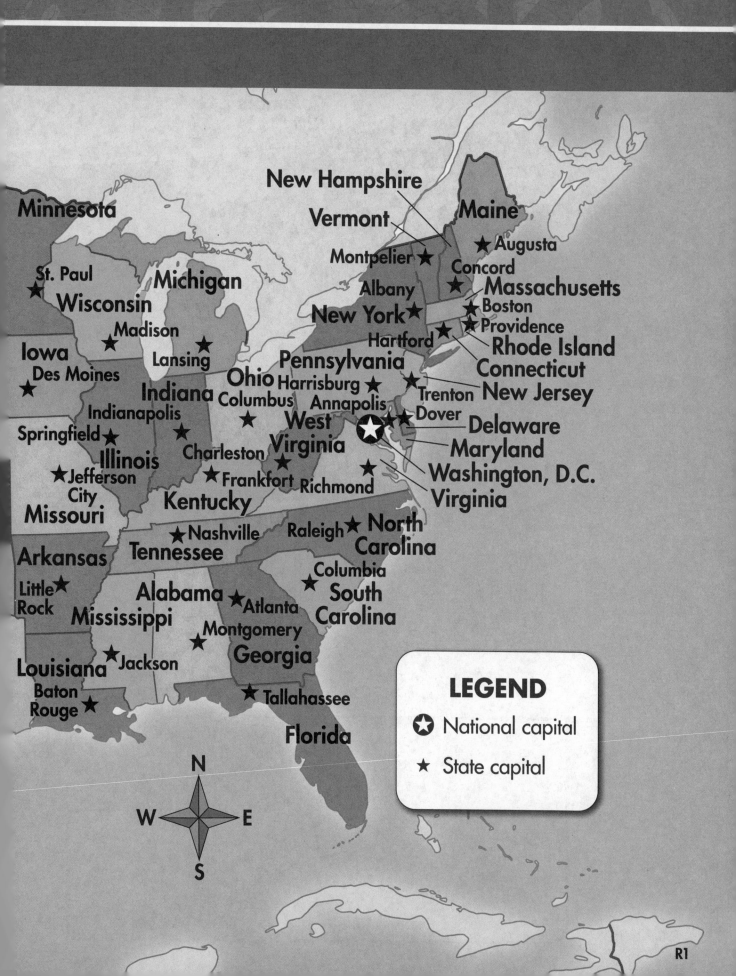

Minnesota

St. Paul ★
Wisconsin
Madison ★

Michigan

Iowa
Des Moines ★
Lansing ★

Indiana

Springfield ★
Illinois
Indianapolis ★

Jefferson ★
City
Missouri

Charleston ★
Frankfort ★
Kentucky

Nashville ★
Tennessee

Arkansas

Little ★
Rock

Alabama ★
Mississippi
Montgomery

Louisiana
Baton ★
Rouge

Jackson ★
Georgia

Tallahassee ★

Florida

New Hampshire

Vermont
Montpelier ★
Albany ★
New York

Maine
★ Augusta
Concord ★
Massachusetts
★ Boston
★ Providence
Rhode Island
Connecticut

Hartford ★

Pennsylvania
Ohio Harrisburg ★
Columbus ★
Annapolis

West ★
Virginia
Charleston ★
Richmond ★

Trenton ★ New Jersey
Dover ★
Delaware
Maryland
Washington, D.C.
Virginia

Raleigh ★ North
Carolina

Columbia ★
South
Carolina

Atlanta ★

N
W ⬥ E
S

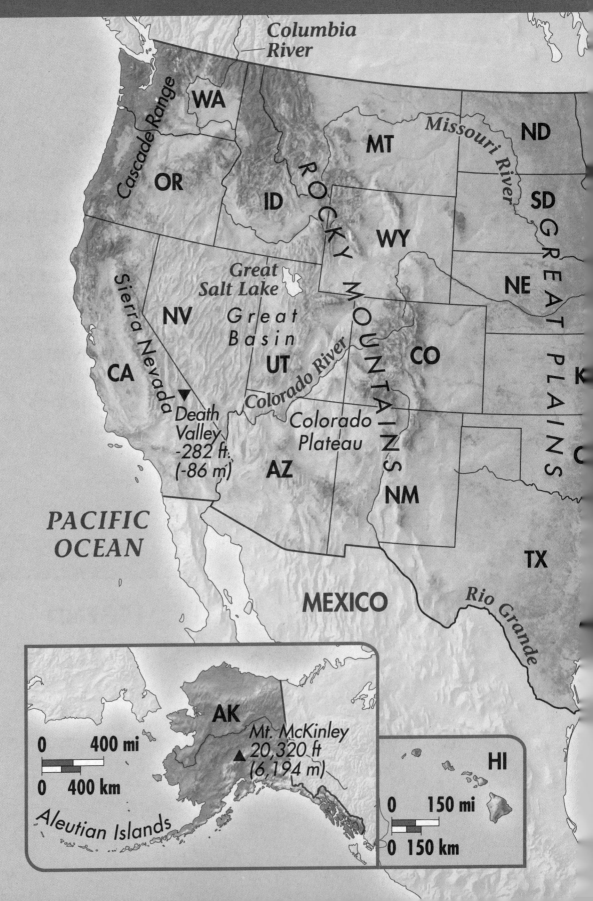

Columbia River

WA

Cascade Range

OR

ID

Missouri River

ND

MT

SD

ROCKY MOUNTAINS

WY

NE

Great Salt Lake

Great Basin

NV

UT

CO

GREAT PLAINS

Sierra Nevada

Colorado River

CA

Death Valley -282 ft. (-86 m)

AZ

Colorado Plateau

NM

TX

PACIFIC OCEAN

MEXICO

Rio Grande

AK

Mt. McKinley 20,320 ft (6,194 m)

0   400 mi

0   400 km

Aleutian Islands

HI

0   150 mi

0   150 km

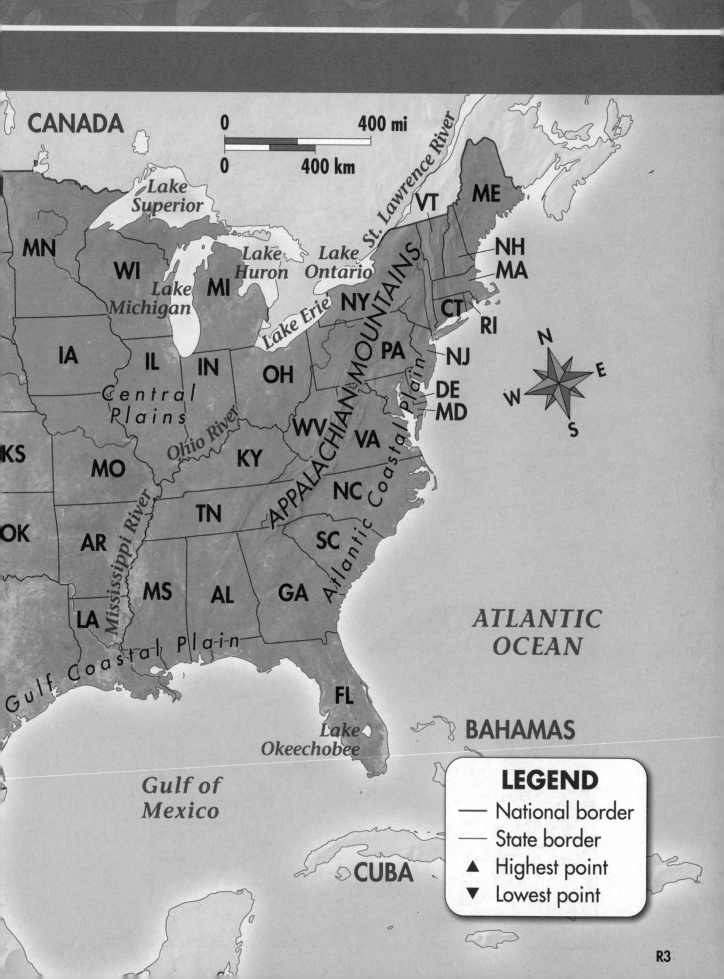

CANADA

Lake Superior

MN

WI

Lake Michigan

MI

Lake Huron

Lake Ontario

St. Lawrence River

VT

ME

NH

MA

Lake Erie

NY

APPALACHIAN MOUNTAINS

CT

RI

IA

IL

IN

OH

PA

NJ

Central Plains

DE
MD

Ohio River

WV

VA

Atlantic Coastal Plain

KS

MO

KY

NC

OK

AR

Mississippi River

TN

SC

LA

MS

AL

GA

Gulf Coastal Plain

FL

Lake Okeechobee

Gulf of Mexico

ATLANTIC OCEAN

BAHAMAS

CUBA

0   400 mi
0   400 km

N
E
W
S

LEGEND
— National border
— State border
▲ Highest point
▼ Lowest point

The World

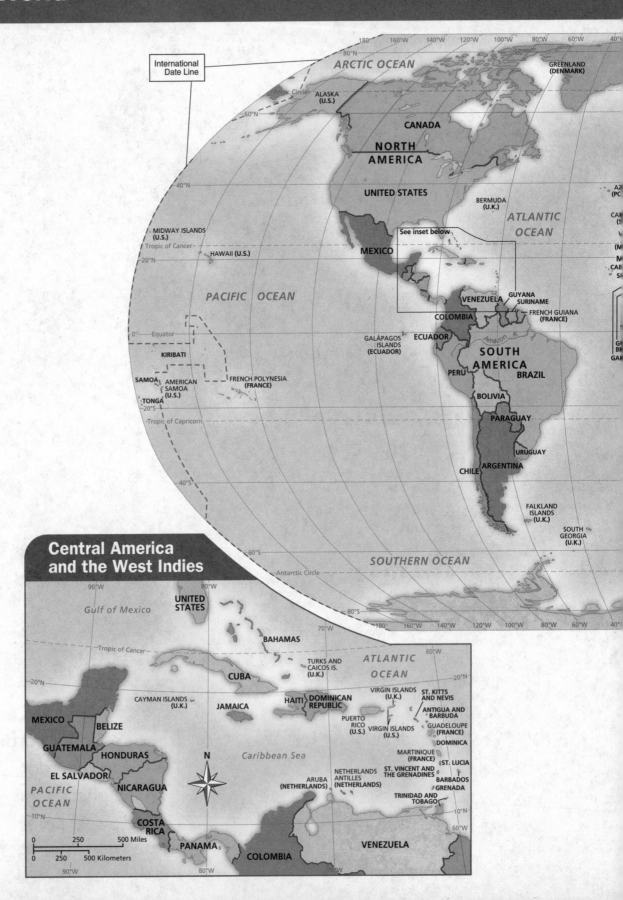

International Date Line

ARCTIC OCEAN

GREENLAND (DENMARK)

80°N

Arctic Circle

ALASKA (U.S.)

60°N

CANADA

NORTH AMERICA

40°N

UNITED STATES

BERMUDA (U.K.)

ATLANTIC OCEAN

AZ (PO

MIDWAY ISLANDS (U.S.)

Tropic of Cancer

HAWAII (U.S.)

20°N

MEXICO

See inset below

CA (S

M

CAB S

PACIFIC OCEAN

VENEZUELA

GUYANA SURINAME

FRENCH GUIANA (FRANCE)

COLOMBIA

GALÁPAGOS ISLANDS (ECUADOR)

ECUADOR

Amazon R.

G B GA

0° Equator

KIRIBATI

SOUTH AMERICA

BRAZIL

SAMOA

AMERICAN SAMOA (U.S.)

FRENCH POLYNESIA (FRANCE)

PERU

TONGA

20°S

BOLIVIA

Tropic of Capricorn

PARAGUAY

URUGUAY

CHILE

ARGENTINA

40°S

FALKLAND ISLANDS (U.K.)

SOUTH GEORGIA (U.K.)

60°S

SOUTHERN OCEAN

Antarctic Circle

80°S

180   160°W   140°W   120°W   100°W   80°W   60°W   40

Central America and the West Indies

90°W   80°W

Gulf of Mexico

UNITED STATES

BAHAMAS

Tropic of Cancer

70°W

ATLANTIC OCEAN

60°W

20°N

CUBA

TURKS AND CAICOS IS. (U.K.)

20°N

MEXICO

CAYMAN ISLANDS (U.K.)

JAMAICA

HAITI

DOMINICAN REPUBLIC

VIRGIN ISLANDS (U.K.)

ST. KITTS AND NEVIS

BELIZE

PUERTO RICO (U.S.)

VIRGIN ISLANDS (U.S.)

ANTIGUA AND BARBUDA

GUADELOUPE (FRANCE)

GUATEMALA

DOMINICA

HONDURAS

N

Caribbean Sea

MARTINIQUE (FRANCE)

ST. LUCIA

EL SALVADOR

NICARAGUA

ARUBA (NETHERLANDS)

NETHERLANDS ANTILLES (NETHERLANDS)

ST. VINCENT AND THE GRENADINES

BARBADOS

GRENADA

PACIFIC OCEAN

10°N

TRINIDAD AND TOBAGO

10°N

COSTA RICA

0   250   500 Miles

0   250   500 Kilometers

PANAMA

COLOMBIA

VENEZUELA

60°W

90°W   80°W   70°W

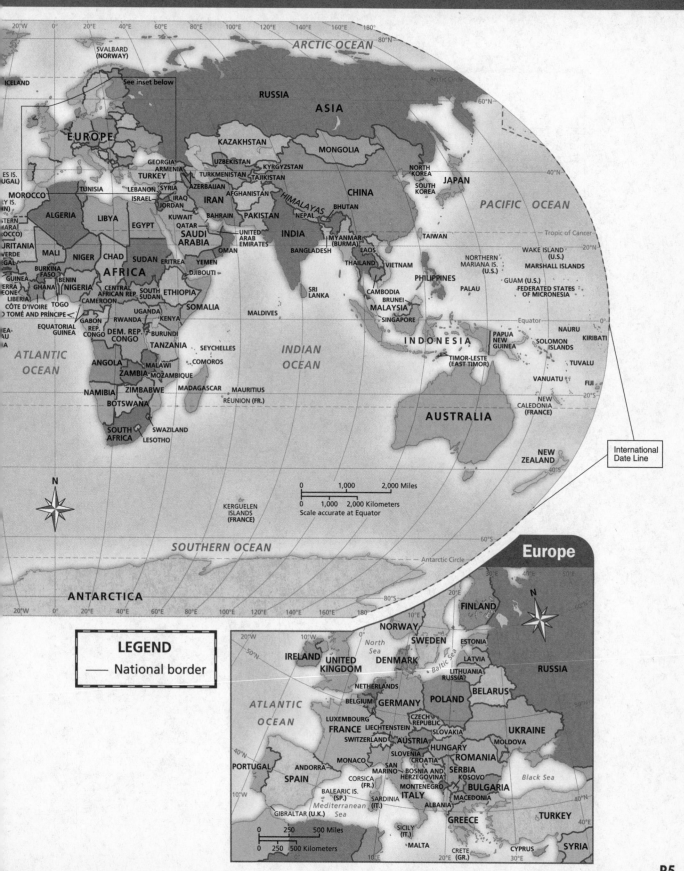

ARCTIC OCEAN 80°N

20°W 0° 20°E 40°E 60°E 80°E 100°E 120°E 140°E 160°E 180°

SVALBARD
(NORWAY)

ICELAND

See inset below

RUSSIA

ASIA   60°N

EUROPE

KAZAKHSTAN

MONGOLIA

GEORGIA
ARMENIA
TURKEY

UZBEKISTAN

KYRGYZSTAN

NORTH
KOREA

JAPAN   40°N

ES IS.
UGAL)

TUNISIA

LEBANON
SYRIA

AZERBAIJAN

TURKMENISTAN

TAJIKISTAN

CHINA

SOUTH
KOREA

PACIFIC OCEAN

MOROCCO
TY IS.
N)

ISRAEL

IRAQ
JORDAN

AFGHANISTAN

HIMALAYAS

IRAN

BHUTAN

ALGERIA

LIBYA

EGYPT

KUWAIT

QATAR

PAKISTAN

NEPAL

MYANMAR
(BURMA)

TAIWAN   Tropic of Cancer

RITANIA
VERDE
GAL

MALI

NIGER

CHAD

SAUDI
ARABIA

UNITED
ARAB
EMIRATES

OMAN

INDIA

BANGLADESH

LAOS

THAILAND

VIETNAM

NORTHERN
MARIANA IS.
(U.S.)

WAKE ISLAND
(U.S.)   20°N

MARSHALL ISLANDS

BURKINA
FASO

SUDAN

ERITREA

YEMEN

GUAM (U.S.)

GUINEA

BENIN

AFRICA

CENTRAL

DJIBOUTI

PHILIPPINES

PALAU

FEDERATED STATES
OF MICRONESIA

ERRA
EONE
LIBERIA

GHANA

NIGERIA

AFRICAN REP.

SOUTH
SUDAN

ETHIOPIA

CAMBODIA

CÔTE D'IVOIRE
TOGO

CAMEROON

BRUNEI

O TOMÉ AND PRÍNCIPE

EQUATORIAL
GUINEA

GABON
REP.
CONGO

UGANDA

RWANDA

DEM. REP.
CONGO

BURUNDI

KENYA

SOMALIA

MALDIVES

MALAYSIA

SINGAPORE

Equator   0°

NAURU

KIRIBATI

EA-
AU

TANZANIA

SEYCHELLES

INDONESIA

PAPUA
NEW
GUINEA

SOLOMON
ISLANDS

ATLANTIC
OCEAN

ANGOLA

MALAWI

ZAMBIA

MOZAMBIQUE

COMOROS

INDIAN
OCEAN

TIMOR-LESTE
(EAST TIMOR)

TUVALU

NAMIBIA

ZIMBABWE

MADAGASCAR

MAURITIUS

VANUATU

FIJI   20°S

BOTSWANA

RÉUNION (FR.)

NEW
CALEDONIA
(FRANCE)

AUSTRALIA

SOUTH
AFRICA

SWAZILAND

LESOTHO

N

International
Date Line

NEW
ZEALAND   40°S

0   1,000   2,000 Miles

0   1,000   2,000 Kilometers
Scale accurate at Equator

KERGUELEN
ISLANDS
(FRANCE)

SOUTHERN OCEAN   60°S

Antarctic Circle

80°S

ANTARCTICA

20°W 0° 20°E 40°E 60°E 80°E 100°E 120°E 140°E 160°E 180°

LEGEND

National border

Europe

30°E 40°E 50°E

FINLAND   N

20°E 10°W 0°

NORWAY

North
Sea

SWEDEN

ESTONIA

60°N

IRELAND

UNITED
KINGDOM

DENMARK

Baltic
Sea

LATVIA

RUSSIA

50°N

LITHUANIA
RUSSIA

BELARUS

NETHERLANDS

BELGIUM

GERMANY

POLAND

ATLANTIC

LUXEMBOURG

CZECH
REPUBLIC

UKRAINE

OCEAN

FRANCE

LIECHTENSTEIN

SLOVAKIA

MOLDOVA

SWITZERLAND

AUSTRIA

HUNGARY

ROMANIA

40°N

SLOVENIA

PORTUGAL

ANDORRA

MONACO

SAN
MARINO

CROATIA

BOSNIA AND
HERZEGOVINA

SERBIA

KOSOVO

Black Sea

SPAIN

CORSICA
(FR.)

MONTENEGRO

BULGARIA

40°N

BALEARIC IS.
(SP.)

SARDINIA
(IT.)

ITALY

MACEDONIA

ALBANIA

GIBRALTAR (U.K.)

Mediterranean
Sea

GREECE

TURKEY   40°E

SICILY
(IT.)

CRETE
(GR.)

CYPRUS

SYRIA

MALTA

20°E 30°E

0   250   500 Miles

0   250   500 Kilometers

R5

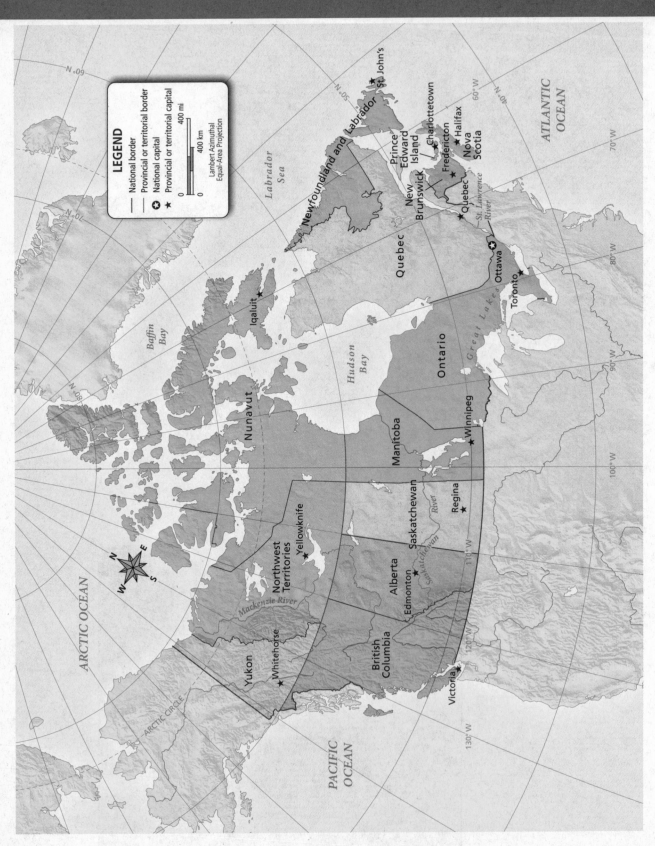

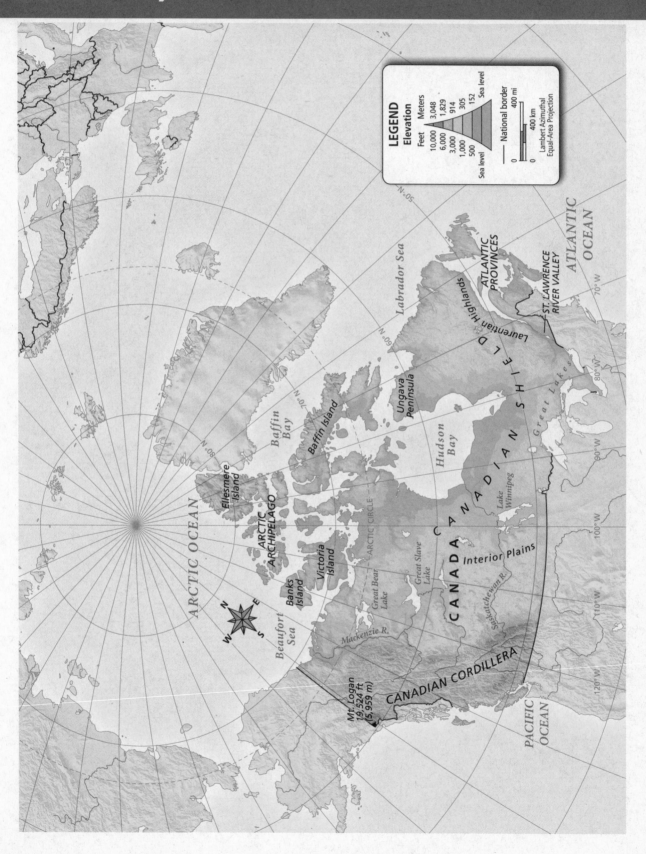

LEGEND

Elevation

Feet	Meters
10,000	3,048
6,000	1,829
3,000	914
1,000	305
500	152
Sea level	Sea level

National border

400 mi

400 km

Lambert Azimuthal
Equal-Area Projection

ATLANTIC OCEAN

ATLANTIC PROVINCES

ST. LAWRENCE RIVER VALLEY

Labrador Sea

Laurentian Highlands

CANADIAN SHIELD

Baffin Bay

Baffin Island

Ungava Peninsula

Hudson Bay

Great Lakes

Ellesmere Island

ARCTIC OCEAN

ARCTIC ARCHIPELAGO

Victoria Island

Banks Island

ARCTIC CIRCLE

Great Bear Lake

Great Slave Lake

Lake Winnipeg

Interior Plains

CANADA

Saskatchewan R.

Beaufort Sea

Mackenzie R.

Mt. Logan
19,524 ft
(5,959 m)

CANADIAN CORDILLERA

PACIFIC OCEAN

70° W

80° W

90° W

100° W

110° W

120° W

50° N

60° N

70° N

80° N

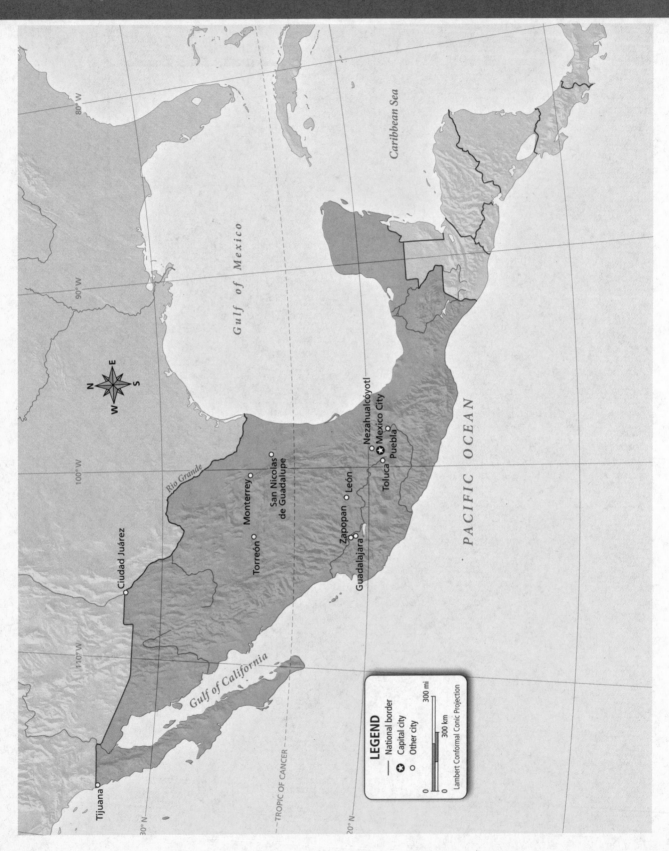

Caribbean Sea

Gulf of Mexico

Rio Grande

Ciudad Juárez

Monterrey

San Nicolas
de Guadalupe

Torreón

Zapopan León

Guadalajara

Toluca Nezahualcóyotl
Mexico City
Puebla

PACIFIC OCEAN

Gulf of California

Tijuana

TROPIC OF CANCER

80° W

90° W

100° W

110° W

30° N

20° N

LEGEND
National border
Capital city
Other city

300 mi

300 km

Lambert Conformal Conic Projection

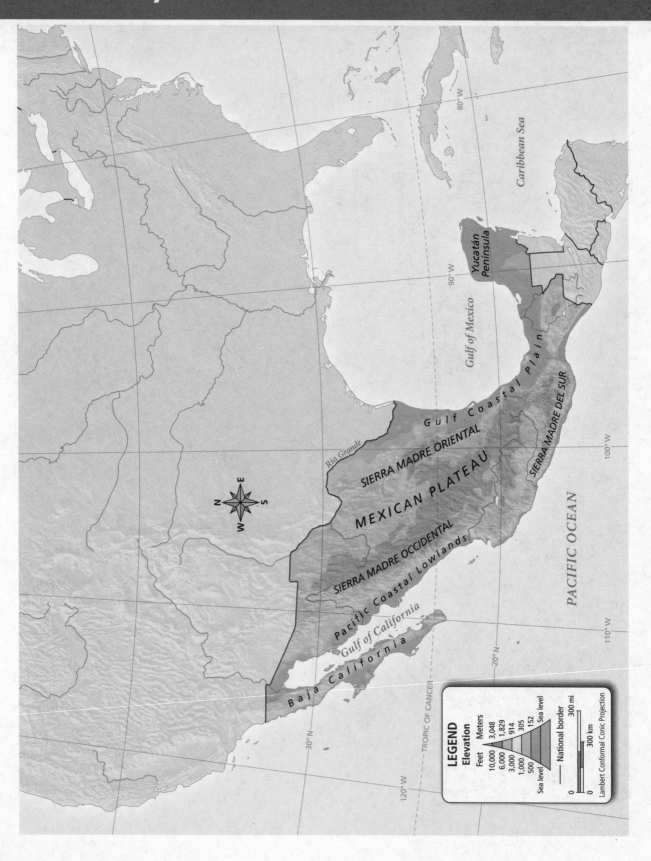

Caribbean Sea

Yucatán Peninsula

Gulf of Mexico

Gulf Coastal Plain

SIERRA MADRE ORIENTAL

SIERRA MADRE DEL SUR

Rio Grande

MEXICAN PLATEAU

SIERRA MADRE OCCIDENTAL

PACIFIC OCEAN

Pacific Coastal Lowlands

Gulf of California

Gulf of California

Baja California

TROPIC OF CANCER

LEGEND

Elevation

Feet	Meters
10,000	3,048
6,000	1,829
3,000	914
1,000	305
500	152
Sea level	Sea level

National border

300 mi

300 km

0

0

Lambert Conformal Conic Projection

80°W

90°W

100°W

110°W

120°W

30°N

20°N

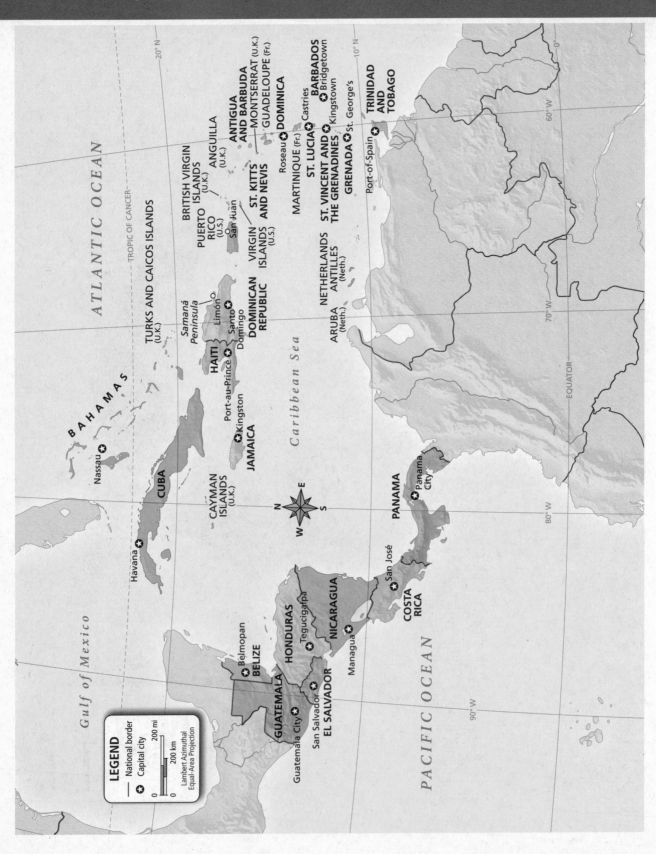

ATLANTIC OCEAN

TROPIC OF CANCER

20° N

10° N

ANTIGUA
AND BARBUDA
MONTSERRAT (U.K.)
GUADELOUPE (Fr.)
DOMINICA
✪ Roseau

ANGUILLA
(U.K.)
BRITISH VIRGIN
ISLANDS
(U.K.)
ST. KITTS
AND NEVIS
PUERTO
RICO
(U.S.)
San Juan
VIRGIN
ISLANDS
(U.S.)

MARTINIQUE (Fr.)
ST. LUCIA ✪ Castries
BARBADOS
✪ Bridgetown
ST. VINCENT AND
THE GRENADINES ✪ Kingstown
GRENADA ✪ St. George's

TRINIDAD
AND
TOBAGO
✪ Port-of-Spain

60° W

TURKS AND CAICOS ISLANDS
(U.K.)

Samaná
Peninsula
Limón
Santo
Domingo ✪
DOMINICAN
REPUBLIC

NETHERLANDS
ANTILLES
(Neth.)

70° W

HAITI ✪
Port-au-Prince ✪

ARUBA
(Neth.)

Caribbean Sea

B A H A M A S

✪ Nassau

Kingston ✪
JAMAICA

CUBA

CAYMAN
ISLANDS
(U.K.)

N
E
S
W

PANAMA
✪ Panama
City

EQUATOR

80° W

✪ Havana

Gulf of Mexico

San José ✪

Belmopan ✪
BELIZE

Tegucigalpa ✪
HONDURAS

NICARAGUA

COSTA
RICA

GUATEMALA

Managua ✪

PACIFIC OCEAN

San Salvador ✪
EL SALVADOR

Guatemala City ✪

90° W

LEGEND
National border
✪ Capital city

200 mi
0

200 km
0

Lambert Azimuthal
Equal-Area Projection

Texas, Physical

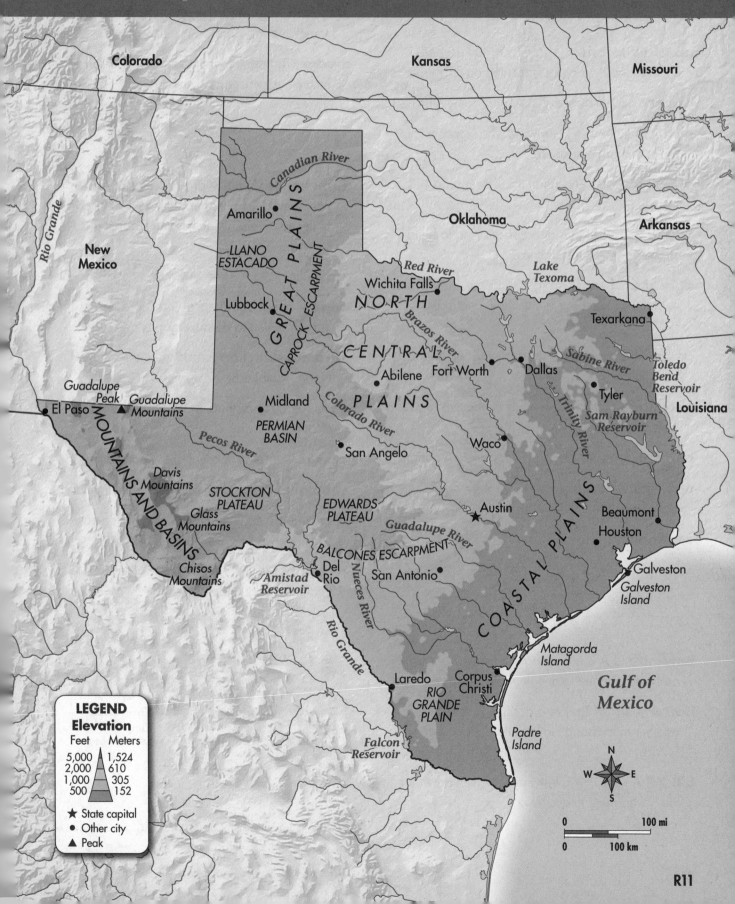

Colorado

Kansas

Missouri

Rio Grande

New
Mexico

Canadian River

Amarillo

LLANO
ESTACADO

Lubbock

GREAT PLAINS

CAPROCK ESCARPMENT

Oklahoma

Arkansas

Red River

Wichita Falls

NORTH

Lake
Texoma

Texarkana

Brazos River

CENTRAL

Abilene

Fort Worth

Dallas

Sabine River

Midland

PLAINS

Colorado River

Tyler

Toledo
Bend
Reservoir

Louisiana

Guadalupe
Peak

Guadalupe
Mountains

El Paso

PERMIAN
BASIN

Pecos River

San Angelo

Waco

Sam Rayburn
Reservoir

Trinity River

MOUNTAINS AND BASINS

Davis
Mountains

STOCKTON
PLATEAU

Glass
Mountains

Chisos
Mountains

EDWARDS
PLATEAU

Amistad
Reservoir

Del
Rio

BALCONES ESCARPMENT

Guadalupe River

San Antonio

Nueces River

Austin

COASTAL PLAINS

Beaumont

Houston

Galveston

Galveston
Island

Rio Grande

Laredo

RIO
GRANDE
PLAIN

Corpus
Christi

Matagorda
Island

Gulf of
Mexico

Falcon
Reservoir

Padre
Island

LEGEND
Elevation

Feet	Meters
5,000	1,524
2,000	610
1,000	305
500	152

★ State capital
● Other city
▲ Peak

N
W   E
S

0	100 mi
0	100 km

Glossary

A

absolute location (ab′sə lo͞ot′ lō kā′shən) Where exactly a place is located on Earth.

abundance (ə bun′dəns) A lot of something.

activist (ak′tə vist′) Someone who works to make a change happen.

adapt (ə dapt′) To change the way you do something.

adobe (ə dō′bē) Sun-dried bricks used to build shelters and other buildings.

agricultural region (ag′ri kul′chər əl rē′jən) A place where there is much flat land and rich soil.

amendment (ə mend′mənt) A change to a constitution.

ancestor (an′ses′tər) A relative who lived long ago.

anthem (an′thəm) A song of loyalty to a nation.

arts (ärts) Paintings, sculptures, songs, stories, and dances.

assembly line (ə sem′blē līn) Each worker does only one part of a job.

B

bank (bank) A business that keeps, exchanges, and lends money to people.

barter (bärt′ər) To give a good or a service to another in exchange for a different good or service.

bill (bil) An idea for a law that is written down for the government to decide on.

boycott (boi′kät′) When people refuse to do something for a reason.

budget (buj′it) A plan that shows a person's income, expenses, and savings.

C

Cabinet (cab′ə nit) A group of advisors, or people who tell a leader, such as the United States president, what they think about a subject.

canal (kə nal′) A waterway that is dug by people.

capital resource (kap′ət ′l rē′sôrs′) Something that is needed to produce goods and services.

cardinal direction (kärd′′n əl də rek′shən) North, south, east, or west.

cause (kôz) Something that people feel strongly about.

census (sen′səs) A count of the population.

chaplains (chap′ləns) Ministers in the military.

citizen (sit′ə zən) An official member of a community.

civil rights (siv′əl rīts) Rights of all citizens to be treated equally under the law.

Pronunciation Key

a in hat	ō in open	′l in cattle
ā in age	ô in order	′n in sudden
ä in father	o͞o in tool	th in weather
e in let	u in cup	zh in measure
ē in equal	ʉ in reverse	
i in it	ə a in ago	
ī in ice	e in agent	
o in hot	o in collect	
	u in focus	

climate (klī′mət) The weather that a place has over a long period.

colonize (käl′ən īz′) To settle lands for another country.

colony (käl′ə nē) A place ruled by another country.

communicate (kə myo͞o′nə kāt) To pass thoughts or information to others.

community (kə myo͞o′nə tē) A place where people live, work, and have fun together.

confederacy (kən fed′ər ə sē) A formal agreement or treaty between groups to work together.

Congress (kän′grəs) The legislative branch of United States government.

conserve (kən sʉrv′) To save and protect something.

constitution (kän′stə to͞o′shən) A written plan of government that explains the beliefs and laws of a state or nation.

constitutional republic (kän′stə to͞o′shnəl ri pə′blik) A form of government in which people are ruled by leaders they elect.

consumer (kən so͞om′ər) A person who spends money to buy things he or she needs or wants.

continent (känt′′n ənt) One of the seven largest land areas on Earth: Asia, Africa, North America, South America, Antarctica, Europe, and Australia.

convention (kən ven′shən) A large meeting.

cooperate (kō äp′ər āt′) To work together.

council (koun′səl) A group that makes laws.

credit (kred′it) A promise to pay for something.

credit card (kred′it kärd) A card used in place of money that lets the cardholder buy things and pay for them later.

cultural heritage (kul′chər əl her′ ətij) Describes the traditions, customs, and artifacts of a cultural group. Some examples of cultural heritage are stories, dance, art, and buildings.

cultural region (kul′chər əl rē′jən) An area where people who share a similar culture live.

culture (kul′chər) The way of life of a group of people.

current events (kur′ənt ēvents′) Things that happen in the present, or now.

custom (kus′təm) A special way of doing something that is part of a person's culture.

D

debt (det) Money that is owed to another person.

deed (dēd) An action.

delegate (del′ə git) A person chosen to act for others.

demand (di mand′) The amount of goods or services that people want and can buy.

deposit (dē päz′it) The money a person puts in a bank.

diverse (də vʉrs′) Different.

diversity (də vʉr′sə tē) When there are many differences among people.

division of labor (də vizh′ən əv lā′bər) When a project is divided, or broken down, into smaller jobs.

drought (drout) A period of time when there is not enough water.

E

ecosystem (ē′kō sis′təm) An area where all living things, such as the plants and animals, interact with each other.

elevation (el′ə vā′shən) The height of land above sea level.

entrepreneur (än trə prə nur′) A person who starts a business.

equal rights (ē′kwəl rīts) When all people have the same rights.

erosion (ē rō′zhən) The washing away of soil by rain, wind, and nearby rivers.

exclusion (eks klōō′zhən) Keeping people out of a place.

executive (eg zek′yōō tiv) Describes the branch of government that enforces, or carries out, the laws.

expedition (eks pə dish ′ən) A trip made for a special reason.

explorer (ek splôr′ər) A person who travels looking for new lands and discoveries.

export (ek spôrt′) To send products and resources from one country to another country.

F

fort (fôrt) A strong building or area that can be defended against enemy attacks.

free enterprise system (frē en′tər prīz′ sis′təm) An economy in which people and private businesses, not the government, decide what goods to make and buy.

frontier (frun tir′) A region that forms the edge of a settled area.

G

gold rush (gōld rush) A time period in the late 1840s when thousands of people came from around the world to California to search for gold.

goods (goods) Things that people make or grow and then sell.

government (guv′ərn mənt) A system of ruling people.

governor (guv′ə nər) The head of a state's executive branch who is elected by the people in a state.

H

harvest (här′vist) The crops gathered at the end of the growing season.

hemisphere (hem′i sfir) A part into which Earth is divided by lines of latitude and longitude.

homestead (hōm′sted′) An area of land that includes a house and its buildings.

human resource (hyōō′mən rē′sôrs′) A person who makes products or provides services.

I

immigrant (im′ə grənt) A person who moves from one country to settle in a different country.

import (im pôrt′) To bring products and resources into one country from another.

independence (in′dē pen′dəns) Freedom.

industrial region (in′dus′trē əl rē′jən) A place where many kinds of factories are located.

interdependence (in′tər dē pen′dəns) When people depend on each other to get the things they need and want.

interest (in′trist) The money a bank gives a person for letting it hold his or her money.

intermediate direction (in′tər mē′dē it də rek′shən) Northeast, southeast, northwest, or southwest.

interpreter (in tʉr′prə tər) A person who helps people who speak different languages understand each other.

invention (in ven′shən) Something that is made for the first time.

irrigate (ir′ə gāt′) To bring water in through pipes.

judicial (jo͞o dish′əl) Describes the branch of government that makes sure laws are fair.

landform (land′fôrm′) The form or shape of part of Earth's surface.

landmark (land′märk′) A building or other structure that is important to a culture.

legend (lej′ənd) A traditional, fictional story.

legislative (lej′is lāt tiv′) Describes the branch of government that makes laws.

legislature (lej′is lā′chər) A part of government that makes laws.

liberty (lib′ər tē) Freedom.

loan (lōn) The money a bank lends to people.

location (lō kā′shən) A place where something is.

longhouse (lông′hous′) A Native American home that is longer than it is wide.

mayor (mā′ər) A leader of a community.

mine (mīn) To dig for materials.

mineral (min′ər əl) A resource that does not come from an animal or a plant.

mission (mish′ən) A settlement that has a church where religion is taught.

modify (mäd′ə fī′) To change something, such as the physical environment.

motto (mät′ō) A saying.

natural resource (nach′ər əl rē′sôrs′) Something found in nature that is useful to people.

needs (nēdz) Things you must have to live.

nonrenewable resource (nän ri no͞o′ə bəl rē′sôrs′) A natural resource that takes a long time to replace or cannot be replaced after it is used.

opportunity cost (äp ər to͞o′nə tē kôst) The value of the thing you give up when you choose one thing over another.

P

patent (pat/'nt) A document that gives a person the right to be the only one making or selling an invention.

patriot (pā/trē ət) A person who loves and defends his or her country and upholds people's rights.

physical geography (fiz/ i kəl jē äg/ rə fē) The land, water, and other resources of an area.

pilgrim (pil/grəm) A person who travels for a religious reason.

powwow (pou/wou/) A Native American gathering.

producer (prə dōōs/ər) A person who makes a product or provides a service.

profit (präf/it) The money that businesses have left after their costs are paid.

protest (prō test/) To complain.

Q

Quaker (kwā/kər) A follower of a religion that believes in peace and equal treatment for all people.

R

recreation (rek/rē ā/shən) A way of enjoying oneself.

recycle (rē sī/kəl) To use an item again.

region (rē/jən) An area with common features that set it apart from other places.

relative location (rel/ə tiv lō kā/shən) A description of where a place is in relation to other places.

renewable resource (ri nōō/ə bəl rē/sôrs/) A natural resource that can be replaced in a short time.

represent (rep/ri zent/) To speak for others.

representative (rep/rə zen/tə tiv) A person chosen to speak for others.

reservation (rez/ər vā/shən) Land that the United States government set aside for Native Americans many years ago.

revolution (rev/ə lōō/shən) When people want to take over the government that rules them and create a new one.

route (rōōt) The course you take to get somewhere.

rural (roor/əl) Describes a community in the countryside where there is plenty of open space.

S

savings (sā/vings) The money a person earns but does not spend.

scarcity (sker/sə tē) When there is not enough of something to meet people's needs and wants.

segregate (seg/rə gāt/) To separate.

service (sɨr/vis) Work that one person does for another.

specialization (spesh/əl ə zā/shən) When each person in a group has a special skill and does one job or one part of a project.

strike (strīk) When workers stop working until things change.

suburban (sə bur′bən) Describes a community near a large city.

suffrage (səf′rij) The right to vote.

supply (sə plī′) The amount of goods or services that people can sell.

symbol (sim′bəl) On a map, a small picture or shape that stands for a specific location, settlement, or building.

tax (taks) Money paid to a government.

technology (tek näl′ə jē) The scientific knowledge about how things work.

telegraph (tel′ə graf′) A machine that sends and receives signals through a thin wire.

territory (ter′ə tôr′ē) An area of land owned by a country either within or outside the country's borders.

toll (tōl) Money that is paid for using a road.

trade (trād) To use money to buy and sell goods and services.

tradition (trə dish′ən) A special way that a group does something that is part of its culture.

transcontinental (trans′kän tə nent′′l) Across the continent.

union (yōōn′yən) A group of workers that joins together.

urban (ur′bən) Describes a community in a large city.

vaccine (vak sēn′) A shot with a weak virus that helps people's bodies fight off disease.

value (val′yōō) What an item is worth to a person.

vegetation (vej′ə tā′shən) Plant life.

veto (vē′tō) To reject.

volunteer (väl ən tir′) A person who improves the community and helps others.

wagon train (wag′ən trān) A group of covered wagons that travels together for safety.

wants (wänts) Things you would like to have but do not need.

weather (weth′ər) The daily conditions outside.

Index

This index lists the pages on which topics appear in this book. Page numbers followed by *m* refer to maps. Page numbers followed by *p* refer to photographs. Page numbers followed by *c* refer to charts or graphs. Page numbers followed by *t* refer to timelines. **Bold** page numbers indicate vocabulary definitions. The terms *See* and *See also* direct the reader to alternate entries.

Credits

Text Acknowledgments

Grateful acknowledgement is made to the following for copyrighted material:

Page 45
Cousteau Society

"National Geographic and The Cousteau Society Present Rediscovery of the Mediterranean" from cousteau.org, July 2, 2010. Copyright © Cousteau Society.

Page 294
North Carolina Press

The Poems of Phillis Wheatley edited and with an introduction by Julian D. Mason Jr. Copyright (c) 1966 by the University of North Carolina Press, renewed 1989. Used by permission of the publisher.

Note: Every effort has been made to locate the copyright owner of material reproduced in this component. Omissions brought to our attention will be corrected in subsequent editions.

Maps

XNR Productions, Inc.

Photographs

Photo locators denoted as follows: Top (T), Center (C), Bottom (B), Left (L), Right (R), Background (Bkgd)

Cover

Front Cover (TL) Public Safety Officer, Jacky Chapman/Alamy; (TR) Parade float, Jill Stephenson/Alamy; (CL) Bullock Texas State History Museum, Alamy; (CC) San Antonio firefighter, James Southers/Alamy; (CR) Skateboarder with helmet, dfstyle/Fotolia and Jeff R Clow/Flikr/Getty Images; (BC) Children on beach, David R. Frazier Photolibrary, Inc./Alamy.
Back Cover (TC) People canoeing, Witold Skrypczak/Alamy; (CL) Football, idimair/Fotolia; (CR) Chili festival, Ana Ramirez/Conroe Courier/AP Images; (BL) Girl gardening, Pearson Education; (BC) DART train in Dallas, SuperStock/Glow Images.

Text

Front Matter

x: Look Photography/Corbis; xi: Brian Cook/Alamy; xii: North Wind Picture Archives/©Associated Press; xiii: Jon Spaull/©DK Images; xiv: JLP/Jose L. Pelaez/Corbis; xv: Mary Evans Picture Library/Alamy Images; xvi: Pearson Education; xvii: Peter M. Fredin/©Associated Press

Celebrate Texas and the Nation

001: AdStock RF/Shutterstock; 002: GPI Stock/Alamy; 002: scis65/Fotolia; 003: donna day/Big Cheese Photo/Corbis; 004: AP Images; 004: Library of Congress Prints and Photographs Division Washington, D.C.[LC-USZ62-78987]; 005: Library of Congress Prints and Photographs Division Washington, D.C.[LC-DIG-ppmsca-18548]; 006: Enigma/Alamy; 006: Matt Slocum/AP Images; 007: John Zellmer/E+/Getty Images; 007: Library of Congress Prints and Photographs Division Washington, D.C.[LC-USZ62-137628]; 008: Mark Wilson/Getty Images; 008: NASA Collection/Alamy; 009: GL Archive/Alamy; 010: Kevin Dietsch/UPI/Newscom; 010: Action Plus Sports Images/Alamy; 011: Helen Wright/NASA Images; 011: Naashon Zalk/Corbis; 012: AP Images; 012: Tommy Hultgren/AP Images; 012: ZUMA Press, Inc./Alamy; 016: Luc Novovitch/Alamy; 016: Yadid Levy/Alamy; 017: Cyril Hou/Alamy; 017: Frans Lemmens/Superstock; Alamy

Chapter 01

019: Pearson Education; 020: Comstock/Thinkstock; 020: Pearson Education; 021: Fackler Non CC/Alamy; 021: Jupiterimages/Thinkstock; 021: Pearson Education; 022: Bruce Leighty/Ticket/Photolibrary; 023: William Roy Lawrence Collection/Ohio Historical Society; 024: Grafton Marshall Smith/Flirt/Corbis; 024: Joe Sohm/VisionsofAmerica/Getty Images; 025: Jim West/Alamy; 029: BMD Images/Alamy; 040: Chad Ehlers/Alamy; 040: dbimages/Alamy; 041: Lived In Images/Alloy/Corbis; 041: DK Images; 042: Glowimages/Getty Images; 042: White/Photodisc/Photolibrary; 043: Hemera/Thinkstock; 044: Liane Cary/Age Fotostock/Photolibrary; 40, 41: Stephen Saks Photography/Alamy; Lauren Orr/Shutterstock; Luc Novovitch/Alamy; Morgan Lane Photography/Shutterstock

Chapter 02

054: Antoine Beyeler, Shutterstock; 054: Antoine Beyeler/Shutterstock; 054: NASA/Corbis; 054: Peter Harrison/PhotoLibrary; 056: Mike Norton, Shutterstock; 056: Mike Norton/Shutterstock; 057: N/A, Shutterstock; 057: Benn Mitchell/The Image Bank/Getty Images; 057: John Elk III/Alamy; 057: Nagel Photography/Shutterstock; 058: Caitlin Mirra, Shutterstock; 058: Caitlin Mirra/Shutterstock; 058: Jeff Banke/Shutterstock; 059: Patrick Eden/Alamy; 060: Martin Harvey/Corbis; 060: Peter Kirillov/Shutterstock; 060: Stephan von Mikusch/Fotolia; 062: Global Warming Images/Alamy; 064: Brian Cook/Alamy; 064: Papilio/Alamy; 070: Galyna Andrushko/Shutterstock; 070: Lonely Planet Images/Alamy; 072: Hemera/Thinkstock; 073: moodboard/Alamy; 074: Commercial Eye/The Image Bank/Getty Images; 074: Morgan Lane Photography/Shutterstock; 076: Lazar Mihai-Bogdan/Shutterstock; 078: Chad Ehlers/Alamy; 078: Danita Delimont/Alamy; 079: Yvette Cardozo/Alamy; 082: Andy Z./Shutterstock; 083: Ivan Bondarenko/Shutterstock; 084: Disney Channel/Getty Images; 085: Daniel Grill/Tetra Images/Corbis; Catmando/Shutterstock; Louis DeLuca/Dallas Morning News/Corbis; Mark Rightmire/Zuma Press/Newscom; Mike Theiss/Ultimate Chase/Corbis News/Corbis; Robert Nickelsberg/Getty Images; Underwood & Underwood/Bettmann/Corbis; Uppa/Photoshot